CW00684646

Twilight of the Hellenistic World

Twilight of the Hellenistic World

Bob Bennett and Mike Roberts

Pen & Sword
MILITARY

First published in Great Britain in 2012 by
Pen & Sword Military
an imprint of
Pen & Sword Books Ltd
47 Church Street
Barnsley
South Yorkshire
S70 2AS

ISBN 978-1-84884-136-9

The right of Bob Bennett and Mike Roberts to be identified as Authors of this
Work has been asserted by them in accordance with the Copyright, Designs
and Patents Act 1988.

A CIP catalogue record for this book is available from the British Library.

Typeset in 11pt Ehrhardt by
Mac Style, Beverley, E. Yorkshire

Printed and bound in the UK by
CPI Group (UK) Ltd, Croydon, CRO 4YY

Pen & Sword Books Ltd incorporates the Imprints of Pen & Sword Aviation,
Pen & Sword Family History, Pen & Sword Maritime, Pen & Sword Military,
Pen & Sword Discovery, Wharncliffe Local History, Wharncliffe True Crime,
Wharncliffe Transport, Pen & Sword Select, Pen & Sword Military Classics,
Leo Cooper, The Praetorian Press, Remember When, Seaforth Publishing and
Frontline Publishing.

For a complete list of Pen & Sword titles please contact
PEN & SWORD BOOKS LIMITED
47 Church Street, Barnsley, South Yorkshire, S70 2AS, England
E-mail: enquiries@pen-and-sword.co.uk
Website: www.pen-and-sword.co.uk

Contents

Maps and Battle Plans

Map 1: Western Greece.

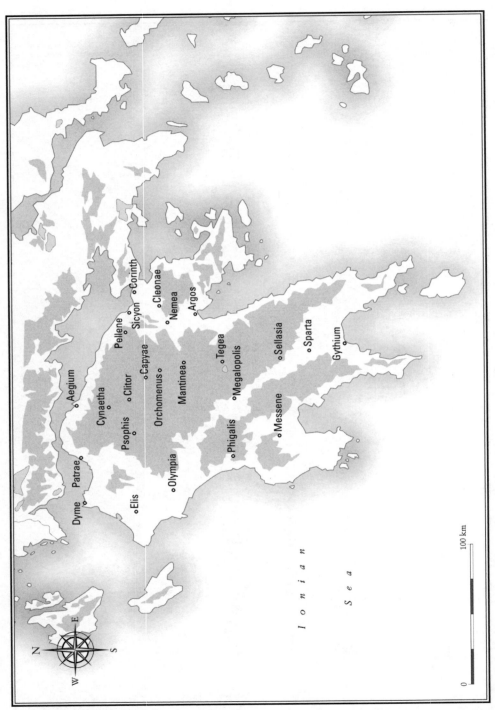

Map 2: Eastern Greece.

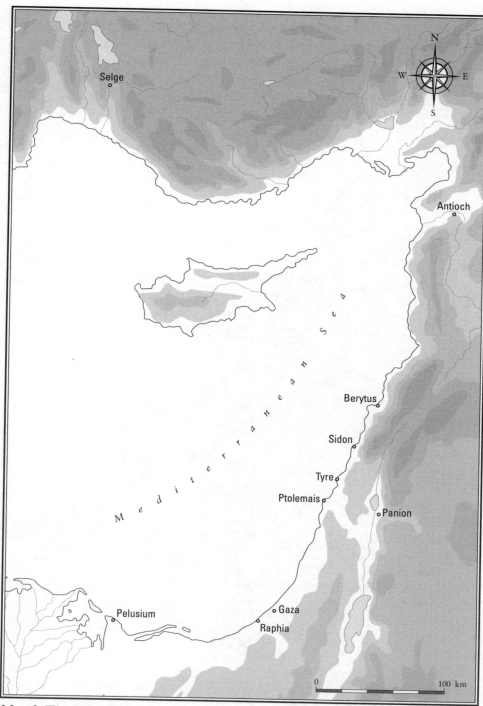

Map 3: The Poloponnese.

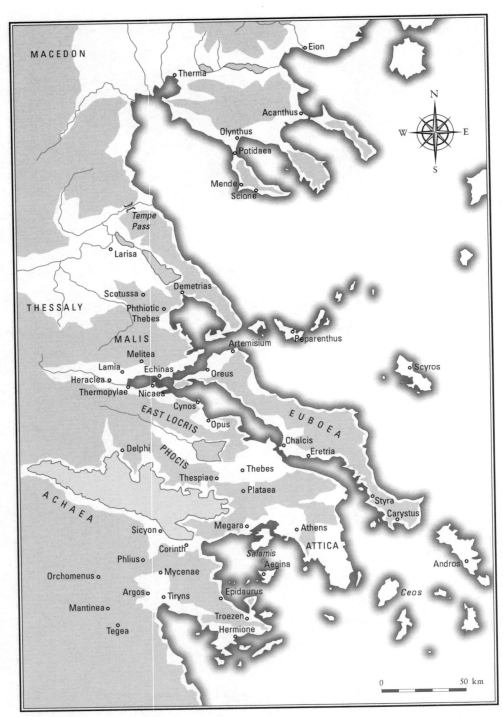

Map 4: The Eastern Mediterranean.

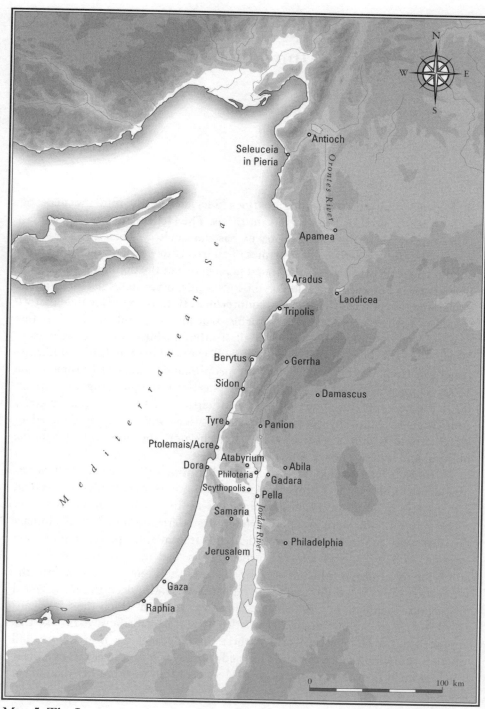

Map 5: The Levant.

Introduction

This project we are submitting to the reader fits neatly into the dialectic. Indeed, it is a carefully constructed antithesis. The Hellenistic World in the last thirty or so years of the third century BC has almost always been discovered as a preparation for the arrival of the armies of an irresistibly expanding Rome. This should be no surprise, as it is the stated perspective of the dominant source, the disingenuous but indispensable Polybius, who purposely states his intention of explaining this process to his fellow countrymen. But, the opposite pole that we intend to balance upon is just as arguable, that for the people of the time this was not how they perceived things at all. To the inhabitants of the Hellenistic World, the early years of the Second Punic War would have looked a bit like the American Civil War as perceived by the peoples and powers of Europe in the 1860s. Government and citizen alike knew there was an epic struggle going on off to the west, but very few would have anticipated that the country, generally considered as culturally backward, over the water and currently deluged in blood, would within a relatively short time become the dominant economic, political and military power over their own lives.

To continue the analogy of the USA and Europe in the second half of the nineteenth century, the Europeans knew huge events were under way. Great armies were involved in mega campaigns but to them it was still far away and there were few who were prescient enough to understand how it might impact on their own continent. How ascendant the transatlantic power would soon become. And, even after we know what history had in store we still do not subscribe to a European historiography that sees the Franco–Prussian War, the unification of Italy and Germany, the Balkan Wars and indeed the First World War as just incidents in a timeline leading to a world in which the Americans ruled the roost. So, one questions whether it is reasonable always to take this approach to the Hellenistic World in these three decades down to 200 BC, and whether something more might be learned from eyeing up the era from a place much more in the centre of the eastern Mediterranean world rather than off to the west.

This is surely realistic; to share a perspective with the Hellenistic public that saw the power players of their own time as much the same as those who had shaken out after the death of Alexander the Great, plus a few others who had emerged over the intervening years. The kingdom of Pergamum, the Aetolian League, maritime powers like Rhodes, the great old cities like Athens or Sparta – not what they had been but still needing to be noted. Others would wax in power in the period we are considering, like the Achaean League, and others would fade, like the realm of Epirus, but even by the turn of the century, it was only the very far-sighted that imagined that this structure would crumble and alter under pressure from altogether another power from the west.

The interests of some Hellenistic peoples and their leaders were perhaps purely Peloponnesian, or for others attention was confined to the Greek peninsula. Certainly the great territorial kings had wider horizons west, east and south, but still most attention was given to the centre, where their borders and spheres of influence collided. The king of Macedon might interfere in Illyrian matters, a policy that brought them cheek by jowl with Rome; they might even ally with Carthage, but it is not credible that there was real ambition beyond some influence over the Adriatic coast. And the ruling elite at Pella had little enough understanding of what cataclysmic forces they were inviting in when they let themselves be involved on this western frontier. As for the Seleucids, they had a mess of centrifugal tugging to deal with before the greatest king since their founder turned east not west to encompass the greatest achievement of his life and won for his name the appendage of 'Great' and finally concluded a long line of Syrian Wars to his advantage. His enemy in these wars, the Ptolemies of Egypt, although early in their significant intercourse with Rome, still their main interests were far away from the west, first successfully contesting the war for Coele Syria but then finding themselves so riven by domestic strife that they managed to lose all they had won in the next round of fighting. The Nile valley, inner Iran, Afghanistan, the Chersonese, Thrace, Anatolia, and at the most Illyria; this was what the kings thought about while a menace grew over the western horizon, a menace that was seldom perceived as critical. To get an accurate view of the motives, strategies and policies of Antigonus Doson, Philip V, Antiochus III, the Ptolemies, the Aetolians, the Achaeans and the Spartans, these must be the focus of our concentration, not what was a happening hundreds of miles away over the Adriatic.

It is not just that there is an opening for a different perspective; there also seems to be a gap in modern detailing of these years, one that seems strange not to have been filled. This is not a period like the first three-quarters of the third century or the second half of the second when good source material peters out. There is plenty here, admittedly most of it based on just one voice, but still there is enough flesh on these bones that it is surprising that this space has not been filled recently. And exploring this fissure, both from written records and on the ground, is not as difficult as with many other projects. The regions where the events we are considering took place are very accessible. Much occurred in Greece, Turkey and Egypt, places both very familiar to the original sources and also readily accessible to the modern traveller, avoiding the problems of having a centre of activity in Iraq, Iran and Afghanistan, places that were both *terra incognito* to most ancient authors and that have been difficult for outsiders to visit in safety for some considerable time.

Some years have passed since serious attempts have been made to tell the story of Cleomenes, Philip V, Aratus or Philopoemen. Antiochus the Great, with his bitty source attestation, is almost less embraced, the solitary recent major work dealing only with his encounters with Rome and eschewing much of interest in the first half of his reign. Articles, of course, continue to appear but pretty sparsely, although occasionally something substantial is vouchsafed, like a recent work on the Aetolian League. There are certainly some excellent general histories available, but the breadth and depth of the subject matter means this is not wholly satisfying to those who want more details on the individual careers, conflicts and local developments.[1]

Nor is this so difficult a stretch. The overriding source, Polybius, despite his Tiber-centric position and pro–Achaean bias, sniffing slightly of a quisling aroma, still held a declared manifesto to write a history of all the world. He covers in good detail much of what happened in Greece, Anatolia, Egypt, Mesopotamia and further east, and some of this still remains. And, even if the legions had long conquered in the time of others of the ancient writing pantheon, like Plutarch, Appian and Pausanias, they can still see a world where Sparta, Alexandria and Antioch loom as large as the city on seven hills.

Polybius dominates not just because of what is left to us but also because many who came after used his works as the basis of their efforts. He saw himself as a teacher of future leaders, as befitted a man who mixed with Scipio Aemilius, son of the victor of Pydna. A self-accredited didact, he took himself pretty seriously, earnestly criticizing, if not always avoiding, the failures he saw in others. He condemns lost toilers like Phylarchus, Theopompus, Zeno and Timaeus as having picked up some very bad habits that he did not want to reproduce. He described at length, and in detail, an intention to get back to a serious kind of history without the rhetorical flourishes and tragic tantrums that had marred these others. Also, he did not want to just be a library historian but to reclaim the ground Thucydides had stood upon by going where things had happened and talking to those who had been involved. This attempt to get back to clean Thucydidian lines was based on a real experience of warfare and statecraft, but still his inability to appreciate others does not make the man more congenial. If this is perhaps understandable with respect to some of the rhetorical or tragical extravagances that had been peddled as history before him, his refusal to accept the importance of telling a good story sends him down to us looking extremely po-faced indeed.

Polybius himself was from Megalopolis in Arcadia, but at the time he was born it had become part of the Achaean League. Not only that, he was the son of a prominent Achaean commander. Together with his use of Aratus as a source, it is perhaps no great surprise that we find him delivering verdicts on the Achaean League such as: 'one could not find a political system and principle so favourable to equality and freedom of speech, in a word so sincerely democratic as that of the Achaean League.'[2] Later, he excuses the League's habit of forcibly incorporating cities by informing us that 'those whom it forced to adhere to it when the occasion presented itself suddenly underwent a change and became quite reconciled to their position'.[3] Not possibly the observations of an unbiased commentator.

Mixing with the great, he saw them as the engine of events. It was Philip V or Hamilcar Barca that caused their countries' wars with Rome, rather than any other underlying factors. And the unpleasant toadying to the powerful is only slightly appeased by his belief that chance (*tyche*) also pressed some of the buttons of causation. Crucially, he was wonderfully near to things, although perhaps not as contemporary as Thucydides. Still, anything with his stamp on it does benefit from coming, if not exactly on the heel of events, then very soon after. His contemporaries would all have had parents or grandparents that lived through the events he chronicled. Indeed, he could have met very old men who when young would have been there at the proceedings he recounted. This is a special quality, as for the hundred and fifty years before there are no writers who are both extant and historically close to what they are describing. The years of Philip, Alexander, the Diadochi and the first Hellenistic kings are depicted by historians who lived hundreds of years after, as far distant as the days of Pitt the Elder or the Duke of Marlborough are from us.

The period he recounted was an age of kings; the Successor monarchs of Alexander's empire dominated the world. The framework was provided by the direct rule or spheres of influence of polities, now several generations deep. Leagues, cities and tribes might huff and puff but it was still the kings with their great standing armies and resource-sucking bureaucracies who really called the shots. As will be seen, it would only be when these lesser powers forged alliances that they could have any chance of standing toe to toe with a Seleucid, an Antigonid or a Ptolemy. It is not a period that resonates snugly in the way that the Classical Age does, and this is not just because the primary source does not stand up to Herodotus or Thucydides as either great writer or epic historian. Certainly, it is a time when something had very definably been lost, even before the grim intrusion of Roman might, though perhaps not the independent power of the city states of Athens, Sparta and Thebes; that was long gone. But still something that was so obviously culturally valuable and intellectually interesting that it would, under Roman tutelage, re-emerge in a sort of theme park Greece, a Hellenistic 'Disneyland' that every senatorial bigwig would visit with more or less understanding and interest.

War was perennially at the centre when still so much prestige and power came with the profession of arms, whether it be as a citizen phalangite or a conquering king in the Alexander mould. Hellenistic citizens conducted their business, whether economic, domestic or political, in the shadows of statues lining the marketplaces and other public spaces that might just as likely be of some warrior hero as of an all-powerful deity. And the spectacles on offer to a demanding audience were frequently martially based, from the local gilded youths and their cavalry exercises to huge parades of regal military power at Daphnia and Alexandria; these were just as much part of the calendar of entertainment as athletic, artistic and religious events. War was attention-grabbing because it was so dynamic, one of the few factors that would subvert the traditional range of social interaction. The pressures of war might see the bluebloods contemplating radical debt cancellation, to allow an increase in the citizen pool that supplied the warriors. Cities, when threatened by extinction, could free slaves to boost their defensive forces and even the involvement of women in fighting could be contemplated. Foreigners might be brought into the citizen fold if their assets made the difference in a fight for survival. Even the pantheon might be adjusted; kings were most often raised to the status of saviour gods by their decisive efforts in martial matters. Much could be changed because movement of people is always socially dynamic and war always moved people. Whether they were mercenaries mobilized by greed, ambition and thirst for adventure, or enslaved prisoners dragged from their homes, all meant great shifting of population in the Hellenistic era.

The three great kingdoms of the Hellenistic World were what events were really about in the time we are intending to describe. Many other polities will be mentioned, some familiar from centuries before and others new, but they were all structured around the great threesome. They will also to a considerable degree enforce the structure of this book. Our chapters are neither strictly chronological nor strictly regional. We defiantly, on occasions, jump between the Balkans and the Levant with occasional expeditions to Bactria and Anatolia, aiming to paint a picture that is both explanatory and entertaining. To be completely regional would lose some of the unity of the world we are describing, and in some ways we would have ended up with separate stories just welded together, whilst to be completely chronological would require jumping about in a very unhandsome manner.

The headline stories will range from the ascent of Achaea under Aratus to an ebullient and socially radicalized Sparta rising only to fall at the battle of Sellasia. There is the story of Philip V of Macedonia's attempt to resurrect the Empire of greater Macedonia of Philip II in the Balkans, with the Aetolian League always eager to place pitfalls in his way. Illyrians, the new kings of Pergamum and the Romans shuffle and rustle on the sidelines, and Dardanian and other wild raiders have their say. But still most events centre around the

Peloponnese and the Malian Gulf, the hunting ground of Greek and Hellenistic hard men from mythical times to Xenophon, Epaminondas, Philip and Alexander. Then there is another huge patch of action that sees two great kingdoms going head to head over ownership of Coele Syria when they were not distracted by local difficulties in the Nile Valley or, in the case of the Seleucids, by difficult relatives or rebellious proconsuls in Anatolia and Mesopotamia. And, of course, the great adventure in the lands of Iran and Afghanistan cannot be left un-noted, despite the scarcity of sources, as it did give the vaunted title of 'Great' to one monarch of our period.

We have tried to write, as many authors have said before, the book we would like to read on the subject. We think we can assume from our reader a general knowledge of the east Mediterranean world during the Classical Age, the rivalry of Sparta and Thebes, the rise of Macedonia and the conquest of Persia by Alexander the Great. If not superbly written, such a summary of centuries, often found in other volumes, can be frustrating to plough through. The years from Alexander's death and the Diadochi Wars down through most of the third century is less well known so we have touched on it, but in general we have tried to get straight into the meat of our story. The same is true of the military dimension; we have avoided a résumé of Classical hoplite fighting and the development of the Macedonian phalanx, although we will have discussions referring to both these matters and many others that were significant in the world of the high Hellenistic kingdoms.

But the book that we would like to read, while looking at the details of campaigns and the intrigues at the courts of Antiochus, Ptolemy and Philip, still must have a shot at understanding what life was like for the participants, whether by getting inside the heads of the old guard who tried to influence Philip V when he first came to power or the power brokers of Achaea, or else the more regular fellows who haggled in the market or strutted in garrison towns, playing out the role of both defender and oppressor. And this impulse to understand an era so long in the past is bound to involve making comparisons with our own world, and certainly there seem parallels to be drawn between the supposed waning of the Classical World into its Hellenistic by-blow and what has occurred during the last century of our era. All such comparative analysis is, of course, deeply questionable, but none the less irresistible. Indeed, the feet of clay of the process are always exposed by how often any era in the past is trotted out as mirroring the author's own days. Yet this does not disqualify the practice because all are considering aspects of human development, while human imperatives remain, human partiality remains, human self-delusion remains. And if, for example, the excellent Barbara Tuchman can throw up the late fourteenth century as a 'Distant Mirror' to her own time, we are following a vogue that has borne good fruit before.

There is certainly a dourness in the great Greek cities of the pre-Hellenistic Age that recalls to some extent the post-Second World War years in Britain. There is an epic that has been played out, but in its wake is an era bathed in a depressing aura. In our own time the cloud of drabness that hovered over the years immediately after 1945 has to some extent dissipated with a culturally mixed, much more interesting townscape emerging in Britain in the last few decades, just as it also surfaced in the age we are considering. The Hellenistic Age loved its food where Sparta only had its gruel, and even the Athens of Pericles' day was not much better. It also saw an enjoyment and cherishing of people, women as well as men, and even of strangers who had been dragged into the orbit of the new, expanded world in a way that is reminiscent of our own times. The era of open racism, misogyny and homophobia of Britain in the 1950s, 1960s and 1970s has largely changed into something more light and interesting, and this was also true as the Hellenic changed into the Hellenistic Age. The corollary was then, as it is now, that old certainties were gone, so old authorities held not the same unreasoning sway. In such a more interesting world, the one unfortunate result, struggled with in both eras, is that public political participation has considerably decreased. People don't go to union meetings or support political parties in the way they did even thirty years ago, and in the Hellenistic Age the depth of communal involvement was just not what it was.

Longevity was always an ace in the hole for any ruler of the pre-modern world. The first three decades of the third century BC saw the start of three reigns, all of which would last a very long time, while all concerned were adults with good groundings in power when they came to the throne of a great Successor kingdom. The first to establish himself did so in Egypt. It was a rough enough ride for Ptolemy II to get to the throne; he had elder half brothers that had to be got off the scene before the regnal transition from father to son could be smoothly accomplished. He had a short period as co-ruler with his father but finally took full control of the reins in about 283 and, as he died in 246, it meant he contrived a personal government of nearly 40 years. A good long time in a polity which had advantages that some of its competitors did not. Egypt, the heartland, had been a state with settled government with effective communal relations between its constituent parts for millennia. It was not just rich and organized; it was also very defensible, with outposts of power all round the Eastern Mediterranean and a navy powerful enough to keep the whole lot stitched together. The first Ptolemy had chosen well when he picked the country as his prize in the lottery at the death of Alexander, and his son continued the cautious and pragmatic policy of that ruler and scribbler. The most noticed developments are at the city of Alexandria, where boom times funded the extraordinary flowering of Hellenistic culture at the Museum and Library. But, power politics counted too and the second Ptolemy took his part in Syrian Wars against the Seleucids and frequently financed trouble for his Macedonian rivals through proxies in Sparta and Athens.

The next to establish firm roots was Antiochus I, son of Seleucus. He did not have siblings to fight for the prize; his place in the dynastic arrangements could not have been clearer. Indeed, he had led his father's armies at least since the battle of Ipsus in 301 and by the 290s was established as the real ruler of the eastern half of the Seleucid realm. His interest in that area never diminished; he is noted as the ruler of Bactria and built the great defensive walls at Merv. But, instead of sibling rivals, he had to face the disruption caused when the first Seleucid, who looked set to gain control of all of Alexander's empire outside of Egypt, was despatched by the assassin's blade of Ptolemy the Thunderbolt. This crumbled all the old man had built in the west of his empire, and the situation was only made worse by the eruption of hordes of Galatian invaders whose wanderings took them as far as central Greece, Thrace and Anatolia. From his power base in southern Mesopotamia and with the resources of the upper satrapies to call upon, Antiochus took up the challenges to his power. But it took years to re-establish real government in most of the places where his father's writ had run. Indeed, he never fully succeeded. If the elephant victory of 273 imposed some discipline on the Gallic intruders, it was not possible to put back in the bottle the genie of an independent Pergamum. Just before he died, Antiochus had tried to bring Pergamum under control but lost in battle near Sardis to Eumenes I. In Anatolia, the reality was that Bithynia, Cappadocia and Pontus meant he was not all powerful there. He overplayed his hand against Ptolemy II in the first Syrian War, where, if initially successful, he ended losing what he had gained and holdings in Caria and Cilicia as well. And he never even attempted to pass the Hellespont into the Balkan lands that Seleucus claimed at the end of his life after his victory over Lysimachus. The realm he left to his son in 261 included an unfinished war with Egypt, but Antiochus II wound it up with no great difficulty and it was a reasonably stable package that had been handed on. Antiochus' reign might not have been quite as extravagantly long as his compatriot kings but, when it is acknowledged that for many years he ruled jointly with his father, it is clear he was around long enough to bed his dynasty in what was the biggest and most centrifugally inclined of the Hellenistic kingdoms.

Chapter 1

Rise of Aratus

After Ptolemy II and Antiochus I, the last and longest lived of the three great Hellenistic kings hung his hat at Pella. Antigonus Gonatas, the son of Demetrius I Poliorcetes, after many vicissitudes, had firmly established the Antigonid dynasty in Macedonia by 271.* He lasted until 239 and must have been nearly 80 at his death, the very age his grandfather was when he perished at the battle of Ipsus in 301. It might have seemed that the Macedonian homeland was a secure place to put down dynastic roots but, in fact, it was a ruptured polity wracked after many years of turmoil. Civil war, multiple monarchs and Galatian invasions had cut away at foundations that were, anyway, far from tried and ancient. A Galatian Thracian state was a new threat to the east and Pyrrhus, king of Epirus, back from Italy and Sicily, had ousted the newcomer, at least temporarily, before that stormy petrel was seen off by an old lady with a roof tile in Argos. Still, by the end of the 270s, Antigonus had finally secured himself on the throne his father had lost in such an undignified manner only a few years before.

He had pressed his cause with a phalanx in one hand and a bevy of stoics in the other. His public relations offensive was ably led by the incredibly ancient Hieronymus of Cardia, and Demetrius' son pushed a policy that had been at the heart of the Macedonian approach at least as far back as the time when Antipater ran the state from Pella, whilst Alexander adventured in Asia.[1] Garrisons, tyrants, dictators and oligarchs held in thrall many of the communities in Greece, bending them to the will of the government of the northern kingdom in return for their own security in domestic affairs. Meanwhile, rivals, usually of more democratic bent, were either at home or in exile, perpetually looking for a chance to topple them. Better to be sure with paid swords or dependent but unpopular enforcers than to risk a popular assembly turning away from friendship and alliance when offered material blandishments and dreams of lost imperial glory by agents from Alexandria, Antioch, Pergamum or other great power centres of the Hellenistic World.

---

* All dates are BC unless specified otherwise.

Antigonus did not have the resources to effectively hold Greece; his primary focus would have been to the north, not the squabbling city states to the south. What he tried to do, however, was secure his position by digging in at the so-called fetters of Greece, namely Demetrias, Chalcis on Euboea and Acrocorinth. These were not arbitrary choices; control over Demetrias, founded by Gonatas' father, gave him a grip on the Thessalian hinterland; Chalcis helped him maintain the sea routes around Euboea, as well as giving him a possibility to influence affairs in central Greece; and control over Acrocorinth gave him a significant lever point in the Peloponnese. In addition, he sought to retain control of Piraeus, the fortress harbour of Athens, not only for its mercantile and naval significance but as a padlock to batten his authority on Athens itself, still regarded by so many as the most prestigious and important Greek metropolis.

Both Athens and Sparta were to pose problems for Antigonus, most notably in the Chremonidean War of approximately 268–263 (the chronology is unclear). Egged on by Ptolemy II Philadelphus of Egypt, the two old warhorses began to dream, yet again, of regaining the lost grandeur of more than two centuries before. Athens, under the stoic philosopher Chremonides, resenting that both Piraeus and Salamis were in the hands of the Macedonians, proposed an anti-Macedonian alliance comprising essentially Athens, Sparta and her allies in the Peloponnese; an association which recalled in the minds of some of the more fanciful participants the famous anti-Persian coalition of 480. Dreams of Marathon, Thermopylae and Salamis aside, the scantily reported war started with some indecisive and minor campaigns but hotted up considerably when Gonatas won a decisive victory at Corinth in either 266 or 265, killing the Spartan king, Areus, in the process. Now, left to its own devices, Athens awaited the inevitable siege, sustained only by the hope of Egyptian aid. Unfortunately, Philadelphus, like his father, Ptolemy Soter, was never going to commit himself decisively so far away from home and the old city finally capitulated in about 263. The Macedonians installed a garrison at the heart of the metropolis. The Chremonidean War had badly backfired and now Macedonian control was more firmly entrenched than ever. Sparta remained unbowed, but Athens, even though the Macedonian garrison was removed in 255, was politically neutered, with the famous Long Walls to Piraeus falling into ruins.

It was to be others who would take up the challenge to Macedonian hegemony, most notably the Aetolian and Achaean Leagues. There had been other Leagues before, such as that of Corinth set up in 338 by Philip II, but these had been essentially vehicles for Macedonian imperialism. The Aetolian and Achaean Leagues were of a different order altogether. They were examples of 'federalism' where the *polis* was subsumed under what was regarded, certainly in the case of the Aetolians, as an ethnic group.

Although the Achaean League had an earlier history, its real importance dates from about 280 when it was reformed, the first four Achaean towns Dyme, Patrae, Pharae and Tritaea federating with each other in a bid to throw off the Macedonian yoke. But, it was to reach its greatest influence in the mid third century thanks to one powerful figure from a non-Achaean *polis*, Aratus of Sicyon, who, although a largely forgotten figure now, was deemed worthy of a life by Plutarch.[2] He was the driving force behind the Achaean League, thrusting it into prominence during the third century. Furthermore, he wrote his memoirs, now unfortunately lost, on which Polybius and Plutarch drew heavily by their own admission.[3] Indeed, Polybius states that he will deal with Aratus' career 'quite summarily, as he published a truthful and clearly written memoir of his own career.'[4]

Aratus was born in 271 in Sicyon. Of aristocratic birth, he was the son of Clinias who was governing the *polis* as one of the elected magistrates. His gymnasium can still be seen amongst the ruins of ancient Sicyon. In 264, the city was the subject of a coup by one Abantidas, who had Clinias murdered; he also sought to have the seven-year-old Aratus extinguished but he escaped. The boy had, in the confusion, strayed into the house of his aunt, Soso, who also happened to be the sister of Abantidas. Despite this connection, she took pity on Aratus, hid him till nightfall and then smuggled him out of Sicyon to be raised in exile by friends in Argos. There, Aratus made something of a name for himself. Educated in a 'free' city by the 'liberal' friends of his father, he won a reputation as an orator and athlete, winning the Olympic pentathlon once. However, he was consumed by a burning desire to win back freedom for his home city.

Despite his youth, this resolute character seems to have been early on accepted as the leader of the exiles' party. These included more than just Sicyonians; a man from Megalopolis is explicitly mentioned and, as is the norm amongst these groups both ancient and modern, there were deep conflicts over strategy. Aratus, we learn, was something of a hothead who worried older hands in his youthful zeal for action.

In Sicyon itself, faction strife dominated during the years of Aratus' youth, with Abantidas cut down by rivals. All this laid the city open to depredations from aggressive neighbours, so there was strong feeling towards the exiles, who it was thought might bring some stability and security. This might seem parochial to Sicyon, but Aratus was clearly seen by many as a major player. Already, as a young man, he had corresponded with the kings of Macedonia and Egypt, and even if they gave him little practical help at that juncture the fact that he was in communication with such people indicates he was a high-stakes operator. In fact, we are told the main reason the tyrant of Sicyon, who was then Nicocles, was worried about the young man was his elevated connections.

In 251, Aratus, no longer able to bear inaction, decided to take and hold a fortified post near Sicyon from where he could raid his enemies' property and where sympathizers could join him. But before he put this plan into action a man arrived who opened up completely new possibilities. A political prisoner who had recently broken out of the tyrant's prison in Sicyon arrived at Argos with interesting news. He was a brother of one of Aratus' group and explained that the escape route out of Sicyon that he had taken could easily be retraced by men with scaling ladders who could probably enter over the defensive walls by which he had left unnoticed, because the place 'was almost level with the ground on the inside, where it had been attached to steep and rocky places, and that on the outside it was not at all too high for scaling-ladders.'[5]

The possibility of a coup rather than a drawn-out war of raids appealed to Aratus and he sent his people to scout the route the refugee had proposed. They returned to report that the only real obstacle was a 'fierce and savage dog' owned by the gardener, whose plot abutted the wall at the point identified. Aratus armed his men and ladders were constructed, but all needed to be done in secret as the tyrant of Sicyon's spies kept a keen surveillance on the exiles. Aratus, hot on security, did not even tell the men who assembled what their target was, particularly as they included not only 30 of his own servants and 10 each from the other prosperous exiles but also some mercenaries, to give a professional edge to the enterprise under Xenophilus, described as the 'foremost of the robber captains'. Precautions were taken as small groups slipped out of Argos to rendezvous in Sicyonian territory at a tower well known as a landmark. And, on the night of the attempt, Caphisias, with four followers, was sent first to lock up the gardener and his dogs while the rest followed with the ladders concealed in boxes on wagons.

Nicocles' people had been keeping their eyes open in Argos and a real shadow play was needed to keep security uncompromised. Aratus sported at the marketplace and gym and made obvious preparations for a fiesta on the day he had decided on for his coup. It worked, and when he knew the spies had left Argos convinced he had nothing under hand, he breakfasted and sped off to join his men at the tower of Polygnotus. From there they marched on towards Nemea; at this advanced base he gave a pep talk and, declaring the watchword to be 'Apollo Victorious', he led them down the road to Sicyon, intending to get to the walls when there would still be a little light.

As they approached the garden, Aratus met Caphisias, who reported failure. The dogs were still free, although he had secured the gardener. This worried the men but Aratus encouraged them on. The ladders were brought to the walls despite the dogs barking and harassing the first group led by Ecdelus, the Megalopolitan. They began to climb the ladders, but near the top of the wall they saw the watch coming to investigate the noise. Crouching down on the ladders under the wall, they managed to avoid being seen. When the sentries passed, they mounted the wall and waited for the rest. Technon, a servant of Aratus, had been sent to bring them on, and led by Aratus they got up and over. Now, more dogs in the watch tower almost blew the cover of these men following up. They started barking at their approach and, for a second time, a cacophony threatened to expose the attempt, but when the town watch approached, the keeper of these dogs stated they had only been excited by the previous commotion. The man's motivation is not explained but it thoroughly bucked up Aratus' men who assumed he was a friend facilitating their enterprise. Now, the rest followed and all had entered by the time the sun came up and the city shook itself into life.

With dawn breaking, the intruders rushed the tyrant Nicocles' house and the barracks, capturing all the mercenary guards who lodged there. Nicocles himself managed to escape by an underground passageway. Rumours soon spread about what was happening and a crowd thronged to the theatre before setting Nicocles' residence on fire; the flames could allegedly be seen from Corinth, seven miles away. Aratus did not intervene to stop the looting, letting the citizens assuage their fury after thirteen years of tyranny. Remarkably, when calm was restored, the successful coup proved to have been almost entirely bloodless, with no one killed. It was 251 and Aratus was just twenty years of age.

His first act was to restore the exiles to Sicyon, eighty who had been banished by Nicocles and, if we are to believe Plutarch, another 500, some of whom had been absent from Sicyon for up to 50 years. They, not unnaturally, wanted to claim their own property back, and the prospect of a civil war began to rear its ugly head. Antigonus Gonatas, observing the coup in Sicyon with some alarm, offered Aratus twenty-five talents as a personal gift and goodwill gesture (no doubt hoping Aratus would prove a useful Macedonian puppet in the Peloponnese).[6] However, he was to be sorely disappointed, as not only did Aratus allegedly give the money away to his fellow citizens but took the monumental decision to attach Sicyon to the Achaean League, probably also in 251, a decision which changed the course of Greek history for the next 30 odd years. It was the first time the League had admitted a non Achaean *polis* (Sicyon was Dorian) and the ramifications of this new pan-Hellenic organisation were to be profound indeed. Aratus, also, by this decision, showed that rare quality in a politician, patience, as he must have known he was too young to serve in any position in the League.

In the meantime, he undertook an epic voyage to Egypt to seek the alliance of Ptolemy Philadelphus. Sicyon was still in economic turmoil and he needed aid. Having burnt his bridges with Gonatas, he had little option. The inevitably colourful tale in Plutarch has Aratus forced to land on Andros in the Cyclades before eventually hitching a lift with a Roman vessel and eventually, by way of Caria, disembarking in Egypt. Aratus and Sicyon were both in good odour there as he had, apparently, been instrumental in sending various works of art from

Sicyon to Ptolemy. It was a leading arts centre in the Greek world and Aratus, supposedly, one of its finest connoisseurs. Notwithstanding this *Antiques Road Show*, Aratus soon returned with forty talents and a promise of a further 110 in instalments. Back home, he refused the office of independent arbiter of the exile question and how to distribute the Ptolemaic money and insisted on having a committee of himself and fifteen others to do the job. Be that as it may, with the Ptolemaic money he was able to ameliorate the political problems in Sicyon and the grateful citizens erected a brass statue of Aratus.[7] The rest of the period between 251 and 245 is obscure, though he served for four or five years as a dutiful cavalryman in the Achaean militia.

In 245, Aratus was elected *strategos* (chief executive and war leader) of the League for the first time, a position he was to hold every two years until his death, with one or two exceptions (the constitution prevented a *strategos* serving consecutive years). From the outset, his watchword was expansion. His first campaign included pillaging the countryside of Locris and Calydon just over the Gulf of Corinth from Patrae, and he even led a force, claimed as 10,000 strong, to help the Boeotians who had been thumped by the Aetolians. But it was closer to home that his heart's desire lay, at that beetling fortress of Acrocorinth. The city itself was at the door of the Peloponnese, a trading Mecca, with access to both the Saronic and Corinthian Gulfs. It was built on the flat but above it, rising to a great rock nearly 2,000 feet high, was a fortress that had few equals in Europe, with a fresh water source, steep cliffs all around, topped off with a massive walled citadel.

> The Isthmus, rising like a bank between the seas, collects into a single spot and compresses together the whole continent of Greece; and Acrocorinth, being a high mountain springing up out of the very middle of what here is Greece.[8]

Antigonus Gonatas had, after some chequered times, got this place firmly back into his hands by a combination of marriage, diplomacy and trickery. And he now held it firm with a strong garrison under a philosopher–soldier called Persaeus. But in 243 opportunity came knocking for Aratus. According to Plutarch, there were four Syrian brothers living in Corinth, one of whom, Diocles, was a mercenary employed as a guard in the Acrocorinth. The brothers were in the habit of stealing gold plate from their employer and ventured to a banker in Sicyon to dispose of it. The banker, Aegias, discovered that one of the brothers worked in the citadel and it was reported to him that there was a fissure in the cliff, upon which the Acrocorinth was situated, conveniently just where the wall was at its lowest. Aegias made the following memorable crack to Erginus, the brother he was most acquainted with:

'Do you, then, best of men, thus for the sake of a little gold plate rifle the king's treasures, when it is in your power to sell a single hour's work for large sums of money? Don't you know that burglars as well as traitors, if they are caught, have only one death to die?"[9]

Aratus knew Aegias and so he became aware of all this and was soon in negotiations with the brothers. He agreed to give them sixty talents if he could successfully capture the citadel and, for security, gave the banker most of his plate and his wife's gold rather than risking public funds. And, after an unlikely tale of mistaken identity involving another of the four brothers, only retrieved by the quick footwork of the servant Technon, Aratus was ready in midsummer to undertake his coup.

Aratus had raised a major force from the Achaean cities to push this enterprise, although we are not told exactly how many. But certainly most of the main body was left to spend a tense night on the road between Sicyon and the target with sword in hand while a 'forlorn hope' stepped out to follow Aratus. With these four hundred men, he made his way to the temple of Hera, near the gate of Corinth, on a night of the full moon. However, very conveniently, cloud began to envelop the city, and after Erginus and seven followers had made their way to the gate and slaughtered the guards on duty, Aratus and 100 hand-picked men climbed their ladders barefooted to avoid making any noise. They were only at the gate and still had to climb to the citadel and had a narrow escape when they ambushed a night watch of four men. Three they killed but the other escaped to raise the alarm. Just when it seemed Aratus' party would get lost on the dark track leading up to the citadel, the clouds parted and the moon revealed the fissure they were looking for. In the meantime, the other 300 men had climbed the ladders over the wall, got into the city and were trying to locate Aratus. But, in the confusion of a dark and disturbed city, all they could do was reach the cliffs below the Acrocorinth and there they took shelter, confused and aimless, although ultimately their presence was to prove decisive. Above them, Aratus' men found themselves in great difficulties under the citadel walls. As they tried to assail them, climbing the ladders they had laid up against the ramparts, the defenders rained down missiles on their exposed side. And there was an even greater danger. A Macedonian commander in the city, Archelaus, was now thoroughly awake and had organized a large force to take Aratus' men in the rear. He led his soldiers up from the city to the attack but, as the clouds had come over again, he passed by the 300 Achaeans who huddled under the Acrocorinth cliff. The Achaeans observed them and acting decisively fell on their unshielded side and drove them off in rout. This bloody business in the dark was fraying nerves and nobody was quite sure who were friends or foe. Everything seemed un-coordinated and it looked distinctly possible the whole attack might unravel. But, Erginus saved the day; he stumbled onto the 300 Achaeans and delivered a desperate message from Aratus that he and his men were engaged with the enemy on the heights. They were defending themselves vigorously on the citadel wall, and if his attack was to succeed there was need of speedy help. The 300 hurried forward in the dark and:

> the light of the full moon also made their arms appear more numerous to the enemy than they really were, owing to the length of their line of march and the echoes of the night gave the impression that the shouts proceeded from many times the number of men there really were.[10]

The Macedonians were suitably dismayed, and Aratus' united companies clambered up the ladders and over the walls, driving the garrison back. Again, it was desperate fighting in the dark, but they held their ground till daylight when the balance of the Achaean army waiting outside hurried up the road to secure the town and citadel. The coup at Sicyon had been something, but now Aratus had achieved what few apart from Demetrius the Besieger had accomplished, the taking of the extraordinary, defensible Acrocorinth by escalade. It had been that most difficult of military operations, a night assault against the most formidable of defences. That it had worked had been due in part to good luck, but also to planning and nerves of steel in the execution. Aratus had done something extraordinary and his stock with his people now took an upturn that almost nothing could erode. And he did not let the grass grow but took Lechaeum, Corinth's port, and 25 of Gonatas' warships docked there, all good realizable assets, and apart from a League garrison of 400 he also installed 50 guard dogs and their handlers at the Acrocorinth.

The capture of the Acrocorinth was a staggering achievement, probably the crowning glory of Aratus' whole career. In a highly dramatic gesture he handed over the keys of the gates and Corinth was free from foreign control for the first time in more than 100 years. In gratitude, it joined the League and soon afterwards Megara, Troezen and Epidaurus followed suit. The League's new place in the world was confirmed when Ptolemy III Euergetes (Philadelphus had died in 246) was elected *hegemon*, a largely honorific position (which Ptolemy by his subsequent inaction did little to change). Because of Aratus, the League was now a major player. The lines were being drawn and both Macedonia and the League found somewhat unlikely allies. Antigonus was forced into the arms of the Aetolian League as they made grandiose plans to dissolve the Achaean League and split the territories between them. As for the Achaeans, they decided to chance an alliance with that most unpredictable of *poleis*, Sparta.

In Aratus' third term as *strategos* in 241, the Aetolians (the Macedonians being content for them to do their dirty work for them) decided on an invasion of the Peloponnese. Aratus and the Spartans were to hold the line at the Isthmus of Corinth. But, there was disagreement about strategy between Aratus and the Spartan king, Agis IV, the latter wanting to confront the Aetolians there and then and Aratus wishing to avoid a battle and arguing that the Aetolians could do little damage as the crops had already been harvested. Whether this was because Aratus genuinely believed this or was regretting the League's alliance with Sparta is unclear. It could also be one of those perplexing episodes which punctuate Aratus' military career; for among many highlights there are a number of times when he seems to lose his nerve. Alexander he was not.

Aratus was a very able statesman but, if we are to believe Plutarch, not a man whose mastery extended to the battlefield where 'he always had cramps in the bowels when a battle was imminent.'[11] However, he appeared to be a master of the surprise attack and his career is littered with successes; although their details are often suspiciously similar. He appears to have been fairly incorruptible and seems to have started out with a genuine desire to rid Greece of its tyrannies and finally break free of Macedonian control. However, *real politick* was often to make its presence felt.

Whether or not Aratus' talents or failings had a bearing, the end result was the same and the Spartan army marched back home; the alliance was at an end. The impact of Agis' departure was immediately felt as the front could no longer be held and the road from Megara through the Geraneia hills was open to the Aetolians. They soon took it and entering eastern Achaea captured Pellene, one of the early members of the Achaean League. But, to confound his critics, Aratus now showed a completely different face; without delay he marched after the enemy with just the soldiers he had with him. He discovered the Aetolians in complete disarray; 'while the leaders and captains were going about and seizing the wives and daughters of the Pellenians, on whose heads they put their own helmets, that no one else might seize them.'[12] The Achaeans easily routed the enemy they found carousing outside the walls before bursting into the town and cutting down those Aetolians who had occupied it. Seven hundred of them were slain as Aratus pulled off this sudden attack and recaptured the town.

By 240 it was apparent to a weary and old Gonatas that the Aetolians were perhaps not the best of allies and he sued for peace with the Achaeans. A peace, however, that was not destined to last, as little over a year later the eighty-year-old 'stoic philosopher' king died. He was succeeded by his son Demetrius II, who had held a number of military commands, including in Epirus. But, as with so much of his life, the details are obscure; he may have been co-regent with his father for the last years of Gonatas' reign.

The occasion of Gonatas' death brought about that most unlikely of alliances between the Achaean and Aetolian Leagues. The reasons for this are obscure in the extreme and, in reality, never had any lasting viability; it was only ever a marriage of political convenience.[13] The result of all this was the so-called war of Demetrius from 239 to 229, of which again we have little detail. However, Plutarch fills us in on some of Aratus' activities during these years. Despite the Achaeans' alliance with the Aetolians, he remained more concerned to free more

Greek *poleis* from tyranny, most notably Argos, Athens and Megalopolis. In Argos there was already some domestic resistance eager to act against their oppressors, but they had no weapons. So Aratus first turned arms smuggler, hiding daggers in packsaddles brought into the city by confederates posing as merchants. But the plotters fell out; tense times turned one, a soothsayer called Charimenes, traitor, and he peached on his comrades just as the coup was under way. So the plot to kill the tyrant in the marketplace was foiled, but if the insurgents were thwarted at least most got away to Corinth. Now what the Argives could not do for themselves, Aratus decided he would do for them. He tried a hallmark raid with all the Achaeans of military age available, but on nearing Argos found the people unwilling to join him.

Still, Aratus remained determined in this drive to emancipate his neighbour, despite threats to his life, apparently ordered by the Argive tyrant in tandem with the king at Pella. After several other efforts, in 235 he yet again attempted to free the city, then under Aristippus. Yet another night-time assault found him inside the walls of Argos, but to his chagrin found the Argives again completely unenthusiastic about being 'freed'. According to Plutarch, 'the Argives, as though it were not a battle to secure their liberties, but a contest in the Nemean Games of which they were the judges, sat as just and impartial spectators of what was going on without lifting a finger.'[14] The men who had scaled the city walls on ladders were prepared for a bloody action and in the street fighting that followed Aratus led his soldiers well but was wounded in the thigh by a spear point. Injured, and with his men fighting in heavy armour and distressed by thirst, Aratus was forced to withdraw, and he led his disconsolate troops out onto the Argive plain. This was very unfortunate timing as the tyrant was just about to flee for his life and had already sent his valuables down to the harbour to be loaded on boats in preparation for his escape. But now Aristippus took courage and led out his army and prepared for battle near the River Xerias.

Aratus' presence in the Argive farmland ensured battle lines were drawn. It was a combat of two wings, a not unusual occurrence in Greek phalanx warfare. On one side, the Achaeans hunkered down behind their hoplon shields and levelled their spears. Their blood must have still been up from the fight in the city streets because they drove the Argives opposite them back until their phalanx fractured and they pursued them from the field. But Aratus, commanding on the other wing, was again wounded and, clearly shaken rather than stirred by the previous fighting, retreated with his men back to the security of their camp. This incensed the soldiers on the victorious flank when they came back from chasing the enemy; his action had allowed the undefeated half of the Argives to retain the field and raise a victory trophy. Shamed by his angry troops into battle the following day, Aratus drew the army up again in battle array in the very shadow of the Argive edifice. But when the men saw that the enemy had been much reinforced and was larger than their own they withdrew again. But, if this explained why they repented of their bellicosity and accepted a truce, presumably Aristippus agreed because he was glad to be rid of these troublesome intruders. However, Aratus managed to spin his behaviour to most people's satisfaction and he also succeeded in taking the town of Cleonae on the Corinth–Nemea road. Here, he celebrated the Nemean Games and sold any Argives he found into slavery despite the protection usually afforded to travellers around festival time.

Aristippus was having none of this Achaean intimidation and determined to get Cleonae back; this was clearly becoming something of a personal duel. When Aratus heard news of the tyrant's intention he was at Corinth but acted straight away. 'He assembled an army by public proclamation', presumably mobilising all who were on hand and prepared to volunteer. The Argives were now fearful to move on Cleonae while the Achaeans were encamped at Corinth from where Aratus could easily descend on Argos if the defenders left. But Aratus, eager to get them into the open again, tried a ploy; he moved off to Cenchreae, southeast of Corinth, hoping this would encourage Aristippus to jump because the Achaean army seemed to be out of the way. And it worked; he marched on Cleonae with his main force. Aratus, kept well informed, now led his men through the evening back to Corinth and then on to Cleonae and entered the town in the middle of the night. In the morning he drew up his phalanx inside the city gate and with trumpets sounding charged out against an astonished enemy. The Achaeans routed the Argives who had not time to take up their formations, and the whole kit and caboodle were pursued more than six miles as far as Mycenae and, in the chaos, Aristippus himself was killed by a Cretan soldier in Achaean pay. In all, more than 1,500 men fell, a huge butcher's bill for these small wars, particularly as it is implausibly claimed the Achaeans lost no men at all. But, for the larger picture Aratus' luck was out as Aristippus' brother, Aristomachus, got back into Argos and proclaimed himself the new tyrant.

Megalopolis was to prove a much different matter – a city founded in 371 as a bulwark against Sparta by the great Theban general Epaminondas. As befitted a 'new town' it was built on a grand scale with many magnificent public buildings. Megalopolis, under its tyrant Lydiades, had remained close to Macedonia, but seeing which way the wind was blowing, with Aratus rampaging around the Peloponnese, the death of Aristippus and with great concerns about what was happening in Sparta, he agreed to lay down his power and join the League in 235. This seemingly selfless act had major ramifications. Orchomenus and Mantinea soon followed Megalopolis' example and also joined the League. It was now at its greatest extent and greatest power; a truly pan–Peloponnesian entity. Aratus had achieved great things. Even accepting a bias from a trumpet-blowing memoirist, it has to be agreed that it was he who had been the driving force. From Dyme to Acrocorinth, the north Peloponnese was now controlled by a powerful federation with organized armed forces and the tax funds to sustain them. A reward for Lydiades' actions was soon to follow, as the year after he took Megalopolis into the League he was elected *strategos* (presumably this was part of the deal for their admission). This was the first of three *strategoi* he was to hold in alternate years to Aratus; the start of a tradition of Megalopolitans holding the position of *strategos* in the years to come, most notably Philopoemen.

The realization that, with the addition of Megalopolis, the League was now a serious force to be reckoned with stirred Demetrius into action, and in 233 he sent a force under the general Bithys into the Peloponnese, where he succeeded in beating the Achaeans at Phylacia, probably near Tegea. Details of the battle, and indeed its precise location, are predictably obscure. Apparently, Aratus escaped and made his way to Corinth, but reports began to circulate that he had either been killed in battle or taken prisoner. Such was the enthusiasm with which this news was greeted in Athens that 'the Athenians, carrying their flattery of the Macedonians to the highest pitch of levity, crowned themselves with garlands as soon as they heard that Aratus was dead.'[15] Even given Plutarch's gift for hyperbole, this suggests that the Athenians were not too kindly disposed towards Aratus.[16]

In any case, the Macedonian guardian at Piraeus, Diogenes, at once despatched orders to Corinth that the Achaean troops should evacuate the city. Aratus received the summons in person and the suitably abashed couriers were sent on their way. Plutarch, somewhat confusingly, also reports that Demetrius sent a ship from Macedonia to bring back the captured Aratus in chains. It is exceedingly unlikely that both stories can be correct, but the end result was the same, as Aratus, annoyed by the Athenians' attitude, mounted a punitive expedition into Attica but turned back when he reached the Academy one mile outside the city walls. The reasons for this are unclear; he could have been driven back by force or perhaps been perturbed by hearing that Bithys was on his way back north.

Demetrius has been seen by some as one of the most inactive Macedonian kings of all time, but this is perhaps unfair and his perceived lack of action is the result of our fragmentary sources.[17] What is certain was that he was unlucky. With Bithys' success and his own in Boeotia, he looked set fair to make some impact in the Peloponnese. But, that bane of Macedonia, a tribal invasion from the north intervened again. This time it was the Dardanians, a tribe on the Thracian and Illyrian borderlands (present day Kosovo) who were the intruders. Called back to deal with it, he was defeated and killed in battle.

Athens, emboldened by news of his death, now felt in a position to expel its enfeebled Macedonian garrison. Aratus, although not *strategos* (Lydiades was), and ill, 'was carried in a litter to help the city in its time of need, and joined in persuading Diogenes, the commander of the garrison, to give up Piraeus,

Munychia, Salamis, and Sunium to the Athenians for 150 talents, twenty of which Aratus contributed himself.'[18] Diogenes, this time, dismissed his troops and Athens was completely free once more for the first time since 294. But, despite accepting Aratus' money and now released from the Macedonian yoke, they refused to join the Achaean League.

> They took no part in the affairs of the rest of Greece, but were profuse in their adulation of all the kings, and chiefly of Ptolemy, consenting to every variety of decree and proclamation, however humiliating, and paid little heed to decency in this respect owing to the lack of judgment of their leaders.[19]

Macedonia's sole remaining ally in the Peloponnese, Aristomachus of Argos, bowed to *force majeure* and finally joined his city to the Achaean League. This happened after some wrangling between Aratus and Lydiades over who should take the credit, and a payment of fifty talents from Aratus so Aristomachus could disband his army. Yet another example of how money greased the palms of so many in these times. Aristomachus fitted himself seamlessly into the League and was predictably made *strategos* the following year, 228.

The League needed all the help it could get as it began to face new foes both to the north and south. The alliance with the Aetolians fell away, the only surprise in this being that they had managed to stay onside for almost ten years. In Macedonia, after Demetrius II's death, Antigonus Doson, grandson of Demetrius Poliorcetes and cousin of his predecessor, took charge as regent for the child king Philip V. He first shored up the crumbling position in the north and then contrived a treaty with the Aetolians in about 228. But the next few years were to transform his fortunes completely as a threat to the Achaean League, gestated in the far south, risked turning the whole of Greek politics upside down. It came from Sparta.

Chapter 2

Converging on Sellasia

Of the heritage that ancient Greece has bequeathed the world, two names stand out: Athens and Sparta. And it is arguable that it is Sparta that resonates the most down the centuries. It did not produce any philosophers or playwrights of note, they did not leave any fine buildings for posterity and, indeed, Sparta is a sad, forlorn and melancholy ruin today. Yet two common words in everyday use, spartan and laconic are familiar from any dictionary. No such vocabulary is available to sum up the essence of being, say, Theban or Athenian. The reason for this is the remarkable society that the Spartans created and their incredible stubbornness at maintaining it against the outside world.[1] In many ways, a byword for cruelty and militarism, equally they have been acclaimed for their heroism. Economically, the early Spartans gloried in their backwardness, using barter and iron bars as currency. The singular ordering of Spartan society have made it a source of fascination over the years for feminists and Marxists alike, and even the crazed ideologues of Nazi Germany. It continues to fascinate up to the present day, and apart from the political dimension, there have been any number of sporting teams called the Spartans who have hoped to catch in the name some of their aura of prowess, strength, and discipline.[2]

Sparta was just another unremarkable Greek settlement in the eighth century. However, it then took the extraordinary decision to permanently annex the neighbouring territory to the west, Messenia, and as a result doubled the land mass it could exploit, and even more remarkably chose to permanently enslave the locals. Both they and the non–Spartan Laconians they had already brought into bondage, now collectively known as helots, were to remain in subjugation for hundreds of years. To cement their new slave empire, far reaching measures both political and military were instituted.[3] Spartan landholding was split into lots (*kleroi*) and each male Spartan citizen was entitled to one. With this allotment went the responsibility to train as a hoplite spearman full time, which was the basis for Sparta's unmatched military reputation in Greece. Helots were attached to the land and expected to do all manual work needed, while the Spartan males lived in military barracks. The number of *kleroi* is unclear, but as the citizens numbered approximately 9,000 at Sparta's peak this presumably corresponds to the number of lots. Apart from this military political elite (*Spartiates*) who alone had the right to vote in the citizen assembly, there were the so called *perioeci*, freemen of Sparta's territory (but not citizens) who received smaller plots of land and carried out the tasks of trade and commerce that full Spartans disdained in order to concentrate on the military life.

The key to the socialising of the full Spartiates was the *agoge*. Young boys were taken from their parents at the age of seven and put into 'herds' where the most promising were groomed for leadership. Progressing satisfactorily at 18, they became reserve members of the Spartan army and at 20 eligible for full military service. Anyone who did not pass the *agoge* was denied citizenship. Even then, only at the age of 30 could they become full citizens, members of the assembly and were allowed to leave the barracks, marry and raise a family. Military service went on to the age of 60 when those who survived might become members of the *gerousia*.

Politically, Sparta also differed, as from the start they had had two kings taken from two separate lines (the Eurypontids and Agiads). Their power was never absolute, diluted by the influence of the Spartan assembly and the *gerousia*, a kind of Spartan senate. This last consisted of the two kings and twenty-eight other male members for life, who had to be more than 60 years of age, from the leading families. The *gerousia's* main purpose appears to have been to introduce proposals to the full assembly, whose powers, although poorly understood, could both veto and approve decisions of the *gerousia* and who elected the *ephors*, who in many ways were the real rulers of Sparta. Five *ephors* were elected by the assembly, each for a year, and they controlled education and the infant selection process. They could even remove one or both of the kings if necessary.

One of the celebrated peculiarities of Spartan societal arrangements was the position of women; they occupied a visible role wholly unlike that enjoyed in any other Greek communities. They were allowed to own property and, most importantly, could inherit land from their father if there was no male heir. Indeed, Aristotle asserts that by the fourth century Spartan women owned nearly two fifths of all land and property.[4] In addition, they exercised full control of their husband's property when they were away at war. Young females of the elite also trained in public like the boys to ensure they attained the physical attributes necessary to produce the next generation of warriors.

All this had been the basis of Spartan military proficiency that had made them such big hitters in the days of the Persian Invasion, the Peloponnesian War and, indeed, the brief period when they themselves held sway over most of south and central Greece. But, the demands of constant war and imperial defence increased the pressure on the state's declining manpower, and actual Spartiates often, except for the major battles, acted more as an officer corps leading forces made up of *perioeci*, helots and allies who might be armed as hoplites, peltasts or light infantry, dependent on need and resources. By the middle of the Peloponnesian War even helots were being recruited and armed as hoplites.

But much had changed in the century and a half since then. One major blow to the system was the loss of the Messenian lands, which had been given their independence after the Spartans' Greek hegemony went down in blood at the hands of the Thebans under Epaminondas in 371. But this was not all. The number of Spartiates had fallen drastically. From perhaps a maximum number of 8,000 to 9,000 at about the time of the Persian Wars, by Agis IV's accession in the 240s it had plummeted to about 700, with the concomitant disastrous consequences for the strength and morale of the armed forces, and, indeed, the *agoge* itself seems to have fallen into disuse over time. There were a number of factors behind this decline in numbers. An economic system originally built on barter had gradually buckled under the influx of gold and silver after the Peloponnesian War. The resultant money economy had led to inevitable inequalities, with land ending up in fewer and wealthier hands. Another factor was the rise in the numbers of Spartans becoming mercenaries and leaving their native land and usually disposing of their *kleros*, which again only tended to concentrate the land in fewer and fewer hands. The attraction of this life was the high wages paid for experienced soldiers in the armies of Egypt and Asia, and the men who went were unlikely to be the rich Spartiates but more probably those who had over the years already mortgaged their *kleros*. Thus, by the 240s not only were there some extremely wealthy men in possession of large tracts of land, there were also a number of wealthy women. Indeed, Plutarch tells us in his life of Agis that 'Now, at this time the greater part of the wealth of Sparta was in the hands of the women, and this made the work of Agis a grievous and difficult one.'[5] This concentration, in turn, led to there being less and less land available for potential Spartiates. Also, by the late third century there were estimated to be something like 2,000 so-called 'inferiors' who for one reason and another were unable to keep up the Spartiate lifestyle, so were no longer available to serve in the ranks of the military elite. King Agis IV who had attained the throne in 245 intended to do something and what he proposed was startling.

What Agis proposed was to cancel all debts and arrange a redistribution of public land into equal allotments. Not only was it intended the land should be allocated to the existing Spartiates and the 'inferiors' but land was also to be given to those *perioeci* who were considered suitable for full Spartan citizenship. By this measure, Agis hoped to have 4,500 *kleroi* and thus the equivalent number of Spartiates, so increasing by more than six fold the existing number of full citizens and soldiers.[6] He also sought the re-imposition of the full *agoge* and its mess system. The question of what the Spartan revolution was really about has exercised many an academic mind as well as inspiring a classic novel.[7] An interesting and vexing problem, but what was certain was that the reaction to Agis' proposals would be fierce. There were too many vested interests to allow them to go through without a colossal fight. At the first attempt, the initial step of debt cancellation was defeated by the very slimmest majority. Opposition had been organized by Agis' co-king Leonidas, but his removal was soon engineered and he fled to exile in Tegea, and, with some further re-jigging of the *ephors*, Agis was able to have his measures passed. But opposition had not ceased, and, if anything, it increased after the cancellation of debts, which may well have suited many Spartans far more then the proposed redistribution of land.

This was the situation when Agis had marched to defend the isthmus line with Aratus against an Aetolian army intent on invading the Peloponnese, egged on by the Macedonians. In this campaign, Agis IV gained no glory as the Spartans were dismissed from the allied army by Aratus without having even come into contact with the enemy. So it was in no great standing that the king returned home to find his reform plans in tatters. Leonidas had had himself restored to the kingship and yet another new set of *ephors* had been installed. Agis found his base would not stand and that he could not compete with the new power in the state. He feared for his life and sought sanctuary in the temple of Athena while his supporters fled the city. But, he did not stay safe for long; he was betrayed, thrown into prison and executed after a show trial.

And there the matter of reform may have stood if it was not for yet another extraordinary Spartan twist in the tail. Although the next five years from 240 to 235 are exceedingly obscure, by the end of this period another remarkable king was to emerge. This was Cleomenes III, the son of Leonidas, but who was married to Agiatis, the widow of Agis IV. Whether, as has been suggested, Cleomenes got his radical ideas from her is unknown, although Plutarch apparently thought so: 'And he, as soon as Agiatis was his, became passionately fond of her, and in a way sympathized with her devotion to the memory of Agis, so that he would often ask her about the career of Agis, and listen attentively as she told of the plans and purposes which Agis had formed.'[8] But, despite all this hyperbole, Plutarch still knew what this revolutionary stuff was all about: the need to increase the pool of warriors. He twins Agis and Cleomenes with the Roman Gracchi who also were essentially 'Tory' reformers who worried that the middling farmers who had traditionally provided the legions that won the wars were in rapid decline. But, at least, in Rome there was an alternative: to militarize the non-property owners and make greater demands on allies for troops. For Sparta, that was not an option; it was from their own ranks they must recreate a large core of national troops or accept virtually complete regional insignificance. Ten thousand of the best soldiers in the world might dominate the Peloponnese, 700 would not, and Sparta was truly reluctant to consider a life as a marginal player in the way Athens had finally been prepared to. Whatever, Cleomenes was to carry the mantle for an even bolder version of Agis' reforms.

Unfortunately, the first six years of Cleomenes' reign from 235 to 229 are again almost a complete blank in terms of information. But, in 229 matters began to really heat up. Argos, one of Sparta's age-old enemies, joined Megalopolis in the Achaean League and the Aetolians allowed Cleomenes to take over three Arcadian towns – Tegea, Orchomenus and Mantinea – in obscure circumstances.[9] Whatever the motive, the acquisition of the towns was strategically significant as possession of them gave Sparta the means to cut off communication between its great foes Argos and Megalopolis.

The stage was set for what was to become known as the Cleomenean War, which was to last from 229 to 222. But, though it was to bear his name, the initial stages were directed by the *ephors*. If true, it shows how Cleomenes' (who by now was probably about 30 years of age) power as king was constrained. In any case, the *ephors* instructed Cleomenes to seize the Athenaeum, a strategically placed fort, which straddled the route from Sparta to Arcadia and was disputed territory, but before Cleomenes' incursion had belonged to Megalopolis. Such an act looked like a declaration of war and the Achaean League duly responded. Aratus, *strategos* once more, tried his old trick of mounting night raids to try and subvert Tegea and Orchomenus. However, his luck was out this time as his partisans in both towns betrayed him and gave notice to Cleomenes of what he had been up to.

The *ephors* now called back Cleomenes to Sparta, presumably because they still wanted to avoid an all-out war. But, it was too late, as in his absence Aratus seized Caphyae, another Arcadian town that had earlier been the subject of an obscure dispute between Sparta, the Aetolian League and the Achaean League. In retaliation, Cleomenes was despatched once more and took over the small Arcadian settlement of Methydrium. But this was only a prelude, as now the Achaeans decided to take decisive action. With Aristomachus, the ex-tyrant of Argos, as *strategos*, the League marched out with an army of 20,000 infantry and 1,000 cavalry in an effort to bring Cleomenes to battle. They converged near Pallantium, somewhere in Arcadia. Cleomenes had only an army of some 5,000 but their reputation was still enough to strike fear into the Achaeans. Allegedly, Aratus, although not *strategos*, dissuaded Aristomachus from fighting, much to the disgust of Lydiades. This sheds an interesting light on Aratus' position in the Achaean League. Prior to the accession of Megalopolis and Argos to the League, he had virtually singlehandedly directed the League's strategy. But, with the powerful ex-tyrants Aristomachus and Lydiades now on board, it was much more difficult for Aratus to get his own way. This is most strikingly shown in the matter of Sparta. It often appears that Aratus' policy was to avoid war with Sparta at any cost, but given Megalopolis' and Argos' age-old attitude to Sparta, this was always going to be a difficult position to maintain. And even given Plutarch's love for a story, the withdrawal at Pallantium does indicate the tensions within the expanded Achaean League.

The next action saw Cleomenes defeat the Achaeans under Aratus at Mount Lycaeum, again in Arcadia. Details are vague but it seems the war had spread to Elis on the western borders of Arcadia where both combatants had been campaigning. Elis had been a Spartan ally and Aratus was in the process of withdrawing from there when he was caught by Cleomenes. The defeat was heavy, with many Achaean losses, but Aratus, after losing his way in the night and once again presumed dead, managed to make some capital out of it by secretly marching to and capturing Mantinea, thus importantly opening up the route from Argos to Megalopolis. From there he marched his men north over the hills to Orchomenus and proceeded to besiege it.

Perhaps the war would have carried on in this comparatively inconsequential tit-for-tat fashion with no great conclusion. Certainly, Aratus' somewhat hesitant approach to the war was matched on the Spartans' side by the seemingly half-hearted attitude of the *ephors* to the conflict as, once more, they recalled Cleomenes after the news from Mantinea. However, two events of moment were to change matters.

First, Cleomenes achieved a victory of great note, having with difficulty persuaded the *ephors* to send him out on campaign again (probably in 227). He determined on a decisive clash with the Achaeans and therefore marched straight for Megalopolis, capturing Leuctra, a fortress seven miles from the city. Aratus responded by coming to the aid of the Megalopolitans, now hard pressed. Cleomenes had drawn up his army not far from the city walls and the Achaeans sallied out and with their light infantry, drove some of the enemy back as far as their own camp. A considerable proportion of the Spartan army were now scattered amongst their own tents, but Aratus would not exploit the advantage and kept the bulk of the army sheltered but quiescent with a ravine between it and the Spartans opposite, ordering his men not to cross.

Lydiades, in front of his own city, was appalled at his leader's lethargy or failure of nerve. Forever at loggerheads with Aratus over the League's policy, now he flagrantly disregarded his orders. While hurling opprobrium at his colleague, he collected all the cavalry he could and launched into a headlong pursuit of the Spartans. He led these squadrons forward against the right wing of the enemy line, which buckled and fled in rout until they reached a small settlement called Ladoceia. Here was 'a place full of vines, ditches, and walls, [Lydiades] had his ranks broken and thrown into disorder thereby, and began to fall into difficulties.'[10] Cleomenes, seeing that Aratus was holding back and that Lydiades was vulnerable, attacked with his Tarentines and Cretans and after a stiff fight they ended defeating Lydiades' men and killing the man himself, almost at the gates of Megalopolis. And, more than this, the surviving men turned and fled, careering back into the main army lines and throwing them into panic and disorder. This inspired the wavering Spartan army, which advanced *en masse* and altogether defeated the Achaeans.

As it turned out, Megalopolis had been saved, but it was at a heavy cost and the death of Lydiades brought further scorn onto the head of Aratus. A hastily convened Achaean assembly, at Aegium, even voted not to give him any more money. Aratus, although 'smarting under this insult, he resolved to give up his seal at once, and resign the office of general, but upon reflection he held on for the present,'[11] once more showing his remarkable resilience. He led a troop of Achaeans to Orchomenus where he defeated a Spartan army under the command of Megistonous, Cleomenes' stepfather, killing 300 and taking him prisoner. However, he must have been quickly ransomed as he was to be prominent in Spartan affairs shortly afterwards.

As for Cleomenes, he could now return to Sparta with at last a substantial military triumph. This success would enable him to begin to make his moves to revolutionize the state. Things had already begun to head in his direction. Shortly before the battle, his fellow King Eudamidas III from the Eurypontid line, apparently still a boy, had died, according to Pausanias, by poisoning at Cleomenes' hands.[12] He now recalled from exile in Messenia, Archidamus, the brother of the late King Agis IV. But the luckless man was assassinated very shortly afterwards. Indeed, it is not even clear whether he reached Sparta or who was behind his murder.[13]

Cleomenes was now ready to make his move. He planned it meticulously; first he approached the ransomed plutocrat Megistonous for support and to prepare the ground. Then, fearful of any possible reaction amongst his Spartan troops he left them on exercise following his victory and sped back to Sparta with a handpicked group of mercenaries whose personal loyalty he could be sure of. Once there, he staged a *coup d'état*, murdering four of the *ephors* (the other one escaped) and prepared to put in place a political programme that promised to outdo anything Agis had ever tried. The office of *ephor* was abolished and the *gerousia* replaced by a new body, the *patronomoi*, whose make up is, however, unclear. Cleomenes also exiled eighty of his leading opponents. As for the office of king, in succession to the murdered Eudamidas III and Archidamus V, he simply appointed his brother Eucleidas. Although this maintained the fiction of two kings, for the first and only time in her history Sparta had two kings from the same Agiad line. Of course, in reality, it was much starker than that because, in effect, Cleomenes was now the sole ruler of Sparta.

As with Agis, all debts were again cancelled and all the land (including that of Cleomenes and his family) was divided into four thousand equal plots. These were distributed not only to the disenfranchised Spartiates but to the most promising candidates of the *perioeci*. The *agoge* was resuscitated under the aegis of the Stoic philosopher Sphaerus who had been Cleomenes' tutor. Sphaerus had been taught in Athens by no less a person than the founder of Stoicism, Zeno of Citium. That Sphaerus, a native of the Bosporus, and the author of more than thirty books, had such a prominent role in Spartan affairs says much for the mongrel tenor of the Cleomenean reforms.[14]

This mongrel nature was to carry over much further into the military reforms because although the *agoge* was to be revivified the army was to be refitted in the most radical fashion. The original army had been based on the Spartiates as the best trained hoplites in Greece fighting in a traditional phalanx, usually eight deep, seconded by large numbers of *perioeci* as hoplites, peltasts or light infantry, and even helots acting as something between servants and skirmishers. They were now to use 'a long pike, held in both hands, instead of a short spear, and to carry their shields by a strap instead of by a fixed handle.'[15] Hundreds of years of Spartan tradition were overthrown and the Macedonian *sarissa* (a very long, heavy pike) somewhat belatedly introduced. Cleomenes' New Model Army with a 4,000 strong phalanx was now a potent tool in his hands, unfettered by any restriction from the *ephors*.

As the campaigning season of 226 opened, the citizens of Mantinea appealed for help to the Spartans. In a surprise night attack, Cleomenes managed to expel the Achaean garrison and restore to the Mantineans their old constitutional rights. According to Polybius, the Mantineans also massacred the garrison, an act which he strongly disapproved of. 'It is not easy to name any greater or more atrocious act of treachery than this. For in resolving to foreswear their friendship and gratitude, they should at least have spared the lives of these men and allowed them all to depart under terms.'[16] Next on the list was Tegea, and then north onto the Achaean city of Pharae. Carrying all before them, Cleomenes and his new army were determined to bring the Achaean League to decisive battle.

This he eventually succeeded in doing, and the Spartans and the Achaean League met in pitched battle at Hecatombaeum near Dyme on the northwest coast of Achaea. The strategies of either side are unclear but the siting of the battlefield suggests that Elis was the main factor; perhaps the Achaeans were invading and Cleomenes was coming to the defence of his allies. Whatever the strategic thinking, the battle was fought in autumn 226 but unfortunately again we have very little detail on the clash. The League forces were commanded by the otherwise unknown *strategos* Hyperbatas. They had camped outside Dyme when Cleomenes arrived on the scene. The Spartans were not willing to camp between the Achaean army and Dyme for fear of being trapped; presumably there must have been another significant force in the city. Instead, they boldly advanced and forced Hyperbatas' Achaeans to fight. The key to the battle was the clash of heavy infantry and in this, its first test, the reformed Macedonian-style phalanx routed the opposition, causing a great many casualties and taking many prisoners.

The aftermath was to prove intriguing. The Achaeans, heavily shaken by their crushing defeat, were in desperate straits and sued for terms. Cleomenes, from his position of strength, demanded no less than being made *strategos* of the League, a demand only slightly ameliorated by the concomitant offer of handing back the prisoners and strongholds he had taken. The League, no doubt playing for time, suggested a conference to discuss terms, to be held in Lerna on the Gulf of Argos probably in January or February 225. What this conference would have settled is a very moot point as it is difficult to envisage Aratus relinquishing his hold on power. In the event, Cleomenes, perhaps conveniently, was taken ill, suffering a haemorrhage after drinking too much water following a strenuous march. Prominent Achaean prisoners were restored but the conference itself was postponed and Cleomenes returned to Sparta to convalesce.

Aratus, though no great general, more than made up for this deficiency by being an astute politician. He had recognized the potential problem of Cleomenes some years back and had, through the offices of Megalopolis, approached, of all people, the Macedonians for an alliance. This has occasioned much surprise and almost as much academic controversy as the Spartan revolutions but, in reality, Aratus had increasingly little choice. A rampant Sparta would have undone all he had tried to achieve in the last few years. The League did not have the military resources to face Cleomenes alone, whereas with Macedonia's help the tables would be reversed. Macedonia, in the person of its king, Antigonus Doson, would extract a price, but it may well be a price worth paying. Megalopolis was chosen as a go-between as it had been a long-standing friend of Macedon. Doson was not unreceptive to their overtures and promised to consider aid if a direct request came from the League. There the matter had rested, but now was the time to try and resuscitate the idea. An embassy, including Aratus' own son, was fitted out and sent once more to Macedonia. Doson again proved far from unfriendly but, this time, laid out the real cost of his alliance; he demanded the Acrocorinth; a price the League was not yet prepared to pay.

It was time for the rearranged conference (spring 225). Whatever the outcome of the Macedonian negotiations, Aratus had reasserted his suzerainty over the League and they began to make demands of Cleomenes prior to the conference. Depending on which Plutarch (Aratus or Cleomenes) you believe, he was told either to come with only 300 men but 'if he was distrustful he should be given hostages by the Achaeans'[17] or to come alone and be given 300 League hostages for his safe conduct, or alternatively meet with the League outside the city at the gymnasium. None of these demands were likely to be ones Cleomenes could accept and an angry and personally insulting exchange of letters ensued between Aratus and Cleomenes before the Spartan king formally declared war. However, it was a high-risk strategy Aratus was maintaining, as the League was not yet sure of the Macedonian alliance and Cleomenes was likely to prove as irresistible as he had at Hecatombaeum.

So it was to prove, as the campaigning season of 225 opened. Cleomenes went straight for the jugular and attacked Aratus' home *polis* of Sicyon, calculating that if he took it the whole League may fall apart, for certainly there appears to have been much disunity within their ranks. Many were unhappy with Aratus' Macedonian strategy, and there also must have been many tempted by Cleomenes' policies in Sparta and hoping that he would do the same for other debt-ridden and land-starved people. Although there was a fifth column in Sicyon, Cleomenes was foiled. It seemed to matter little as he turned west and took Pellene, Pheneus and Penteleum in short order.

Even worse was to follow, for now Cleomenes managed to take Argos. The League, divided amongst itself, had sent out some troops from Argos to Corinth and Sicyon to quell any hint of dissension while the rest of the League was celebrating the Nemean Games. Cleomenes, taking advantage of the revelry, decided to make his move. Leading his army in a night raid, he managed to occupy the southern slopes of the acropolis directly above the theatre. His sudden arrival disconcerted the Argives and he swiftly imposed a garrison. The Argives, never the most enthusiastic members of the Achaean League, agreed to ally themselves with Sparta and gave Cleomenes complete command. Not surprisingly, several modern commentators find this tale from Plutarch a touch implausible as it stands and sense the hand of the ex-tyrant Aristomachus in these shenanigans.[18]

The League was now in chaos. To combat the crisis, Aratus was given plenipotentiary powers. Thus armed, he set off for his home town of Sicyon and promptly executed the ringleaders of the dissidents. From there, he moved on to Corinth where he found the situation very different. Here news that the Acrocorinth was likely to be handed over to Antigonus Doson as a price for his support in the war against Sparta would now have been well known. A crowd of angry Corinthians gathered in the temple of Apollo determined to seize Aratus. It was only with great difficulty that he managed to make his escape and ride off back to Sicyon with just a bodyguard of thirty men. The Corinthians pursued him to no avail but they now decided to offer their city to Cleomenes. But, just as Corinth posed difficulties for Aratus so it did for Cleomenes. To take over Corinth would only hasten the coming of Antigonus, which Cleomenes was understandably anxious to avoid. Furthermore, there was the not inconsequential matter of the Acrocorinth, which was still in the hands of an Achaean garrison. Notwithstanding this, Cleomenes had no real option but to respond and he began to make a rather circuitous way there from Argos, capturing Troezen, Epidaurus and Hermione *en route* to secure the coast of the Argolid.

There was another stab at negotiations with Cleomenes, who seems this time to have instigated them. He sent his stepfather Megistonous to Sicyon with the offer of a sum of money for the surrender of the Acrocorinth. Aratus peremptorily refused and apparently wrote in his memoirs that 'he did not control affairs, but rather affairs controlled him,'[19] remarks of a wily and obfuscating politician. Cleomenes now belatedly entered Corinth and began to invest the Acrocorinth. One final attempt at peace was made when Cleomenes sent a further envoy to Sicyon. The offer this time was slightly different; he proposed that the citadel be jointly garrisoned by the Achaeans and the Spartans and that Aratus be offered 'double the stipend which he was receiving from King Ptolemy.'[20]

The Ptolemy in question was Ptolemy III Euergetes (247–222) who had been sending a subsidy of six talents a year to Aratus. Like his grandfather Ptolemy Soter, he was not averse to fiddling in the affairs of Greece, particularly to the detriment of Macedonia, while making sure he never had to commit himself other than financially. Euergetes' father, Ptolemy Philadelphus, had pledged aid of 150 talents to Aratus back in the heady aftermath of his taking of Sicyon and attaching the *polis* to the Achaean League in 250. Later Euergetes had been elected *hegemon* of the League after the freeing of Corinth in 242. Concomitant with this honour, Euergetes had been paying the stipend but had contributed little else.

In any case, the offer of a private pension of 12 talents a year did not appear to attract Aratus. By now, he must have realized that the only sure way to eliminate Cleomenes and the dangers he posed to the Peloponnese was the Macedonian option, so he chose to refuse the offer. Furious at Aratus' rejection, Cleomenes set off for Sicyon and began to ravage the surrounding countryside and then laid siege to the city itself. The siege was to last for three months. Shortly before it began, Aratus and the League's leaders finally bowed to the inevitable and called for the aid of Antigonus Doson and arranged for the handing over of the Acrocorinth. Aratus even sent his son as one of the hostages that Doson was demanding.

Antigonus Doson was ready and waiting; he had an army of 20,000 foot and 3,000 horse. It was the end of 225; Cleomenes, on hearing the news that Doson's army was on the move, immediately gave up the siege of Sicyon and shifted to the Isthmus of Corinth where he would be better placed to resist the intruder from the north. Antigonus found himself delayed when the intransigent Aetolians refused to let him through the pass at Thermopylae, but he circumvented this by simply sailing round to Euboea.[21] Aratus now ventured out to meet him at Pagae on the Gulf of Corinth. Aratus had been a power now for more than thirty years and he was not looking forward to the meeting.

He had no very great confidence in Antigonus, and put no trust in the Macedonians. For he knew that his own rise to power had been a consequence of the harm he had done to them, and that he had found the first and the chief basis for his conduct of affairs in his hatred towards the former Antigonus [Gonatus]. But seeing how inexorable was the necessity laid upon him in the demands of the hour, to which those we call rulers are slaves, he went on towards the dread ordeal.[22]

In the event, they apparently got on well; they were both hard-headed realists and such was the intimacy and understanding they achieved that at one point, at a banquet where it was cold, they even shared the same blanket to keep warm.

Antigonus, after the convivial summit, marched out to confront the Spartans. Cleomenes had constructed a real Maginot Line of defence south of the Acrocorinth running down over the ridge of Mount Oneion, which forms an east–west barrier against any direct route from the isthmus. The defences were designed to block access to invaders coming down the Megara road, and Cleomenes further secured the gap by putting in palisades and a trench. On the other side, west of the Acrocorinth, there were fifth-century defensive walls running down to the port of Lechaeum, on the Gulf of Corinth side that blocked off any infiltration north of Corinth itself.

It was an extremely effective defence and managed to withstand Doson for some time and, indeed, he lost men trying to force his way past Lechaeum. At one point, he was contemplating transporting his troops across the gulf to Sicyon, a potentially time consuming and hazardous undertaking. However, salvation was at hand. A delegation from Argos arrived asking for help from Aratus as they were disillusioned with Cleomenes' takeover of the city. An illustration that Cleomenes' ideas of emancipating the poor did not stretch much beyond Sparta for 'the multitude were easy to persuade, being incensed because Cleomenes had not brought about the abolition of debts which they expected.'[23] Aratus, with 1,500 Antigonid troops, sailed over to Epidaurus to approach Argos from the east behind Cleomenes' line. But events moved quickly and before Aratus could arrive a revolt began. The Argives besieged the Spartan garrison in Argos' citadel, the Larissa, and help also arrived from Sicyon where Timoxenus, the *strategos* of the Achaean League, brought over a force. Cleomenes, suitably alarmed, despatched 2,000 men under Megistonous, while himself remaining at the isthmus line. Disaster was to follow as Megistonous was defeated and killed in battle. Cleomenes was now in something of a cleft stick; to abandon the isthmus would be to give a virtually free hand to Antigonus Doson. On the other hand, the loss of the beleaguered garrison at Argos would open the road to Sparta, which Cleomenes had left undefended. The latter option was too awful to contemplate, and Cleomenes reluctantly abandoned his position at Corinth and returned south to Argos. His worst fears were soon realized as Antigonus quickly moved in, garrisoned Corinth, and took over the Acrocorinth as had been promised him.

As for Cleomenes, he had moved his forces by night and with some difficulty scaled the walls of Argos and made contact with his garrison. He had some further success at regaining part of Argos using his mercenary Cretan archers to clear the streets and retake control. But, it was all to be in vain, as when he saw Antigonus and his phalanx entering the Argive plain fresh from their success at Corinth he realized the game was up. He retreated back to Sparta. Cleomenes, in just a few months, had gone from being virtually supreme master of the Peloponnese back to just another king of Sparta.

If this was not bad enough, worse was to follow, for as he was on his way back to Sparta, news was brought to him that his wife Agiatis had died. The ex-wife of Agis, she had clearly been a profound influence on him and his ideas and there is no reason to doubt their depth of feeling for each other. Dejected, he prepared to winter in Sparta and, in his present predicament, decided to seek help from Ptolemy, who by now must have ended his stipend to Aratus now that he was in cahoots with Macedon. He listened but demanded hostages as the price of his support. They were not just any old hostages either but Cleomenes' mother and children. After some hesitation they were packed off to Egypt, a decision that would have ramifications for Cleomenes' own future.

As for Antigonus Doson, he was not idle. Arriving at Argos, he arrested their erstwhile tyrant Aristomachus, no doubt with the approval of Aratus, for taking Argos back into the Spartan fold. Aristomachus was led to Cenchreae and racked to death there and his body subsequently thrown into the sea, an act which provoked some criticism for its apparent illegality.[24] Going on to dismantle the forts Cleomenes had imposed on the area, he retired to his own winter quarters near Sicyon. At about the same time he attended the meeting of the Achaean League at Aegium where he was elected *hegemon*, a position previously held by Ptolemy Euergetes. But Antigonus had grander designs than being a mere figurehead and during the winter break formulated plans for a new organization. This was to be a Symmachy (alliance) comprising not just the Macedonians and Achaean League but the Epirotes, Acarnanians, Boeotians, Phocians and possibly the Locrians as well. Although each constituent was to retain its own independence and autonomy, matters of peace and war were to be dealt with by a council, with Antigonus Doson as its president and commander in chief.

As the campaigning season of 224 opened, the situation looked bleak for Cleomenes. He was surrounded by hostile and numerically superior forces. A negotiated settlement was now out of the question and the presence of Macedonia indicated that a solution to the problem of Sparta was going to be bloodily found once and for all. Cleomenes was in desperate straits and needed both troops and money. His solution was to offer helots their freedom but at a price. They had to be able to afford five Attic *minas*, and apparently 6,000 of them did so. Cleomenes, now flush with 500 talents, promptly armed 2,000 in the 'Macedonian fashion' for incorporation into the new-style phalanx. This bold act of manumission has occasioned some debate both on financial and ideological grounds, but Cleomenes seems to have acted solely for military reasons.[25]

Meanwhile, Antigonus had taken control of Tegea only to find that Orchomenus had risen up in his rear and was supporting Cleomenes by sending him troops. Hurrying back, he took Orchomenus by assault and then attacked the Mantineans, who had, of course, in 226, previously handed themselves over to the Spartans and massacred their Achaean garrison. The Symmachy's response was brutal, with the male population either being executed or sold into slavery. Aratus also arranged for its name to be changed to Antigoneia, an appellation it was to bear for several centuries until Hadrian changed it back again in the second century AD. Aratus' treatment of Mantinea aroused some controversy for our main sources. Plutarch saw it as 'neither necessary nor honourable, and cannot be excused.'[26] Polybius, an Achaean remember, took a somewhat different view, feeling that the Mantineans had committed the 'most heinous crimes' when they had slaughtered the Achaean garrison. The response in his view was very moderate 'while nothing more serious befell the Mantineans, in this their hour of calamity, than the pillage of their property and the enslavement of the male citizens.'[27]!

Antigonus and his forces now moved on and took control of two further Arcadian towns, Heraea and Telphusa, where the citizens, no doubt, noting the example of Mantinea, quickly surrendered. Winter was approaching, but it had been a good season for Antigonus and his Achaean allies, although it is noticeable they never seem to have felt strong enough to directly attack Sparta. Even so, it must have been with quiet satisfaction that he discharged most of his Macedonian troops back home. He himself remained in the Peloponnese and settled in Aegium where he could discuss future plans in council with his new allies.

His repose was to be rudely shattered. Cleomenes had been conspicuously quiet during the last campaigning season, only seemingly strengthening his forces in the redoubt that was Sparta. Now he struck in devastating fashion. Knowing that most of Antigonus' troops were in winter quarters, he set out to capture the old Spartan *bête noire*, Megalopolis. Equipping his men with five days' rations, he set off towards Sellasia, hoodwinking his enemy into thinking he was about to attack Tegea, but then veering off to the west to strike at Megalopolis. He was outside the walls in little more than a day and a night, an impressive feat given both the distance (approximately fifty miles) and the season. Despatching two divisions of his troops to the weakest part of the walls, he soon found himself within the precincts of the surprised city. However, all but a thousand of the citizens managed to make their escape to Messene. Negotiations followed, and the upshot was that an offer was sent to the Megalopolitans in Messene, offering to give back the city if they agreed to desert the Achaean League and side with the Spartans.

Even with the impending wreck of their city, the Megalopolitans must have known which way the wind was blowing and refused. The leader who refused Cleomenes was one Philopoemen, a man we shall hear much of in the future. His argument for rejecting the offer was quite sophisticated:

Philopoemen, seeing that the citizens would be glad to accept the offer and were eager to go back home, opposed and dissuaded them from it, showing them that Cleomenes was not so much offering to restore their city as he was trying to win over to himself its citizens, that so he might have the city also more securely in his possession; for he would not be able, Philopoemen said, to remain there and guard empty houses and walls, but the solitude would force him to abandon these also. By this speech Philopoemen diverted the citizens from their purpose.[28]

The refusal, which probably did not surprise Cleomenes, nevertheless infuriated him, and he immediately took revenge. The treasures of Megalopolis, its statues and pictures, were sent off to Sparta and he then completely demolished most of the standing buildings, leaving it uninhabitable. However, as Philopoemen had correctly surmised, the city without citizens was of scant use to Cleomenes, and he had little option but to withdraw and to return to Sparta.

Such vandalism came as a great shock and surprise to the Achaeans and Macedonians holed up in Aegium. A weeping Aratus told them the news at an assembly, and the outrage felt by many spurred on an attempt at reprisals against the Spartans. Antigonus tried to call in his forces from winter quarters but soon realized there was not enough time. Emboldened, Cleomenes now ventured out once more, this time to attack Argos.

Cleomenes and his troops laid waste to the countryside around Argos and finally up to the walls of the city itself. The effect was to make the inhabitants of the Argolid furious with Doson for his lack of action; 'but he, like a true general and prince, paid no attention to anything but a wise conduct of affairs, and remained quiet, while Cleomenes, having carried out his intention of devastating the country and thus striking terror into the enemy and encouraging his own troops to face the coming danger, retired in safety to his own country.'[29] In reality, all Cleomenes had achieved was to antagonize the inhabitants of the Peloponnese, and though he was clearly able to ravage where he wanted to, he was desperately short of allies, as his rebuff by the Megalopolitans had shown all too painfully.

Doson now recalled all his troops from winter quarters and together with his Greek allies amassed a considerable army. He had 10,000 phalangites comprising of two corps, the Bronze Shields (the *Chalkaspides*) and the White Shields (the *Leukaspides*). The exact difference between these two units is unclear, though the bronze shields seem to have been an elite division. In addition, he had 3,000 Macedonian peltasts and 300 horse. His mercenary allies consisted of 1,000 Agrianian light infantry and slingers and the same number of Celtic mercenary swordsmen. After their arrival in about 280, they had become a popular source of mercenaries. Most were javelineers with a characteristic long slashing sword, fighting protected by only a long oval-shaped body shield. Not well disciplined but ferocious, with wild, lime-slicked hair, their initial onrush could be devastating. He had another 3,000 assorted mercenaries and 300 cavalry. As for the Achaean League contingent, this comprised 3,000 elite infantry and 300 horse. There were also 1,000 Megalopolitans (presumably ravenous for revenge) who were 'armed in the Macedonian manner'. There were 2,000 Boeotian foot and 200 horse, 1,000 Epirote foot and fifty horse, an equivalent number of Acarnanians, and finally, 1,600 Illyrians under the command of the rising star, Demetrius of Pharos. How these various infantry were armed is debatable but many would have been so-called *thureophoroi*, who seem to have operated in a role intermediate between skirmishers and the phalanx. The shield that gave them their name was based on the Celtic body shield style, suggesting they were certainly capable of hand-to-hand fighting. They often supported light troops and seemed to be capable of operating in a similar manner to peltasts. All told, Antigonus Doson had a force comprising 27,600 infantry and 1,200 horse; a formidable array indeed, though it is noticeable how few cavalry he had to field.

Cleomenes began to prepare for the assault as best he could. Worse news was to follow as, apparently, ten days before the final battle his paymaster Ptolemy III Euergetes withdrew his subsidies. The account, which derives from Phylarchus, is confusing. On the one hand, he says that this was a massive blow because it meant he would not be able to pay his troops, who might desert. Yet Phylarchus also says that Cleomenes had 6,000 talents from the 'booty' of Megalopolis, which would have ensured he could well afford to fund his army.[30] Whatever the case, Antigonus had been in negotiations with Ptolemy, and the Macedonian pharaoh was surely beginning to realize that backing Sparta against Macedonia and virtually the rest of Greece was not the best use of his money.[31]

Cleomenes decided to stand just north of Sparta at Sellasia. Here, less than a day's march on the Tegean road, was a place that bestrode the main route to the home polis. Cleomenes, showing all his undoubted military talent, chose the strongest possible defensive position. Just north of Sellasia, the River Oinous valley is narrow and the main north-south thoroughfare to Sparta runs alongside the river bank. Overlooking this position were two large hills, Evas to the west and Olympus to the east. Cleomenes sent detachments of his forces to blockade the mountain passes but chose to make his stand on these hills. On Evas, his brother and fellow king, Eucleidas, was posted together with the left flank of the Spartan army. This consisted of the *perioeci* phalangites and what allies he had, whilst on Olympus, Cleomenes took station with the Spartan phalanx and mercenaries. Why Cleomenes split his troops between the two hills in this way is something of a minor mystery and perhaps betrays a lack of faith in his brother's judgement. Both hills were fortified with ditches and palisades whilst down below on the valley floor he posted his cavalry and skirmishers.

Altogether, he had 20,000 troops, a little more than two thirds of Doson's force, but he hoped that his defensive position might yet mitigate this disparity. They not only provided almost impregnable positions but, as they were not mountains but hills with smooth slopes, they also allowed the possibility of downhill charges against the enemy and, if these were used, they might catch Doson in a pincer movement if he tried to force the issue. The troops in the valley floor also meant that the Macedonians and their allies would have difficulty driving their way through, and with the mountain passes covered to prevent outflanking it must have seemed an almost impregnable position. But Cleomenes' main weakness was that of time and how long he could maintain an army there before lack of pay might mean his troops deserting.

This was the situation Antigonus Doson was faced with as he brought his almost 30,000-strong army up the valley. He chose to encamp himself on high ground opposite Olympus with a small river, the Gorgylus, to protect his front. Here matters stood for several days while he tried to provoke the Spartans out of their strong position and attempted to find out the exact details of their deployment. But, like Cleomenes, Antigonus Doson did not have limitless time to spare. He had pressing matters to deal with back in Macedonia and his allies and mercenaries, like those of his foe, were likely to become restless and desert. Accordingly, he realized he had to attack and began to draw up a battle plan. It was July 222.

The plan was carefully thought through. It was decided his right flank would lead the assault on Evas, the smaller hill. Here, Doson placed his best troops, the Bronze Shields phalanx, 5,000 of them. But, instead of being in their usual formation, their lines were interspersed with Illyrian troops under Demetrius of Pharos. This arrangement was designed to give some flexibility to the usual rigid phalanx formation as it advanced up the hill.[32] Behind this line, which apparently was almost 800 yards wide, the second line consisted of the Acarnanians, Epirote and Boeotian forces and was 500 yards wide, while in reserve stood 2,000 Achaean infantry. The whole flank, comprising 12,600 men, was under the overall command of one Alexander.

The centre, occupying the valley floor, comprised Doson's cavalry supported by the remaining 1,000 Achaean infantry and the 1,000 Megalopolitans. They had a frontage of 400–500 yards and were commanded by another Alexander. The left flank, which would try and take on Cleomenes and his entrenchment on Olympus, was commanded by Doson himself. It was drawn up in a different fashion to the right flank. Here at the front were the Agrianian light infantry and slingers, 1,000 strong; immediately behind them came the remaining mercenaries, including the Celtic contingent. Then finally, the remainder of the Macedonian phalanx, the White Shields, drawn up 'in two phalanxes with no interval between, the narrowness of the space rendering this necessary.'[33]

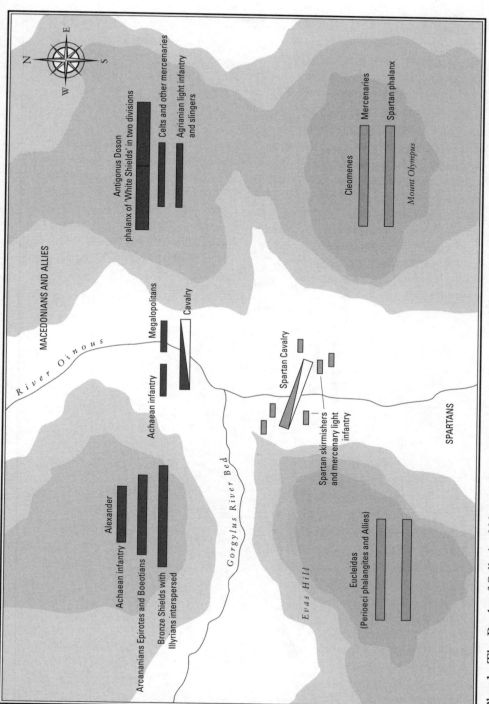

Plan 1: The Battle of Sellasia, 222 BC, initial dispositions.

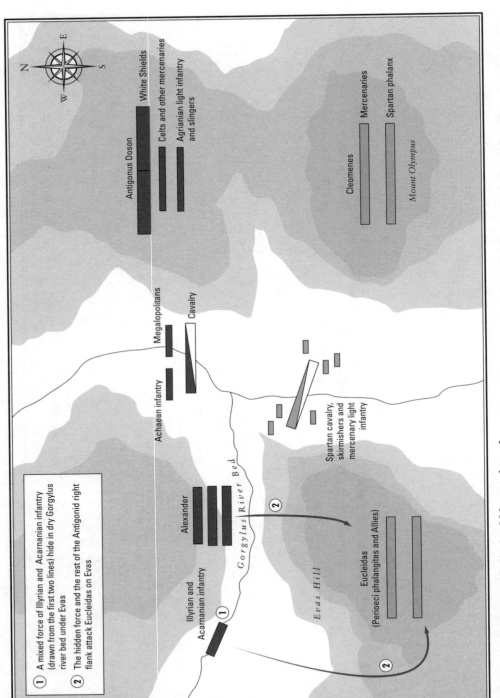

Plan 2: The Battle of Sellasia, 222 BC, phase 1.

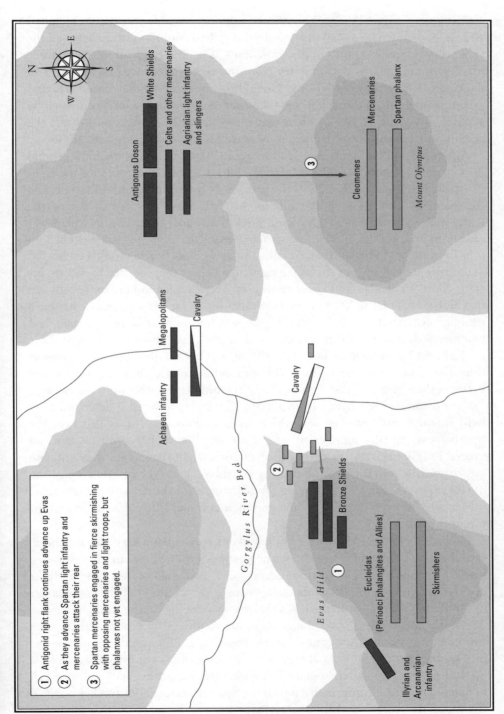

Plan 3: The Battle of Sellasia, 222 BC, phase 2.

The following labels appear within the figure:

N E S W (compass rose)

White Shields
Celts and other mercenaries
Agrianian light infantry and slingers
Antigonus Doson

Mercenaries
Spartan phalanx
Cleomenes
Mount Olympus

③

Megalopolitans
Cavalry
Achaean infantry

Cavalry

Bronze Shields
②
Eucleidas (Perioeci phalangites and Allies)
Skirmishers
①
Evas Hill
Illyrian and Arcananian infantry

Gorgylus River Bed

① Antigonid right flank continues advance up Evas
② As they advance Spartan light infantry and mercenaries attack their rear
③ Spartan mercenaries engaged in fierce skirmishing with opposing mercenaries and light troops, but phalanxes not yet engaged.

Antigonus, together with his officers, who presumably must have included Aratus, had drawn up a plan that required excellent communication between the three very different strands of his battle line.[34] The first requisite was for a force of Illyrian and Acarnanian infantry from the right flank to go under cover of darkness and occupy the dry Gorgylus riverbed under Evas. Having accomplished this, the attack in the following morning was to be coordinated by a series of signals. A flag of linen was to be waved by Antigonus to start the assault on Evas and a red flag was to be waved to signal the centre to advance.

Antigonus, on his flank, managed to get his troops on to some high ground in preparation for the assault on Olympus and then gave the signal for the right to attack. Eucleidas, on Evas, saw the previously hidden column of Illyrians and Acarnanians advancing up the hill on his left, while the remainder of the Antigonid right flank was advancing directly towards him. Doson's plan was clearly to attack Evas and pin down Cleomenes on Olympus, to prevent him offering support to his brother. At first, things went well as his troops on his left and centre moved up, but they then came to a halt as they awaited events on his right. Here, Eucleidas could have torn down his palisades and ordered an all-out downhill attack on the Antigonids. However, this he failed to do and he has been roundly criticized for it. In reality, he was outnumbered two to one and commanded much weaker troops, and a reckless charge may well have precipitated his immediate downfall. But he was not totally helpless, because as the right flank of the enemy inexorably ground up towards him, a gap appeared between their rear and the right of the Antigonid centre, who were still waiting for the command to engage from Doson. Eucleidas ordered a detachment of light infantry and mercenaries, which were stationed in the centre near the Spartan cavalry (the number of whom are not known but probably did not exceed 1,000), to attack the rear of the Antigonid right flank. This they did with gusto, pouring into the gap and causing considerable mayhem. From a position of real exposure, Eucleidas now had the advantage, for the Antigonid right flank was caught between the light infantry in their rear and Eucleidas' troops on the top of the hill.

Disaster loomed for the whole Antigonid enterprise, but a hero was at hand to save the day. This was Philopoemen, the young Megalopolitan. In his first major battle, he was to prove a headstrong commander. Stationed in the centre with the cavalry and his own Megalopolitans, he brought the attention of the commander of the centre, Alexander, to the crisis that was developing on the Antigonid right. Alexander apparently ignored him due to his youth and lack of experience and continued to wait for Antigonus' signal. Frustrated, Philopoemen took matters into his own hands and led a charge of his Megalopolitan contingent against the Spartan cavalry. Alexander, upon realising what was happening, had no option but to follow suit. The ensuing melee forced the Spartan mercenaries and light-armed troops, off the rear of the Antigonid right, to come to the aid of the Spartan horse.

The end result of Philopoemen's charge was that Eucleidas was now doomed. Freed from the assault on their rear, the Bronze Shield phalanx and the Illyrians continued their remorseless climb to the summit. Meanwhile, the Acarnanian and Illyrian infantry had now broken into the rear of the Spartan position on Evas. The hapless Eucleidas and his troops were in chaos, caught with no means of retreat, and were massacred as they tried to flee down precipitous ground.

Elsewhere, the cavalry battle in the centre on the valley floor was raging fiercely, with the light-armed infantry and mercenaries of both sides embroiled. Philopoemen was heavily involved; his horse was killed from under him but he continued the fight on foot. Plutarch tells us that a thronged javelin pierced both his thighs and how Philopoemen reacted:

> now that the battle was at its hottest, the ardour of his ambition made him impatient to join in the struggle, by moving his legs backward and forward he broke the shaft of the weapon in two in the middle, and then ordered each fragment to be drawn out separately.[35]

A frankly incredible story but, miracles of medicine aside, inspired by such apparent heroism, the Antigonid centre gradually pushed back its Spartan counterpart. After the battle, Antigonus queried why the cavalry had gone into action without orders. On being told by Alexander, that Philopoemen 'had begun it contrary to his own judgement, the king said that this stripling in grasping the situation had acted like a good general and Alexander himself, the general, like an ordinary stripling.'[36] Philopoemen's reputation was made and, not surprisingly, he was marked down for future Macedonian service.

Meanwhile, where the battle might have been expected to have been settled, between the two leaders, Antigonus Doson and Cleomenes, very little seems to have happened. The light-armed troops and mercenaries on both sides had become involved in fierce skirmishing but the phalanxes had not engaged. Cleomenes was now, however, becoming seriously alarmed at what appeared to be happening on Evas and the losses in his centre. He proceeded to one last desperate gamble and instructed his troops to tear down the palisades on the top of Olympus and prepare to charge downhill into the face of the Antigonids. He was about to do what his brother had so signally failed to do. At last, in action, the Spartan phalanx, 16 deep, clashed with the Macedonian phalanx, 32 deep, on a frontage of approximately 300 yards. The impact of the Spartan phalanx crashing downhill on to the Macedonians can only be imagined. The impetus of their descent gave them the initial advantage and, fighting not only for their own lives but the very future of Sparta and its glorious military heritage, they forced the Macedonians to give way.

The carnage was appalling and Antigonus must have become seriously alarmed that his seeming triumph on the other flank and centre might come to

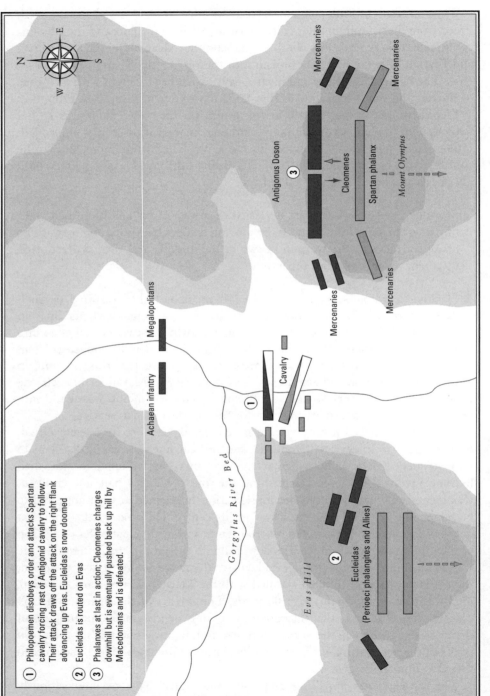

1. Philopoemen disobeys order and attacks Spartan cavalry forcing rest of Antigonid cavalry to follow. Their attack draws off the attack on the right flank advancing up Evas. Eucleidas is now doomed

2. Eucleidas is routed on Evas

3. Phalanxes at last in action; Cleomenes charges downhill but is eventually pushed back up hill by Macedonians and is defeated.

Megalopolitans

Achaean infantry

Cavalry

Gorgylus River Bed

Evas Hill

Eucleidas (Perioeci phalangites and Allies)

Mercenaries

Mercenaries

Mount Olympus

Spartan phalanx

Cleomenes

Antigonus Doson

Mercenaries

Mercenaries

Mercenaries

N E S W

Plan 4: The Battle of Sellasia, 222 BC, phase 3.

naught. But the Spartan momentum eventually slackened as they had to push the Macedonians uphill, and Antigonus, seeing his chance, gave the order for the phalanx to close ranks. This meant closing up into the tightest possible formation with locked shields. The double phalanx was now only 16 deep with each soldier shoulder to shoulder with his neighbour and a frontage of approximately two feet per man. This was a formation usually used in defence and in retreat, but here Doson had other plans.

Propelled by their iron sense of discipline, the Macedonians gradually but inevitably forced the Spartans back up the hill. Each Spartan was now effectively faced by two Macedonians and the effect on their morale must have been catastrophic, especially as they knew the game was up elsewhere on the battlefield. Doson, competent commander that he was, ordered the victorious Illyrians and light infantry, from his right flank, to fall on the back of the retreating Spartan phalanx. Cleomenes and his comrades were done for and the battle ended in complete massacre, with only 200 of the 6,000 strong phalanx surviving, though these did include Cleomenes, himself, who escaped to Egypt.[37]

As for Sparta, Antigonus Doson entered the city in triumph. This was an extraordinary achievement, as no foreign conqueror had ever done so before; not Philip II, Alexander or Pyrrhus. But Doson did not act like an all-conquering warlord; he stayed only a couple of days and treated the city leniently. The *ephors* were restored, the kingship put in abeyance, but he does not seem to have messed unnecessarily with many of Cleomenes' reforms. He was not totally without spite, however, as he installed a governor, Brachyllas, who was from Thebes, a city which had a long history of antagonism to Sparta.

On leaving Sparta, Doson visited Tegea, restored its old form of government and then moved on to Argos to celebrate the Nemean Games in July or August 222. But he did not have long to savour the festivities and all the honours for his famous victory that were no doubt being showered upon him. News arrived of an invasion of Macedonia by the Illyrians, and he had to rush back home to confront them. He was again victorious on the battle field but, during the course of the action, he ruptured a blood vessel, apparently by shouting too strenuously at his troops. Already suffering from consumption, he managed to get back to Pella, but died some months later, probably in the summer of 221.

Beginning with Plutarch, it has not infrequently been suggested that Cleomenes was unlucky and, if he could have survived a little longer, he might have developed a reformed Sparta that could have endured as a key regional power. While containing some elements of truth, this does not take into account the problems Cleomenes would always have had to face. He may have instituted radical reforms at Sparta, but he never seems to have had any serious intention of exporting them elsewhere. The reason for this apparent disinclination to disseminate the social medicine with which he dosed his own people is not hard to find. The aim of the reforms was to militarily reinvigorate Sparta and the last thing he wished for his neighbours was that their armed forces should experience such a fillip, when so many had been rivals in the past and might again be in the future. And, because of this, he experienced the worst of both worlds. He was hated by those who thought he threatened their property while the poor and dispossessed were almost always disappointed in his failure to export the social reforms put in place in Sparta.

Indeed, another 'what if' is perhaps more interesting. Antigonus Doson was only in his mid-forties when he died. By all accounts, he seems to have excelled both in battle and diplomacy and, if he had survived for another generation, he may have been able to position both his own kingdom and his allies in Greece to bat off, or at least absorb with fewer traumas, the intrusion of belligerent Italians from the west.

Chapter 3

Another League

Apart from the Achaeans, another League began a process whereby mountain people of little apparent account became the dominant power of central Greece. Backward, but dangerous, was the common perception of these Aetolians to contemporaries, but then our sources are city folk who are always worried by hill men with strange dialects and different ways of life. Snobbery is at the heart of much history, and the Aetolians, who could be dismissed by Thucydides as raw meat eaters, suffered from this at least until and even beyond the time their efforts against the Galatian attack on Delphi in 279 gave them a new found respectability.

The Aetolian people originally comprised five tribes living around Lake Trichonis and Lake Agelokastro (Lake Lysimachia), who worshipped at the common Sanctuary of Thermus. This temple to Apollo was central to the identity of the people, situated as it was on the border of the lowland and high pasturage where the arable and herding communities comingled. And the organisation of religious ceremony and the accompanying games and markets at Thermus probably acted as something of a state in embryo, kick-starting the process that ended in the Aetolian League as a great power.

When this people organized themselves into a federal League is something of a controversy, but certainly an Athenian decree and a reference in Diodorus suggests the polity was in place at the latest by the 360s.[1] A Spartan who attacked them referred to the Aetolians as shepherds, and everybody emphasized that they beat off the Gauls by harassing tactics, not by fighting properly in stand-up hoplite style. Many certainly must have been shepherds and goatherds; there was little arable farming in the narrow upland valleys, but from the beginning, there were urban communities. By the 280s a number of towns are mentioned in the Achelous valley and around Lake Trichonis. This became even more the case when the League came to dominate the north side of the Corinthian Gulf, where a number of sizable port towns flourished, a process confirmed by an increasing ability to field more hoplites and cavalry. Not that that meant they could not, when necessary, use guerrilla tactics intelligently; even at the time of the Social War, Polybius still claims they were generally equipped and trained for irregular warfare.

Whatever arms they carried or manoeuvres they practised, it was these Aetolians in arms that at two annual assemblies, one in spring and one in autumn, took the key decisions of state; although a *boule* of several hundred with its own subcommittees saw to the ticking over of League affairs between the convocations. The constituent towns retained their own local institutions and each sent annually–elected representatives to the *boule* in rough proportion to their population. Yet, it was still the assembly of warriors that took the final decisions on war and foreign affairs. Aetolian expansion had seen them become more and more important in the Amphictionic League over the third century, and beyond this organisation for the maintenance of sanctuaries and cults (Delphi in particular), their ascendancy leached down to the northern shore of the Gulf of Corinth. By 330 they controlled Oeniadae at the mouth of the gulf and by 280 Naupactus, giving them effective control of what Strabo called 'acquired Aetolia'.

And, more than this march south, there was a push to the east in the era of Antipater and Cassander, when Aetolian armies had frequently closed the road at the 'hot gates' against Macedonian warlords. With the crumbling of the northern kingdom and the Celtic invasions in the first decades of the third century, the possibility of entrenching their power across the whole of central Greece began to be appreciated. The Dolopes and the Ainis joined the League in the 270s, bringing the Aetolians very close to the Malian Gulf. Doris acceded at about the same time and some Malians were officials of the League only a few years later. Heraclea Trachinia was Aetolian by 280; Locris, south of the gulf, joined in the 260s. So by the time Antigonus Gonatas was secure at the tiller in Pella, the Aetolians had a hand clamped across the routes to his garrisons at Corinth and Piraeus. With the death of Demetrius in 229, Macedonia underwent another crisis and allowed the League to push as far as Phthiotis, pressing the leaders there to join the League. Even places in south Thessaly, like Pharsalus, adhered by the 220's, and the League's influence was felt as far as the boundary country around Larissa.

The problems this threw up for the Macedonians were shown when the Aetolians refused to allow Doson to march through Thermopylae in 225; apart from the oppressive reality that now Aetolian Malian Gulf strongholds were almost cheek by jowl with the great Macedonian foundation at Demetrias. After Sellasia, with Corinth back in Macedonian hands and the whole of Greece very much in the sights of the government at Pella, the interaction of the northern kingdom with the Aetolian League was likely to be very fraught indeed. But it was these pushy newcomers that ratcheted up the temperature, not the kingdom of Philip and Alexander. The death of Antigonus Doson looked to the Aetolian leaders like a golden opportunity to destabilize the post-Sellasian settlement.

The changeover of Macedonian monarch had prompted an eclipse in their regional influence in the past, so the Aetolians could expect it to be the case this time again. Surely, this is the only answer to the question of why the Aetolians, who seemed to have so much to lose, did so much to bring on war with so many of their neighbours. Suggestions that they were just a knee-jerk brigand state is as incredible as a recent account that proposed that they were sort of proto-pacifists who attempted good relationships with everybody around but were put upon by a confrontational Achaea and Macedonia.[2] The truth is probably something different. Even if some of the belligerent activity before the outbreak of war was not necessarily official and was carried out by proxies – the wall between peace and war was pretty porous at this time – the extent of Aetolian bellicosity cannot be hidden.

The Aetolians were not fools or mindless pirates; they knew the realities. They did not anticipate an early response from Philip V, and to place a restraint on Messene and establish a position of influence in the central highlands of the Peloponnese warranted the gamble. The places they visited with fire and sword – Cleitor, Caphyae and Cynaetha – were important, because from there they could menace Achaea, in the hope that this fragile vessel might fall apart. Equally, they would be well positioned to combine with the likes of Elis and Sparta.

So now the death of Doson saw Aetolian agents making their presence felt. Phigaleia, twenty odd miles northwest of Messene, on the banks of the River Neda, had been an Aetolian ally since 244, and here a young and ambitious Aetolian, called Dorimachus, began stirring the pot. He was intent on putting pressure on the Messenians, sending men in the summer of 221 to raid their cattle, despite the supposedly general peace. This was intimidation with the intention of bringing Messene into the anti-Achaean camp. The Messenian leaders sent people to Dorimachus to complain about this behaviour and the brazen man even visited the city to discuss the matter, but, while he talked peace, his gang continued to raid the farms of eminent local bigwigs. What Dorimachus' official position was at the time is opaque, but afterwards there is no lack of clarity. He returned to Aetolia to try and persuade his compatriots to make an alliance with Elis and Sparta and to undertake an attack on Messene in real earnest.

But, while the Aetolians were flexing their muscles in an effort to bring waverers on board in the Peloponnese, there was another League that was prepared to push from the other side. Aratus and his colleagues had been stirred and they intended to get the Symmachy underway to put a stop to Aetolian attempts to dislocate the post-Sellasia balance in the peninsula. This Aetolian leadership now chartered out some privateers who evidently cut out and captured a few Macedonian warships they discovered at Cythera, an island off the southern coast of Laconia. Then when they returned, they met up with a squadron of Cephalonian allies and descended on both the coasts of Epirus and Acarnania. Other Aetolian agents heated up some frontier squabbles in the Peloponnese; a small force sent from Aetolia captured the fort of Clarion in the territory of Megalopolis and used it as a base for marauding. The Achaeans responded well enough on this occasion, and with forces brought by Taurion, the Macedonian officer in charge of Orchomenus and presumably Corinth, they besieged the place. At the changeover of the Achaean *strategos*, Dorimachus and Scopas, hoping to take advantage of the hiatus, crossed from Aetolia to Rhium with an army and advanced past the Achaean cities of Patrae and Pharae with the aim of getting to Phigaleia. They still hoped at this time not to make their actions a cause for open war, but could not stop the men from pillaging as they went. After this they turned on the Messenians once more.

In this fraught and difficult atmosphere, the Achaean assembly met at Aegium in 220. The city leaders of Patrae and Pharae brought complaints about their treatment by the Aetolians, and the Messenians too came to implore help against the raiders who were tormenting the people in the countryside around the town, even offering to commit themselves to the Symmachy. But the Achaeans were too worried about their own lack of military readiness to risk immediate war, and it was decided to refer to the full Symmachy assembly the Messenian request to be admitted to the alliance. Aratus, though, at least, was decisive and began to mobilize an army at Megalopolis and he agreed to offer immediate help if Messene consented to leave hostages to ensure they would not, under pressure, renege and come to terms with Aetolians. Aratus now sent envoys to demand the Aetolians desist from raiding Messene and, as they were outnumbered, Scopas and Dorimachus initially concurred. They left for Elis with their booty while Aratus demobilized the main army, only keeping 3,000 foot, 300 horse and Taurion's Macedonians under arms. From Megalopolis, Aratus led his men to Patrae to track the Aetolians. Dorimachus was heading to Rhium now, but when he heard Aratus was nearby he was anxious he might be attacked as he embarked so pulled back to Olympia where he could better defend himself. But, in a few days, Aratus' comparative inaction caused the Aetolians to regain their confidence and they decided to drive away the troops who were threatening them. As Taurion, with his Macedonian forces, was then at Cleitor, the Aetolians advanced to Methydrium in Megalopolitan territory, sitting at a road junction that led south to Megalopolis, east to Mantinea and north to Orchomenus. This dancing round each other in the central highlands of the Peloponnese seemed to be leading nowhere until incompetence by one of the parties engineered a way out of the deadlock:

> The Achaean commanders, when they became aware of the approach of the Aetolians, mismanaged matters to such an extent that it was impossible for anyone to have acted more stupidly.[3]

Taurion and the Achaeans joined forces and marched from Cleitor and camped near Caphyae. The Aetolians had been moving north too, from Methydrium up past Orchomenus, and also deployed in the plain of Caphyae, so there was only a river and some drainage ditches between the two armies. But when the Aetolians moved off towards the Oligyrtus Mountains nearby, Aratus sent out some cavalry and light infantry under the Acarnanian, Epistratus to harass the enemy, and in so doing he allowed the fight to occur in rougher, steeper terrain where the Aetolians were greatly superior. As the Achaean light troops made contact, the Aetolian cavalry slipped away and joined their infantry. Aratus apparently thought they were fleeing, and despatched his 'cuirassed' cavalry from his wings to join the light troops in the attack while he led the main body on at the double. Now, having reached high ground, the whole Aetolian force turned at bay and attacked the Achaean light infantry and heavy horse. Charging from the advantage of an elevated position, they soon won out and put them to flight; the first 500 men who routed infected the rest with panic, and altogether 2,000 light infantry and heavy horse fled. They fell back towards the main body of Achaean heavy infantry looking for protection, but when the phalanx saw them, they too collapsed in disorder, running for the safety of the nearby towns of Orchomenus and Caphyae. This at least saved many lives that otherwise would have been lost but did little to enhance the reputation of either Aratus or the Achaean military. They were not even able to go out to care for their fallen and had to wait for some Megalopolitans, who arrived too late for the fighting, to bury the dead in a trench on the battlefield. The victors now continued their march through the Peloponnese unopposed. They almost captured Pellene, ravaged Sicyon and continued home via the Isthmus of Corinth, absolutely rubbing the noses of everybody in how powerless the Symmachy and the Achaeans were to protect their own.

It was all getting so reminiscent of the middle 220s when a desperate Achaea had to turn to a Macedonian king for succour as a rampant enemy seemed to be able to pursue his policy in the Peloponnese without let or hindrance. But now, at least, the Symmachy was in place to facilitate the process of bringing the northern kingdom in. Even so, at the outset it was not a foregone conclusion. There is certainly evidence that Philip V was not, at first, sure he wanted to go to war with the Aetolians, although it was on him that all depended.

The Aetolians now took advantage of the arrival in Aetolian waters of Illyrians under Scerdilaidas and Demetrius of Pharos, and whilst the latter broke off to turn pirate in the Cyclades, the former with 40 ships hooked up with the Aetolians for a joint invasion of Achaea. This looked like big stuff: Agelaus joined Dorimachus and Scopas, and they called out the general levy that the Illyrians then shipped across the gulf. They headed for Cynaetha, a town in north Arcadia, where certain people had called them in. It had seen much party strife in the past but now the pro-Achaean party was in control. However, they had allowed 300 exiles back, and some of these started plotting to invite the Aetolians in. Those that had the keys to the gates were not interested in half measures; they ensured easy entry by murdering their compatriots, who had been left to man the town's defences. The Aetolians, having been let in, began to slaughter and despoil all and sundry, even the people who had admitted them. After administering this salutary lesson, they left a garrison and marched to Cleitor, which not only resisted their blandishments but also drove off their attack. They then fell back on Cynaetha, where Euripidas took up station after they failed to get the Eleans to take over the place. But their situation was becoming too exposed, and they marched out of a burning ruin, taking the road to Rhium and home, just avoiding being intercepted by the erstwhile pirate Demetrius of Pharos, who had been hired by Taurion to fall on the Aetolian ships as they re-crossed the Corinthian Gulf.

At the same time, embassies had been on the road and filling ports for months all round Greece with articulate Aetolians trying to persuade Achaeans, Epirotes, Eleans and Spartans that their interests did not lie in an allied war against the Aetolian League. Aratus had already sponsored a rack of his guest friends and emissaries to argue just the opposite case over the last months of 220, as well as tempting all who would listen with bits of a dismembered Aetolia as prizes for victory. The Achaeans also despatched embassies to Boeotia, the Phocians, the Acarnanians and the Epirotes as well; while they themselves raised an army of 5,000 foot and 500 horse.

This was the alliance that was preparing to fight the Aetolians and their friends, with military aims that the enemy should both give back any cities or land they had gained control of since the death of Demetrius II. Finally, all this had stoked official war; Macedonia was on board and most of the Symmachy as well. It looked like the Aetolian League was in real trouble, threatened by enemies to the south, east and north in what would be designated the Social War (war of allies). But this was, for at least a time, something of an illusion, only the Acarnanians would be there at the kick-off of the conflict, while even the Epirotes would probably do little until Philip became involved, and the young king of Macedonia still had much else on his plate with Dardanians hustling and bustling up north. The Aetolians realized they had, at least, the winter before they need anticipate a major enemy offensive and they determined to use the time to best effect. And, as well as this window of time, they had achieved important engagements with two Peloponnesian allies.

As the Aetolians disappeared home in 220, the king of Macedon came down to Corinth in response to Aratus' calls for support. As he took the road to Tegea, it became clear that the Spartan dimension had come to the forefront. Some of the elite there had been intriguing with the Aetolians, and Philip and the Symmachy leadership were worried that the monster they thought they had tamed at Sellasia was about to break out again.

The removal of the Macedonian garrison under Brachyllas in 220 had almost led to civil war in the city. The *ephors* had split into factions; the majority were inclined to Aetolia, but when Philip arrived in force they feared for their positions and their lives. They were so alarmed that they even called out the Spartan levy and eliminated the minority who tried to protest against this hostile act. Now, these *ephors* had control, but the state was still near defenceless, so they sent to Philip, blaming the trouble on the men they had killed. The king heard their envoys at Tegea and, advised by Aratus, discounted a complete extirpation of the *ephors* and plumped instead for leniency, only deposing them and putting the administration of Sparta in the hands of 'known friends'.[4]

But this casual clemency only served to exacerbate the contentiousness of the pro-Aetolian party, particularly when it became known that the old enemy Messene had finally joined the Symmachy. They decided on a radical clear-out; the new *ephors* were butchered while in the sanctuary of a temple and anybody else associated with opposition to the Aetolians was driven out of town. Yet more *ephors* were chosen, who committed themselves fully to Machatas, an Aetolian who had been trying to win over the Spartans for some time and who now returned to the city to cement the deal. Many of these hard men, who had published the regime change in blood, were ex-Cleomenists who would have recalled him except that news had just arrived in winter 220 of his death in Egypt. Their solution was to restore the dyarchy of an infant king, Agesipolis III, but the real power was with the other king, Lycurgus, who may not have been of the royal line and possibly bribed his way to power, with a talent to each *ephor*, although this is unclear

The other friends on the ground for the Aetolians were the perennial rivals of Achaea who had worked in tandem with both official and unofficial forces from Aetolia before: 'for Elis is much more thickly inhabited and more full of slaves and farm stock than any other part of Peloponnese.'[5] The opening of the campaigning season of 219 meant that the Aetolians, with Scopas as *strategos*, were able to hit at the Symmachy on several fronts. The first effort was led by Euripidas, from his base in Elis, pushing into the western flank of Achaean League territory. The invaders initially hit Dyme, the westernmost of the Achaean cities, then Patrae and, finally, Tritaea with a raiding force of mainly Eleans. An Achaean response was easily batted off and a fort called 'the wall' was set up near Dyme as a centre for disaffection in a region where the usefulness of being part of the Achaean League was seldom long unquestioned. It had its effect, when Aratus' son (that year's *strategos*) failed to move to their assistance. The towns that had suffered from the Aetolian depredations sundered their ties with the Achaean League, intending to use their tax contributions to organize their own defences. Euripidas, though, was not content with just causing mayhem in west Achaea. He then moved southeast towards Arcadia and Messenia, not far from the places he had established himself the year before, a strategy that had the advantage of not only threatening other parts of Achaea but, equally, making him well placed to support his friends in Phigaleia whose presence kept Messene on a very short leash indeed.

Not that many miles away, to the east of Arcadia, Lycurgus, the Spartan, backed up the Aetolians by attacking Argos and taking several towns in the district east of Mount Parnon, which had been taken from them after Sellasia. In fact, this contribution was unimpressive. Sparta still could not easily be turned in a new direction, and Lycurgus was soon forced to pull back. In the end, the main achievement of this Lacedaemonian intervention was the capture of a fort called Athenaeum that was an important component in the defence of Arcadia and had been the centre of conflict in the past. Apart from this activity in the Peloponnese, another Aetolian probe was led by Dorimachus and an Alexander who came over from Oiantheia across the Corinthian Gulf to attack Aigeira. Although initially successful, when 1,200 men landed in the dead of night and surprised the town's defenders, they were eventually beaten back from the acropolis. Indiscipline and looting meant the invaders were soon enough kicked out of the town, driven back to their ships and across the water to lick their wounds and organize the funeral of General Alexander who had died in the affray.

Although much seemed to have been attempted, the Aetolian League leadership had retained most of its strength for home defence, to face the main threat they knew was coming: Macedonia, with its new young king who possessed considerable talent and certainly had a reputation to make. Philip, back at Pella, now mobilized a considerable army for the war in Greece. Outside the Peloponnese, the anti-Aetolian axis' most enthusiastic members, the Acarnanians, were also its most vulnerable, and so it was in support of them that the young king moved. He had 10,000 phalangites and 5,000 peltasts. These peltasts were clearly elite troops who often worked in difficult terrain in tandem with light infantry, which does not suggest the heavy infantry of the phalanx. Yet, also, they are described locking shields to face off charging cavalry, assaulting city walls, and, when attacking up the slopes of the Menelaion, they are specifically included amongst the heavy-armed. In all this they most resemble the hypaspists of Philip and Alexander's time, and are perhaps best understood as their heirs, deployed as well-armoured frontline infantry in set-piece battle, but versatile enough to adopt looser formations when required. With these were 800 cavalry, and he led them over the Pindus Mountains and into Epirus, a route that took him towards the heart of his enemy's power and meant he could pick up a considerable Epirote army on the road. When he arrived there, 300 Achaean slingers and 500 Cretans rendezvoused with the main body, bringing them up to 16,000 plus men. But, when he left to commence the offensive he had more than 20,000, suggesting that a strong Epirote levy of at least 5,000 men had joined up as well.

Philip, as *hegemon* of the Symmachy, had a credibility that acting just in Macedonian interests could not give him. The Aetolians had offended a sufficient number of the Symmachy members to make them a credible enemy, but this collegiate stance meant Philip had to take notice of the interests of his allies. So his first target was a fort near Ambracia called Ambracus, probably because the Epirotes were concerned about the presence of this enemy strongpoint north of the Ambracian Gulf. It apparently took forty days to winkle out the garrison of 500 Aetolians, a very long interlude considering the speed with which Philip soon began to accomplish things, and then it was onto the ferries and over to Acarnania for the main push of the year. This was a route that avoided fighting their way round the gulf, where the Aetolians controlled a number of defensible strong-points and towns. The Aetolian high command's response was led by Scopas, who will constantly crop up in this story of the Hellenistic World from Thermus to Alexandria and even Palestine. On this occasion, he headed a raid against Macedonia itself. First, he marched east through Thessaly, travelling light, avoiding garrisons and hitting the Aegean coast at the Pieria region near Mount Olympus. Fields were burned and the inhabitants terrorized, but the main target became clear enough when the Aetolians swept into Dium, an important religious centre, which had been for generations the place in which Macedonian armies had gathered prior to marching through the Vale of Tempe into Greece. The town was razed and the sanctuary vandalized, although the temples may not actually have been touched. This is touted as an act of awful sacrilege, but Scopas needed to be noticed if he was to achieve his primary aim of distracting Philip, who was poised to overrun his homeland.

But Philip was not to be sidetracked; he stuck to the task and crossed the mouth of the Ambracian Gulf into Acarnania itself. Two thousand infantry and 200 cavalry came in from the Acarnanian communities to compensate for the Epirote troops that were left to watch the Aetolian forces in Ambracia. With a considerable invasion army, still near 20,000, little time was lost in hitting the main enemy. Phoetiae had been Acarnanian in the past and was the first city to fall after only two days of fighting. The garrison were allowed the honours of war and marched out, but a relief force coming up did not realize the town had fallen, and when Philip got news of their arrival he laid a trap. The Aetolians were completely destroyed, either killed or captured to a man. Next on the invasion itinerary was Stratus, an important place to the east in the valley of the Achelous River. The army was resupplied with local corn, but they found Stratus to be strongly defended and so they ravaged the land but left the town itself alone. The interlopers were not, however, given free rein; local Aetolian gentry had formed up in squadrons to harass them on the march. There was a ford just under two miles from Stratus and they waited there to fall on the Macedonians when they tried to cross, but Philip had a tried-and-tested army under hand, well used to contested river crossings. Peltasts were sent across the river in numbers with shields locked, and the Aetolians could not break them up, in the end having to withdraw behind Stratus' walls.

Philip now feinted towards the Aetolian lake country, looking as if he might take the road to Thermus itself. In fact, it was Oeniadae, an important port at the mouth of the River Achelous on the Corinthian Gulf, which had been much contested in previous years, that he was aiming for. His movements down the river had by now effectively isolated that town and he soon took it. On the way he had besieged Paeonium, which he determined to take not for itself – it was small, only 1,400 yards around – but to tear it down and recycle the wood and stone used in its construction to build up the defences and port facilities at Oeniadae. The building material was then rafted down the river to the mouth of the Achelous and 'Philip fortified the citadel separately and surrounding the harbour and dockyards with a wall he intended to connect them with the citadel, using the building material he had brought down from Paeonium for the work.'[6]

While Philip had been using most of his men in building his base to dominate the Gulf of Corinth, he had kept in touch with his allies, and the Achaeans had sent to try and get him to direct his efforts to the Peloponnese. But he had his own priorities (getting men back for harvest may have been part of it), and any inclination to take notice evaporated when news of more Dardanian activity arrived. Acting quickly, he returned the way he had come back to Acarnania and over the Ambracian Gulf before arriving at Pella via Epirus. His alacrity of response set the Dardanians back on their heels, the threat dissipated; and he was able to spend the rest of the summer at Larissa in Thessaly, where he could prevent Scopas from making any more trouble in the territory around Dium.

In fact, no onslaught developed there, but the Aetolians had been stirred up by the invasion and were inclined to take a whack back. In late September, the new Aetolian *strategos*, Dorimachus, attacked Epirus, raiding from Ambracia up the Arathus River. Dodona, another sacred site, was looted this time and, although the extent of damage and sacrilegious activity is open to debate, it certainly did little to improve the Aetolians' reputation for respectable religiosity. Meanwhile, Euripidas had probed deeper into Achaea. He had 2,200 foot and 100 horse, mainly Eleans and mercenaries, a grand enough force for this front. With these he crossed over into north Arcadia, taking towns and looting as far as Stymphalos, where he was in a position to threaten the main cities of the Achaean League, including Sicyon itself. But, the easy freebooting of this army was not destined to last long. With the harvest in, Philip was free to respond to the Achaeans' appeals as they seemed clearly incapable of defending themselves. And now he began a sequence of military activity that suggested he might become a real figure in the line of great Macedonian kings going back to Philip and Alexander.

As the winter was now advanced, everyone had given up any hope of Philip's reappearance owing to the season, but suddenly the king, taking with him three thousand of his brazen-shielded hoplites, two thousand peltasts, three hundred Cretans, and about four hundred of his horse guards, started from Larissa.[7]

He busied up his regiments, put the men on ships and ferried them to Euboea, then crossed the island and shipped them back to the mainland at Cynus and on through Boeotia, passing Megara and on to Corinth. Thus, neatly sidestepping Aetolian control of the mainland route south, he arrived about the time of the winter solstice, and his presence came as a surprise for friends and foe alike. From Corinth, Philip was determined to force his advantage of numbers. First he tried, while keeping his presence secret, to contact Aratus, and the current Achaean *strategos* to mobilize as much as possible of the Achaean levy. But without waiting for their arrival, he tried a pounce on the exposed company of Euripidas. However, the Aetolian heard news of his enemy as he himself prepared a descent on Sicyon territory. Near Phlious, his men captured some Cretan soldiers, who told him that Philip and a large army was only just down the road. Now he backed off, but the retreat turned into disaster as the Aetolian general tried to push his men through a defile just as the Macedonians were coming up. At first they put up a fight as they thought their enemy were just some troops from Megalopolis.[8] But, when they recognized the presence of Macedonian units, they fell apart and only the leadership, who had fled at the outset, escaped the battle:

all took to flight throwing away their shields. About twelve hundred of them were made prisoners and the remainder perished, either at the hands of the Macedonians or by falling down the precipices, only about a hundred escaping.[9]

Most of what Euripidas had gained was lost, and Philip advanced his army through the snow-covered defiles of Mount Oligyrtus, in the centre of Arcadia, which rises in places to almost 8,000 feet. At Caphyae, northwest of Lake Orchomenus, where Aratus so recently came unstuck, the Achaean troops joined him and raised his army to nearly 10,000 men; there was no one in the vicinity who could counter these kinds of numbers. They then moved quite a way to the west, traversing more very rugged country. This must have been difficult in wintertime but Psophis was eventually reached, an Arcadian town that was allied to the Eleans, whose country it overlooked. It was well protected by both nature and man, with rivers running on three sides, that were deep and fast-flowing at this time of year, with sturdy battlement all around. The only less-protected side was to the north, and even there it was covered by a steep hill with stout walls built at the top. Well garrisoned by both the remnants of Euripidas' army and other Eleans, this barbican was protecting their home territory. The defenders were confident in the integrity of their defences and also, thought the difficulties that Philip would experience campaigning in winter would be bound to decrease his effectiveness. So they felt real surprise when the king led his army over the River Erymanthos by an un-destroyed bridge and marched against the town walls. The defenders' first concern was that some people in the city had arranged to betray them to the attackers but, after these early qualms, they took heart and set themselves to contest with the Macedonians, who were putting up scaling ladders at three spots.

> At first the holders of the city offered a stout resistance and threw down many of the assailants from the ladders, but when their supply of missiles and other requisites began to fall short — their preparations having been made on the spur of the moment — and the Macedonians were showing no sign of fear, the place of each man thrown off the ladder being instantly taken by the man next behind him, the defenders at length turned their backs and all fled to the citadel.[10]

Philip's Cretans were at the front and their blood was up; they hallooed after the defending mercenaries who had thrown away their shields to facilitate flight. The garrison and citizens got to the citadel, but they had no supplies laid up, so a capitulation was soon agreed, with life and liberty assured to all. Winter now did begin to impinge and a snowfall kept Philip pinned down for several days. He utilized the time for some good public relations, ceremoniously handing the city over to the Achaeans.

While Euripidas had slipped away back to Aetolia, Philip headed southwest for Lasion, where the country spread out into easier-going terrain. The Eleans posted there fled, and again the king took possession and handed it over to the Achaeans. From here he took the road down from the central highlands to Olympia, where religious junketing in no way held back the systematic looting of all parts of Elis that his men could reach. They managed a particular coup when large numbers of fugitives, cattle and slaves, and apparently up to 5,000 persons, including 200 mercenaries, were discovered hiding out. All were scooped up with no trouble at all.

With Southern Elis despoiled, Philip moved as if set on evicting his enemy at Phigaleia. The Aetolian alliance had been reinforcing their garrisons, but nothing was about to stop a rampant Philip. He crossed Triphylia, on the coast between Elis and Messene, before heading further inland from near Stratus, via Telphusa and Heraea, and south over the River Alpheus. The defenders there had been reinforced, at the Eleans' request, by Dorimachus, who had sent 600 Aetolians to join 500 mercenaries and 1,000 of the Elean levy and an indeterminate number of Tarentines. After meeting together at Elis, they had been distributed between Lepreum, the most important place in the rich region of Triphylia, Alipheira about six miles to the north east, and Typanae.

Philip dropped his baggage and rushed light-shod against Alipheira, where 500 mercenaries occupied this place with a strong citadel on a precipitous hill. Determined assaults soon took the town, and the garrison, after fleeing to the citadel, arranged surrender as long as their lives were spared. The Aetolians now drew back to Lepreum, evacuating Typanae. Now it and the towns in the surrounding area all came over to Philip and, most importantly, when news of his success reached them, the Aetolians could not even hang onto the city of Phigaleia. The people rose up and threw them out, forcing them to flee for their lives. This latest campaign had apparently taken only six days yet it had removed one of the key Aetolian strongholds, which had acted so long to contain Messene.

The people of Lepreum now also threw out all the Aetolians and Eleans who had been posted there. But they in turn tried to outmuscle the locals and retake control, and only packed up and left when they heard Macedonian troops were on the way. Philip rushed his peltasts and light infantry hot on their trail. He quickly overtook their baggage train and captured it, but their leader and his men threw themselves into Samicum, a handy town on the road. Philip made as if to besiege the place, despite having only a few men with him. The enemy were panicked and surrendered when their tormentors agreed they could march off to Elis.

With winter well advanced, Philip felt he needed to rest the army that had done so much. He marched them to Megalopolis and from there these booty-encumbered combatants advanced to Tegea and then Argos, where they relaxed, counting the spoils of Elis. But Philip was still not finished. He mobilized another force at Aegium and marched west through Patrae to Dyme. Just past the town there were outworks called 'the wall' that the Eleans had dug in at. He took and refurbished it as security for the Dymeans' future. The citizens from that city took over the walls as Philip's men again pillaged Elis. He then returned to Argos, where the king remained, while his Macedonian troops left for home and winter quarters.

In 218 this Macedonian army, which had achieved much in changing the balance of power in the Peloponnese, turned in a new direction to forward the fight against Aetolia. At this juncture, Aratus, despite not being officially *strategos*, showed well. There had seemed to be coolness between monarch and Achaean but Philip laid on the charm at a meeting with Aratus, father and son, at Sicyon. The result was that Aratus led the Achaean assembly in boosting the war budget, voting 50 talents as well as three months pay for the troops and promising corn and 17 talents a month as long as Philip's men remained fighting in the Peloponnese.

As the Symmachy forces mustered again from their winter quarters, it became clear that Philip had decided to transfer the war to the sea:

This, he was convinced, was the only way by which he could himself fall suddenly on his enemies from every side, while at the same time his adversaries would be deprived of the power of rendering assistance to each other, separated as they were geographically and each in alarm for their own safety owing to the rapidity and secrecy with which the enemy could descend on them by sea. For it was against the Aetolians, Lacedaemonians, and Eleans that he was fighting.[11]

A fleet was mobilized, the oarsmen given some basic instruction, supplies and pay distributed, and the army, including 6,000 Macedonians and 1,200 mercenaries, moved along the coast to Patrae. The Achaean leadership still had major concerns over what the Eleans might do, particularly as Scopas and Dorimachus had both arrived there with reinforcements from Aetolia. To counter this threat, a covering force of Achaean mercenaries, some Cretans, 2,000 men of the Achaean levy and some Galatian horse, were left at Dyme, while Philip prepared to lead the main army over the horizon to try and make a more permanent dent in his enemies' arrangements. Allies, including Messenians, Epirotes, Acarnanians and Scerdilaidas (now in Philip's employ) and his Illyrian mercenary squadron, were all instructed to rendezvous at Cephalonia, on which the king had set his sights. This island was a key staging post for forces from Aetolia intervening in the Peloponnese; the islanders provided most of the shipping they needed to make the crossings. In eradicating them, Philip would strike a considerable blow at his main enemies' strategic options. Landfall for the Macedonian forces was at Pronni on the east coast of the island, the shortest sea crossing possible. This place was small but difficult of access, so the invaders pressed on round the coast to Palus on the west side of the island. There were supplies to be had here, so the army encamped and protected the beached fleet with a trench and palisade while they prepared to wait for the allies. Palus was only vulnerable from the south, the direction of the island of Zacynthus, and here the king began to open his siege lines. Allies dribbled in, even the Messenians, now able to join in with Phigaleia no longer a blade pointed at their heart. Ballistae and catapults kept the garrison's heads down as sappers undermined the walls. When a breach was prepared, Philip offered terms, but the garrison was resolute and so the props were set on fire and the walls came tumbling down.

Leontius deployed his peltasts and ordered them forward against the defences, but he kept on holding the men back each time they were on the verge of entering the town. The upshot was a repulse where success had seemed inevitable. Philip, disgusted, had had enough and abandoned the enterprise.

Now both the Acarnanians and Messenians pressed Philip to intervene on their own fronts, while Aratus pushed for an attack on Aetolia itself. The Aetolian command had themselves plumped for another tit-for-tat raid against Thessaly, and Dorimachus, elected *strategos*, was heading there with half the levy. The Aetolian army could not really face the Macedonians in battle, so the only option was to husband their manpower, to defend key spots, while they distracted and punished where else they could. With Philip over the western horizon, Thessaly to the east seemed temptingly open. But this was illusion; two competent Macedonian officers, Chrysogonus and Petraeus, had rounded up the garrisons in the region and prepared to meet the invaders in battle. The Aetolians, intent on easy pickings, were not up for a fight; they 'did not venture to descend into the plain, but kept to the slopes of the hills.'[12] Soon enough, they started for home when they realized that Philip might now himself be heading there.

This Aetolian strategy of pinpricks against their leading enemy could have drawbacks; a powerful beast like the Macedonian military, when bitten hard, might well bite back. And this now came about. Perhaps happy to leave Cephalonia, which had handed him his first setback for some time, Philip shipped his army straight past Leucas Island into the Ambracian Gulf and landed at Limnaia in Acarnania. There he picked up local guides, dumped his heavy gear, joined the Acarnanian levy and the whole headed south of Stratus town and down to the Aetolian lake district. In two days they reached Thermus after a very difficult tramp through rugged terrain around Lake Trichonis and did there what the Aetolians had done at Dium the year before, looting the town and temple precincts. It might be just a raid but the invaders did more than vent their bile, they found useful dumps of corn and valuable booty.

All this was well executed, and, despite being weighed down with booty, when 3,000 Aetolians came to chase him out, they were held off with aplomb. Philip put his heavy troops in front and Acarnanians and mercenaries in the rear and headed for a difficult defile just beyond the town, hoping he could press past it before the enemy struck. In fact, the first Aetolians attacked as the last ranks of Philip's army left Thermus. But, very sensibly, he had left some Illyrians and peltasts posted to help, and when the Aetolians came past them, they were ambushed and driven off, killing more than 100. Philip then marched up the Achelous valley and in a few days got to Stratus, but when the rearguard passed that town, again they were attacked, this time by waiting Aetolian cavalry, reinforced by hired Cretans garrisoning the town. But Philip had kept his Illyrians handy and they drove off the attackers, right back to the gates of Stratus.

The action for the king and Symmachy now returned to the Peloponnese where Sparta became again the progenitor of pandemonium. The new ruler, Lycurgus, had now thoroughly established himself and was set on a course of revenge against the victors of Sellasia. He firstly made a lunge at Messene and got some looting in, then turned north and tried an escalade against Tegea. He carried the town but could not take the citadel and was forced to return to Sparta frustrated. But his Elean allies had done better, pressing on Dyme; they had done real damage to the troops left to defend the place and captured some of the local leaders as well. Philip, in response, sailed from Leucas round to Corinth, pausing to take a swipe at the town of Oeanthe, across the gulf from Aegira. From his landfall at Lechaeum, he sent couriers to call out all the allies to meet him at Tegea. His intention was to hit Sparta hard, hoping that, if he knocked them out, the Aetolian alliance in the Peloponnese would crumble. The Achaeans brought their army to Tegea as requested, so it was in considerable Symmachy panoply that Philip passed the hills bordering Laconia. He wanted to take the Spartans by surprise, so moved through the little-inhabited country east of the Eurotas River, passed round the Menelaion, then south of Sparta itself, and ended up at Amyclae looking down on his enemy from the southwest, less than two miles away. From leaving Aetolia to arriving there, it is claimed only seven days had passed 'so that most of Spartans though they saw what had happened, could not believe their eyes.'[13]

He did not attack Sparta city itself but headed south and ravaged down towards Gythium, the main port on the southern coast of Laconia. Then on until he reached Taenarum, almost the furthermost tip of the mainland, returning to Gythium, then on to the Helos, a fine, prosperous district, and even plundering as far as Boeae, almost down to Cape Maleas. As the campaign began, the Messenians were eager to take a swipe at their old oppressors and mobilized 1,000 foot and 200 horse. They missed Philip at Tegea but followed after as swiftly as they could. In their haste to be in at the kill, they were lax, and on stopping at Glympeis failed to build any camp defences, just bivouacking under the town walls. Lycurgus, who had now recovered from his shock at Philip's arrival, decided that if he was not able to face Philip's 10,000 with his own inferior numbers, he could certainly punish these erstwhile helots who were trailing their coat so appetisingly in front of him. With a force consisting mainly of mercenaries and a few of the main levy, he attacked the Messenians at dawn, drove them inside the town walls, capturing most of their baggage and horses but inflicting few casualties. Lycurgus, with plenty on his plate, was happy to let the Messenians slip shamefacedly back to Argos. Indeed, the Spartans were now contemplating a coup against their main antagonist.

Philip had returned to camp at Amyclae, and Lycurgus had by now bullied 2,000 of his best men into military shape and pushed them out onto the high ground around the Menelaion, a shrine to the deified Menelaus on the left bank of the Eurotas, a couple of miles to the southeast of the city, 'rocky, difficult to ascend, and of considerable height. They absolutely command the level space between the city and the river, which runs close along their foot, its distance from the city being not more than a stade and a half.' (About 300 yards)[14]

The units left in Sparta itself were given instructions, on a given signal, to come out and array facing the Eurotas River just outside the city. To get past them, Philip would have to lead his army between the Spartans drawn up outside the city walls on his left and the river on his right – on the other side of which was Lycurgus on the hill. And this was made all the harder because the Spartans had damned the river and flooded much of the area between the town and the hill. Philip's only feasible route was immediately below the hill where his long-drawn-out column would have to march exactly beneath the 2,000 best Spartans ensconced high above them. He ordered his mercenaries, peltasts and Illyrians to get over the river and drive Lycurgus off the hill. The Spartan leader prepared his own men and signalled his officers still in the town. These deployed their regiments in front of the walls with the cavalry on the right wing.

Lycurgus' heavy infantry, meanwhile, were putting on a good show from the high ground against Philip's mercenaries. But then the king, with greater numbers, got his peltasts and Illyrians in around the enemy flank, and the Spartans began to disintegrate. How exactly this was done is difficult to imagine on the spot as the direct frontal approach to the Menelaion is virtually a sheer cliff. While a few agile men might have climbed up that way, the main body must have marched round the base of the outcrop to approach from the north; here access is steep but feasible. However they accomplished it, apparently 100 defenders were killed and some taken prisoner while the rest got back to Sparta. Philip left his victorious Illyrians on the hills and took the rest back to Aratus who had brought up the phalanx near to the city. Why the Spartans had not helped their comrades on the hill we do not know, unless they were pinned in place by the threat of the phalanx coming up. Whatever, now Philip crossed the river and deployed his light troops, peltasts and cavalry in a protective cordon until the heavy-armed troops had passed between the city and the hills. The Spartans from the city attacked but were kept off, particularly by the peltasts who drove the Spartan cavalry back into the gates. With his men past the bottleneck, Philip camped for the night. He was now well placed to attack the city but he did not, preferring to pull back to Tegea. He encamped on the battleground of Sellasia on the way, making sacrifice there to those who had fallen in victory just a few years before. Certainly, a case can be made that Philip's actions had the requisite effect even without attacking Sparta itself. Soon after, Lycurgus found himself subject to an *ephor*-instigated assassination attempt and was forced to leave the country and find refuge in Aetolia.

Philip returned to Corinth after the Laconia razzia, where he found envoys from Rhodes and Chios, whose trading profits were considerably dented by the raging conflict, proposing to mediate a peace. These intermediaries had successfully opened lines of dialogue; they had been rattling between Corinth and Thermus and were able to report that the Aetolians were definitely ready for some agreement. In September 218, these envoys came up with a proposal for a truce of thirty days, and Philip and the Symmachy leaders were prepared to accept this breathing space.

In the past two years, Philip had been carrying most of the weight of the war, but it had not been an untroubled establishment that had carried it with him. When he picked up the reins of power in 221, a number of officers are mentioned at the head of the administration that had been in place for years under Doson. They were the gate keepers of patronage, and each had a web of family and clients in Macedonia and elsewhere that ensured that they were very powerful indeed in a kingdom where the monarch was young, inexperienced in government and, as yet, had not had time to establish his authority. Apelles seems the most important, but other great men were Leontius, captain of the peltasts, Megaleas as secretary of state, Taurion as commander in the Peloponnese, and Alexander, captain of the bodyguard. Apart from this phalanx of home-grown advisors, Aratus the Achaean had become a very influential figure in the peripatetic court. Doson had been the instigator of his influence; he had brought the teenage prince Philip down to Achaea to drink in the ideals of Hellenism at the knee of the veteran. Indeed, according to Plutarch, the heir apparent had spent the winter of 222 with the Achaean.[15]

Apelles was the driving force amongst those who had served Doson so well. He had not moved away from the traditional stance of Macedonian administrations that their interests lay in directly dominating as much of the Greek peninsula as they could. From Philip's arrival in the south, Apelles' intent was to reduce Achaea to entire dependence on Macedonia. He and his cohorts' tactics in the beginning were crude, nothing more than bullying, throwing Achaean officers out of their billets to accommodate Macedonians and confiscating the Achaean soldiers' booty. Anybody who complained was arrested and mistreated, but what was intended to intimidate had the opposite effect. Some of the younger men went to Aratus with their complaints and he took them straight to Philip. The Achaeans were a vital military partner, so Apelles was told by the king he could only in future give orders to Achaeans through their own *strategos*.

This tension had all boiled up at the end of Philip's winter campaign of 219–218 while the court and army rested at Megalopolis. But when the military caravan left for Tegea and Argos, Apelles targeted Aratus in person. Having attempted intimidation, Apelles tried some politics. He rallied Aratus' local rivals, encouraging them to complain to Philip about Aratus, and also sponsored them in opposing his candidate in that year's *strategos* elections. The result was success for his candidate, Eperatus of Pharae, who pipped Aratus' man, Timoxenus, at the polls.

With ground gained and Apelles on a roll, a campaign was ratcheted up to further undermine Aratus' influence with the king. When Amphidamus, the Elean general, was captured on campaign, Apelles hatched a plot. This man claimed he could persuade his countrymen to desert the Aetolians if he was let go home. But, when this was arranged, he failed to sway his compatriots and Apelles claimed that it was because Aratus had suborned the Elean to really work against peace. The king was shaken by these accusations, but when Aratus demanded the witness be brought back to clear up the matter, Philip acquiesced. Campaigning in Elis soon allowed Amphidamus to be contacted, and he agreed to testify, as his countrymen were far from happy with him and had driven him out of their country to Dyme. Content to be given an exile's billet as the price of giving evidence, the man cleared Aratus completely. Apelles' importance did not seem to be immediately dented, but it must have begun a souring of Philip's feelings for this great officer who had been caught trying to deceive him.

But it was not just Aratus who Apelles was trying to undermine; he was at daggers drawn with certain of his colleagues. We don't know the origins of the divisions, but they are clear enough. Apelles lined up with Leontius, Megaleas and a Ptolemy, but others were rivals from the start. Taurion had been a long-time Macedonian proconsul in the Peloponnese and saw his interests differently from the officers who had just arrived with Philip's court. Apelles hated him as a powerful antagonist and highlighted his local influence to make it seem that he was dangerously independent and powerful. Nor did he leave it there, but began a campaign of gossip against Alexander, captain of the bodyguard, and although we do not know how effective this trashing was, clearly these officers were eager to turn the screw on Apelles and his party when the king disowned them.

In Summer 218, Apelles' behaviour took a quantum leap. He had been competing for influence over the king but, with lack of success, his activity took on a different complexion. Now he contemplated treason; the setting was Corinth, where Philip prepared a considerable naval effort, ordering the Achaeans' ships and his own vessels to concentrate at Lechaeum port. Apelles decided to absent himself from court. Perhaps it was apparent his star was falling, and he made arrangements to be sent to Chalcis, where he could reconstitute his powerbase at this, one of the crucial shackles of Greece. What pretext he used to justify his move is not known but, before he left, Leontius and Megaleas were primed to undermine Philip on the spot, while from Chalcis he would ensure that the supply line for the army was constricted. Clearly, the intriguers had an impact, as it is at this time that we hear Philip had to pawn his own plate to help fund the upcoming campaign. However, even this did not ensure a favourable outcome, as Leontius had made sure the assault on Palus failed in the end.

There was sign of a new mood at court at Limnaia in Acarnania after the invasion of Cephalonia and the attack on Thermus. The king gave thanks to the deities before laying on a banquet to celebrate the raid into Aetolia. But Megaleas, Leontius and a Crinon were of a very different cast of mind, and it seems lack of success was making them desperate. Their failure to dissimulate their disappointment was apparent to all. And more than this, the petulant trio got in their cups and lost control altogether. As the guests were leaving they found Aratus and first threatened, then began to stone the Achaean. An unseemly fracas began that caught the attention of the king. When Philip appeared, Aratus was rescued, while his attackers slipped away from the crowd. Megaleas and Crinon were swiftly arrested and brought before the king but, probably still drunk, they reiterated that they would get Aratus if they got the chance. Philip lost patience and, without benefit of procedure, fined them twenty talents each and imprisoned them until it should be paid. Leontius, still at large, now tried to browbeat the king; he entered the royal tent with some of his own peltasts in tow and demanded to know who had dared lay hands on his friends. But Philip stood firm, forcing Leontius to leave in anger.

Now the court sailed for Leucas with the two men in chains. When they got there, Philip distributed booty to ensure he was in good odour with the army before he had the prisoners formally arraigned in a court of his friends. Aratus took the floor.

> Aratus, who acted as accuser, recounted the malpractices of Leontius and his party from beginning to end... their understanding with Apelles and their obstruction at the siege of Palus, supporting all his statements by proofs and bringing forward witnesses.[16]

The accused apparently had nothing to say; their fines were confirmed, and while Crinon remained in chains, Leontius gave surety for Megaleas, who was released. These men of Apelles' faction had been aiming punches at Aratus, but none had really landed, and the only actual effect of what they had attempted was to alienate themselves from their own king.

At the army camp, now back at Corinth, Leontius, Megaleas, and Ptolemy were getting very desperate and missing the guiding hand of Apelles. Fear spawned recklessness, and they approached the officers and men of the peltasts and the Agema guard, and when these very senior figures started fermenting mutiny they found a receptive audience. They were talking treason but they tickled the soldiers' cupidity by suggesting those who had contributed so much to Philip's victories were not getting their traditional share of the booty. And this soon turned from being just badmouthing, when the younger soldiers decided to take their rightful dues from the tents of the king's friends and the royal headquarters itself. Leontius and his associates had clearly started something big, and the rioting now spread to Corinth itself. The king heard what was happening and rushed up from the port of Lechaeum and, sending out his officers, summoned the army to assemble at the theatre. All was confusion and uproar as the men, those who had rioted and those who had not, pressed to the front of the crowd. Philip's entourage were very worried, and while many suggested arresting the ring leaders, others, realising how ugly things had got, pleaded for the king to offer indemnity to those involved. The king understood the situation could not be settled in the way that Alexander had at Opis, when he jumped in amongst his men to arrest those he considered responsible. He did not have his predecessor's prestige, or perhaps his almost insane lack of caution. In the end he managed to defuse the situation and slipped away to safety. In the light of day, calmer heads in the army prevailed as they considered what they had almost done and where it might lead.

Leontius, realizing that things had gone beyond his own control, sent to Chalcis, urging Apelles to come himself to court. But before he could return, the king made up his mind; he correctly made the connection between the near mutiny and Apelles, and so decided that the time had come to tame this over-mighty subject. Aratus was at the king's elbow as he laid his plans, but though the sources stress his role, this was very much Philip taking his kingdom into his hands. Apelles came hurriedly back to the court, still confident in his influence, and on arrival at Corinth, Leontius, Ptolemy and Megaleas arranged a great reception. He was mobbed by officers and men as he disembarked at the quayside, but when he tried to approach Philip these theatricals cut no ice, and the king's flunkies turned him away. This was an awful rebuff for a man who had been second in the kingdom since the death of Doson, and his followers seeing the way the wind was blowing excused themselves as soon as they could. When Apelles reached his billet, only his children remained with him, even Leontius and the others had left. 'So brief a space of time suffices to exalt and abase men all over the world and especially those in the courts of kings.'[17]

Apelles remained with the king, but he no longer held the levers of power; he was kept at arm's length, and not invited to either royal banquets or councils. When the king's caravan returned to Corinth from Phocis, Megaleas, for one, had seen the abyss and decamped to Athens, leaving Leontius to stand surety for his twenty talents.[18] Apelles was less prescient or was not able to leave, but followed with Philip as he sailed for Sicyon. Here, no doubt was left as to who was in favour; 'excusing himself to the magistrates', Philip turned down public hospitality and lodged at Aratus' private house, while sending Apelles back to Corinth. These machinations were always about what the soldiers would do, and Philip showed he could come out on top in this game. Leontius and his peltasts were the key, and, with Megaleas and Apelles neutralized, he acted. The peltasts were transferred to Taurion's command and ordered to march to Triphylia, in the west, and when they had gone, the king arrested Leontius. This seizure almost brought mutiny, either because they had genuine affection for their leader, or because they realized their own significance was bound up with his. When they heard, on the march, that he was incarcerated, they sent envoys demanding they be present if he was to be condemned and even offered to pay his fine. 'With such freedom did the Macedonians always address their kings.'[19]

But this show of loyalty to their chief only decided Philip to have Leontius executed straight away.

Now the blood was beginning to flow, and it would not stop. Evidence came from Phocis that Megaleas had been in treasonable correspondence with the Aetolians. Alexander, an old enemy of Apelles' party, was sent to Thebes to arrest Megaleas, but the fugitive killed himself before he could be taken. The king, tarring the faction equally, took this as more evidence against Apelles and decided to cut off the head of the movement. He confronted Apelles and 'he placed him in custody and at once despatched him to Corinth together with his son and his minion.'[20] The magnate could no longer have any doubts that he had played his hand and lost; there had been a sea change and it was no longer a 17-year-old boy he was dealing with. Apelles had never lacked courage and he, his son and his lover now killed themselves, and the final line was drawn under these intrigues when, after sailing by the Euripus channel to Demetrias, Philip arraigned Ptolemy, 'the last survivor of Leontius' band of conspirators', before a Macedonian court, where he was condemned and executed.

While these disputative Macedonians had so far, despite their internal turmoil, largely carried the war, the Achaeans had frequently been feeble, and now Philip's agreement to the thirty-day armistice with the Aetolians must have sent a worrying message to his allies. So it is no coincidence that Aratus now put in hand military reforms when he again took over as *strategos*. But if the Achaeans began to be serious about their responsibilities to oppose the Aetolian threat in the Peloponnese, the fact that the Aetolians were equally a danger elsewhere was coming to the forefront of Macedonian minds. Their presence as a power to the south of Macedonian Thessaly could no longer be tolerated. In 217, Philip decided some real work needed to done on his own borderlands. This region had not previously drawn Philip like the Peloponnese, but he had always recognized that the front across Thessaly and the Malian Gulf was important to his position in the whole of Greece. And for the Aetolians, it was not just a defensive advantage; on a number of occasions their control of southwestern Thessaly allowed damaging inroads into the property of the Macedonian's Thessalian friends, and indeed through the Vale of Tempe into the northern kingdom itself. Tearing up Dium was a much more feasible proposition for an Aetolian force base at Phthiotic Thebes than one that would have to fight its way all the way from Thermus.

It does seem Philip's first idea when the war started was to open a western route, and Epirus, Acarnania, Leucas and Cephalonia were the places that drew the Macedonian leadership's attention. But by 217, the idea of a western passage had been ditched and the intention changed to a push on his southern border. Part of this was annoyance at the failure of his Achaean allies. But also, his capacity to carry it out was enhanced by the fact that he had now sorted out the dissension that had wracked his court since the death of Doson. Now it was to the east that he would pursue a route down through Greece. The thoroughfare he wanted to secure was one down from Demetrias and ran north of the Malian Gulf between the mountains and the sea. This was almost as defensible as that through Thermopylae itself, and to get control of the key defended communities along this route was well worth the trouble of coercing or making friends with the town's folk thereabouts.

Before he moved, Philip tided up his northern front, moving forces into Paeonia and taking the town of Bylazora, which effectively blocked the main route usually taken by the Dardanians when they descended on Macedonia. After this, Chrysogonus raised the levies of the upper cantons while Philip organized regiments from Boeotia and the Amphaxites, and all met at Edessa, at the edge of the Macedonian plain, before marching down to Larissa, the usual base for campaigns in Thessaly and Greece. He did not move directly against his main target. Instead, he advanced on Melitia, a town some 20 miles north of Lamia and west of Mount Othrys. Philip's men marched through the night and got there just as day was breaking. This attempt, though successful in surprising the defenders and terrifying the community, was marred by one main factor. The surprise escalade was attempted with ladders brought for the purpose, but they turned out to be too short to reach the top of the walls! Polybius is very sniffy about Philip's lack of planning.[21]

The young king was little daunted and moved the army down by the River Enipeus and sent to Larissa for the siege train of 150 catapults and twenty-five stone throwers that he had had assembled there over the past few weeks. The key target of the campaign now became clear: it was Thebes in Phthiotis, the Aetolians' main fortress for warring against both Macedonian Thessaly and Demetrias, the great base on the bay of Volos.

This proximity of Aetolian power to the prestige foundation of Demetrias had irritated Macedonian imperialists for years and now Philip had made up his mind to scratch the itch. The trench lines were opened against very well-protected Thebes, whose formidable walls can still be just detected on the plateau above the modern town of Mikrotheves. The Macedonians split into three parts and encamped in hills and strongpoints around the town. Between the camps a full line of circumvallation was constructed with manned towers every 100 feet. For three days the Thebans were active and successful in keeping the attackers off with missiles, but constant fighting wore them down. The resultant respite allowed the miners to push forward and in nine days they reached the defences. Then constant digging for three more days and nights prepared a breach under 200 feet of wall. But the attack, when it came, did not go smooth as silk with props breaking before they could be fired. Still, all in all, enough of the defences were damaged for the defenders to lose hope. They parleyed for the surrender, but this time everybody was enslaved, the town emptied and a Macedonian colony named Philippi planted on the spot.

Philip must have thought he was now in a position to push on, and perhaps Heraclea, the main hub just south of the Malian Gulf and over the mountains from Thermopylae, would be ripe for the plucking. But it was not to be, and the king was soon distracted. Scerdilaidas who had, at least since the attack on Cephalonia, been in Philip's hire, had gone off script and taken up his old trade of piracy. The Illyrian was a tricky customer, and he had despatched fifteen galleys to Leucas, putting it about that they had just come to collect the mercenary wages he was owed. Once in the port, they bagged four Macedonian ships they found there, while the rest of the squadron set off for a pirate cruise off Cape Maleas on the southeast coast of Sparta. This defection really infuriated the Macedonian king, and he embarked most of his army: 'he manned twelve decked ships, eight undecked ones, and thirty hemiolii,'[22] and sailed down through the Euripus, the channel between Euboea and mainland Greece, to catch the Illyrians. In fact, the pirates got off before they were caught, but at least Philip now was on the spot and well placed to put some effective pressure on the Aetolians.

Anchoring off Cenchreae, sent off his decked ships with orders to sail round Cape Maleas towards Aegium and Patrae: the rest of his vessels he dragged over the Isthmus, ordering them all to anchor at Lechaeum.[23]

The king, himself, while he waited for his ships to rendezvous in the Gulf of Corinth, left for Argos to enjoy the Nemean festival. The arrival of Philip and his army off their southern littoral certainly made the Aetolians more inclined to peace, particularly when the Macedonians captured 'the castle in Perippia' and made as if to invade Elis again. Philip then moved to a camp at Panormus, a town with a harbour that was directly opposite Naupactus and where a peace conference began to coalesce in earnest.

The Achaeans were happy to consider a cessation because, although the Peloponnese had been by no means quiet, while the waves of war surged around Phthiotic Thebes, nothing in their favour had been decisive. Even during the winter, while Philip was in Macedonia, there had been activity. Eperatus, the Achaean *strategos*, floundered, completely losing the confidence of the citizen levy and even managing to cause a strike by his mercenaries, possibly because they had not been paid since the earlier contributions boycott. He had rendered Achaea in such disarray that Pyrrhias, the Aetolian, hearing word of it and despite the season, could not resist taking advantage. He had 1,300 of his compatriots, the mercenaries retained by Elis and 1,000 Elian foot and 300 horse. With these he attacked the territories of Dyme and Patrae on the coast and Pharae further inland. He then established a defended position on the Panachaean Mountains, which overlook Patrae, and began the organized looting of the regions around Rhium and Aegium. Furthermore, in early summer 217, Lycurgus had been reinstated in Sparta. He was not back for any time at all before he contacted Pyrrhias for a joint descent on Messene. Lycurgus surprized and took Calamae, the most important port in Messene, then moved on to join his ally, but Pyrrhias, who though he marched down the west coast and attacked Cyparissia on the Messene border, was forced to withdraw through lack of troops. The Spartans, on their own, tried to take a place called Andania on the route up from the coast towards Messene. Pausanias mentions it as a mile west of the Carnasian grove, which he claims as second only to Eleusis in holiness in all Greece. There they expected to get news of their allies. When they realized Pyrrhias had gone, it became obvious that on their own they were too weak to make significant progress and so they marched home as well.

Aratus now hurried to take up the post of *strategos* in a situation that seemed no better than it had been at the start of the war. It was decided to raise an army of 8,000 mercenary foot, 3,000 foot and 300 horse of elite Achaeans, 500 infantry from Megalopolis and 50 troopers 'all brazen shielded', and the same number of Argives. Also commissioned were six war ships, three to cruise the coastline of the Gulf of Argolis on the east of the Peloponnese, and the other three to guard the sea lanes by Patrae and Dyme in the Gulf of Corinth. With the creation of this major force in hand, Aratus now acted with the mercenaries and some of the Achaeans that were already mobilized. To put himself between his adversaries, he moved to Megalopolis, sending messengers to the Messenians and to Taurion to send 50 horse and 500 foot. With these forces, he tried to put in place some proper defences for Messenia, Megalopolis, Tegea and Argos; the places most vulnerable to Spartan aggression, although he kept picked Achaeans and mercenaries with himself.

With at least something done, if still left largely untested, Aratus demobbed the Achaean levy and returned to manipulate his political base, the Achaean assembly, giving over command of the mercenaries, the military cutting edge, to one Lycus of Pharae. He soon had to face a severe challenge. The Eleans had not been impressed with the performance of Pyrrhias, so they asked the Aetolians to send Euripidas back to them. This old brigand soon made an impact, with a raiding party of 60 horse and 2,000 foot. They swaggered down the inland road past Pharae where the exasperated citizens on the walls could only watch as the intruders marched into the heart of Achaea, reaching as far as Aegium. But on the way back, on the route leading towards Leontium, up in the high country where rugged roads fit for ambush were the norm, Lycus fell on the booty-laden marauders and gave them a real pasting; the whole force was eliminated.[24]

There were further Achaean successes at sea. A force, how large is not mentioned, landed at Molycria and took off almost 100 slaves then sailed to the island of Chalceia, where, when an enemy squadron came to see them off, they defeated and captured two warships with their crews before heading to Rhium, where another Aetolian galley was captured. And, somewhat later, Achaean ships made a number of descents on the coast of Calydon and Naupactus on the north

shore of the Corinthian Gulf, where they also crushed two Aetolian patrols sent
to safeguard the area. These victories, together with the new army dusting up
the Eleans, showed the Achaean efforts really bearing fruit. And what is
interesting in all this is that it highlights once more the importance of plunder
as the sinews of war. These successes and the booty it brought in allowed the
payment of the troops, arrears and bonuses, with less need for contributions
from the cities. This was always a crucial balance; as if the towns were pressed
to pay too much they might indulge in tax revolts.

Aratus, as *strategos*, was also really getting a grip; he headed off with some
elite Achaean troops to protect the harvest being brought in near Argos, which
also shows how dangerous life still was for League members after two years of
war. The lack of security was only emphasized when Euripidas raided Tritaea,
although here also there was a sound response. Lycus raised the levy at Dyme,
Patrae and Pharae, and with the mercenaries headed into Elis. At Phyxium, they
set themselves up and began to ravage the country, sending out light troops to
forage while keeping their hoplites well positioned to defend their camp.

When the Eleans returned from Tritaea and gathered what men they could,
they began to harry the Achaean raiders and pressed them back towards their
base. But when they approached Phyxium they were disordered and up popped
Lycus and his hoplites and jumped all over them. 'The Eleans did not await the
charge, but turned and ran at once on the appearance of the enemy, who killed
about two hundred of them and captured eighty, bringing in all the booty they
had collected in safety.'[25] But if it was mainly gravy for the Achaeans in the
Peloponnese, there were still threats to other members of the Symmachy.
Agetas, the Aetolian *strategos*, took what is described as the whole citizen force
to ransack Acarnania. This was a major effort, and after despoiling them, they
marched round the Ambracian Gulf to torment the Epirotes. They met with no
resistance at all, and after they had taken as much plunder as they could carry,
the army retired home.

But these mixed results in a war of ambuscades certainly helps us understand
why the Aetolians were so earnest to move the peace process along and, to this
end, they invited the Symmachy leadership and army to come over to the north
side of the Gulf of Corinth near to Naupactus. Although both sides had their
armies cheek by jowl, and this might seem a fraught way to conduct delicate
peace negotiations, it seemed to work. The need was there: Philip with his eyes
on the north, and the key Symmachy players in the Peloponnese worn out and
unhappy, as whatever success they had had still did not seem to promise security.

In the end, whatever the motives of the participants and the nuances of the
negotiations, a peace was brokered on everybody accepting the status quo. An
agreement was reached that gave Philip and the main Symmachy participants
enough; and the Aetolians were perhaps just content to get a breather without
losing more, considering their recent reverses in the Peloponnese, the Malian
Gulf and the Gulf of Corinth.

Chapter 4

Viziers and Rebels

The second half of the third century had been a time of troubles for the descendants of Seleucus Nicator. Family troubles began under the first Antiochus; though his relations with his own father were exemplary this did not push down to the next generation. An eldest son was killed by his father, but this was just scandalous family stuff; in the reign of the younger brother marital incontinence led to tribulations for swathes of people all round the vast but rickety realm. The first wedding adventure of Antiochus II Theos was with his half sister, Laodice, which resulted in a son named Seleucus. But a few years later dynastic imperative, and perhaps a very substantial dowry, bounced a new wife into his marriage bed, a daughter of Ptolemy II Philadelphus called Berenice, and this liaison too led to the birth of another male child. But much was left in the air as neither was declared the designated heir.

Then a fatal sequence occurred, with first Antiochus II dying in Ephesus in 246, and the senior spouse, with a considerable power base in Anatolia, proclaiming her son as the new king Seleucus II. Not prepared to have his inheritance threatened by the child of Berenice, Laodice determined to eliminate the dynastic nuisance in Syria. Before the news of the old king's death could reach Antioch, her agents abducted Berenice and killed her young son. What made this a war of two queens was that Berenice, realising the threat, called on her brother Ptolemy III for help. The resultant Laodicean War or third Syrian War looked for a time to completely upset the power balance in the Hellenistic East. Ptolemy was too late to redeem his sister but found himself well placed to feast on the carcass of a badly ruptured Seleucid empire. He captured Antioch and drove east across Mesopotamia as far as Babylon. Polyaenus even suggests the Ptolemies took control as far as India; a triumph that the military establishment at Alexandria had never contemplated before and would never again. While famous exploits and great reputations were being won by Ptolemaic generals, whose names we do not even know, Laodice's son was preparing. At last, Seleucus II Callinicus, demonstrating the determined mood of the new regime, came south of the Taurus and his followers showed there was still vitality and strength in the dismembered state. Antioch was recaptured, although Seleucia in Pieria, its port twelve miles away, was not. And, by 240, when peace was brokered, Seleucus had reclaimed inland Syria down to Damascus and south to Orthosia on the Phoenician coast.

But, if the 240s had been a time of foreign invasion, the 230s were different. Now it was a war between brothers, the sons of the same Laodice, who had made certain of her bloodline over that of Berenice. Internecine strife began because Seleucus II found himself having to make war with only a rump kingdom, shorn of Mesopotamia and most of its coastal regions. Short-term expediency led him, when pressed by his mother, to install his brother Antiochus Hierax, the Hawk, as a virtual sub-king in Western Anatolia. When the warring parties from the Queens' War pulled out of their sanguine clinch, Seleucus II found that, although much was lost, he was none the less still in control of the heartland provinces where the best of the Seleucid settler soldiers were domiciled. Free to use these martial resources, in about 236 he marched through the Cilician Gates determined to retake his Anatolian lands and reconstitute something like the kingdom his forbears had ruled. Lydia was reached but, although victorious in a battle, he was unable to capture Sardis or Ephesus. Hierax's party regrouped, enrolling Galatian mercenaries and allying with Mithridates of Pontus, and in 235, this powerful axis prepared a defensive cordon in East Anatolia as Seleucus, who was back again, came up from Syria along the Persian royal road to Ancyra. But here defeat left the invader's ambitions in tatters, with the king fleeing in disguise to Cilicia with Hierax threatening to pursue. But if Antiochus had staved off this particular danger, his hegemony was never secure. Still a very young man, apart from a manipulating mother and uncle, there was a mess of out-of-control Gauls, ferocious barbarians who sometimes spearheaded his cause and at others fought as his inveterate enemies. And besides these warrior brigands, a more respectable Hellenic rival had also emerged to plague him.

The genesis of the kingdom of Pergamum had come with the death of Lysimachus in 281 and the quick footwork of his treasurer when the kingdom dissolved. Then a new man had taken that state to a higher level. Born in 269, he was adopted by his uncle Eumenes and made heir to the growing principality, succeeding in 241. Later, after culling some Galatian marauders, he re-designated himself as king Attalus I. Cheek by jowl, Attalus and Hierax inevitably clashed. The war did not begin well for Attalus. An indecisive battle at Aphrodisium, possibly near Pergamum city, suggests the new king was on the defensive. Then in about 228, campaigns were fought in Hellespontine Phrygia, through Bithynia and onto Sardis in Lydia. The pendulum swung Attalus' way and Antiochus lost support when his father in law, Ziaelas, the king of Bithynia, was killed by some of his own Galatians. But though the Hawk was not easily buried, after this he thoroughly overreached himself and invaded his brother's Syrian powerbase. Although initially outflanking the mountain ramparts of Syria via Commagene and finding over the Euphrates an open road to Antioch, he was crushed in battle by the royal army led by Seleucus II's father in law. This was the last throw of the dice for Hierax, who then travelled to Thrace to find refuge with a Ptolemaic garrison. However, this princeling of woes managed first to get himself arrested then escaped, only to encounter a wandering band of Galatians in the mountains of Thrace, who briskly killed him.

The chronology of all this is very difficult. Attalus' first Galatian triumph probably took place in about 236, but his eventual showdown with the Gallic-Hierax axis was certainly consummated almost a decade later. Whether this last campaign preceded or came after the attack on Seleucus II's Syria is again a puzzle. But after that, what was certain was that while one brother was gone another remained. Seleucus II was an energetic prince but, with him, it was always activity not achievement; the victories he won were more to do with the faltering of others than his own use of power to the point. He certainly regained much that had been lost in the Queens' War and stabilized the position in respect of Ptolemy, but the overall impression is that that conqueror had anyway just pushed on too far, and also Seleucus' attempt to restore the dynasty's fortunes in the east does not smell of great success. Even with Hierax no longer a threat, the kingdom of Seleucus was a patchy, unbalanced entity; much of the coastline in both the Levant and Anatolia remained in Ptolemaic control, and Attalus and the kings in Bithynia, Pontus and Cappadocia kept tribute most of the interior west of the Taurus.

In 226, Seleucus II Callinicus fell from his horse and shortly after died of his injuries. He had a son who, on coming to the throne, was not destined to enjoy untroubled longevity; Seleucus III managed only three years. To contemporaries, the circumstances in which the new king found himself might have suggested he ought to concentrate on digging in and retrenchment. But from the start, the energies of his government were bent against Pergamum; several armies were sent to prepare the ground for the main invasion force meant to fashion a decisive conquest. He passed the Cilician Gates at the head of an army recruited from all his empire but when, in the summer of 223, they reached Phrygia the king was murdered by two officers, one called Nicanor and the other Apaturius, a Galatian, who commanded a regiment of his compatriots in the Royal army. A brew of powerful men and an ineffectual monarch had had a toxic outcome, but the two assassins had no follow-up plan. Seleucus II's cousin, Achaeus, the son of Andromachus, the queen's brother, took charge in the camp after the poisoning occurred and, blood ties demanding reprisal, he executed both of the assassins.

High in the hierarchy of power, the troops urged Achaeus to assume the diadem himself but he refused. Instead, he held the throne in trust for the dead king's younger brother Antiochus. Whoever wore the diadem, what was certain was that the invasion was over and the army isolated in the heart of hostile country. We learn that the veteran general Epigenes was most proactive in extricating the kingless army back over the Taurus to Syria, yet Achaeus was still clearly the decisive man in forcing the future. He had Antiochus brought from Babylonia and established him on the throne of his dead elder brother. Achaeus' fealty and lack of personal ambition at this time is applauded, and after the succession was settled, a new thankful monarch returned him to Anatolia with a virtually independent portfolio to regain what had been lost during the Queens' and Brothers' Wars and Hierax's chaotic regime.

The early years of the reign of the king that Achaeus had boosted onto the throne really deserves a Dumas as chronicler, with the contest between Hermeias and Epigenes like an earlier version of Fouquet versus Colbert at Louis XIV's court. Epigenes was an old soldier and a noted orator who had strong support in the army that he had safely shepherded back from its exposed position in Phrygia. However, when Antiochus III had settled on the throne and Achaeus gone back on campaign, Epigenes found Hermeias, a Greek from Caria, established at the head of the Antioch administration and the new king in his pocket. The first head-to-head came very quickly between these two rival servants. When Seleucus III left for the war in Anatolia, a strong faction had been left in control of the eastern provinces, whose leaders were the brothers, Molon and Alexander. The former was satrap of Media and the latter of Persia, and these two were not on good terms with Hermeias, so when they discovered that he was the power behind the new regime, they struck out for independence. News of their rebellion galvanised the court at Antioch; action was clearly required, but the dilemma was that it was not only in the east. There was worrying news coming from the direction of Alexandria, which Hermeias reported as indicating that an aggressive alliance was being fabricated between Ptolemy and Achaeus. He even contrived the discovery of forged correspondence between Alexandria and Sardis to give flavour to these purported machinations.

Early in 222, a council was called, including all the great ministers, military officers and noblemen, in front of the new king to approve the enterprises required to answer the problems brewing all round the young throne. With a number of fronts competing for attention, the scene was set for a fight to the finish to dominate the councils of Antiochus III. Epigenes saw the threat from the east as most deserving of the young king's notice, and he argued that the loyalty of the citizens was such that just the arrival of the legitimate monarch would win the day. Hermeias took the opposing tack, looking for a way to eliminate Epigenes as a rival in council. The Carian's thrust was that Epigenes' policy would put the young king at risk, with a small army in the heart of enemy country. He is reported as getting out of control, unable to contain his anger, and excoriating the general for intentionally wishing to put Antiochus in harm's way. This heated exchange was short-lived, but essentially Hermeias got his way. Whilst the king and the main army concentrated on Coele Syria, a couple of generals called Xenon and Theodotus Hemiolius marched east to try and cope with the Asian rebels.

Whilst they took up this errand, the royal army intended for the campaign against Ptolemy congregated as usual at Apamea before moving on to Laodicea, a place 20 odd miles southwest of modern Homs. From there, Antiochus led them across desert country to gain the road that followed the Marsyas River defile south between the Libanus and Antilibanus mountains. They reached Gerrha, modern Aanjar, where the valley is narrow, and there was at that time a lake that constricted the route even further. There they found themselves faced by defences put up by Theodotus, the Aetolian, Ptolemy's competent general in the region. The Aetolian used methods common in the warfare of his own people, putting up palisades and digging trenches to block the road. This was going to be impossible to get round and very costly to get through, so when news of setbacks in the east reached Antiochus and his councillors they grabbed at this as a good excuse to pull away from what might have easily become an embarrassing reverse.

When he had decided on insurrection in 222, Molon mobilized the settler soldiers in the east by a combination of carrot and stick, the former a guarantee of loot aplenty and the latter consisting of forged letters from Antiochus that promised severe retribution when the king got his hands on them. In concert with his brother Alexander, he also brought on board the rulers of neighbouring satrapies by extensive outlay of 'dousers'. We know little in detail about the principality Molon organized, as our sources are Mediterranean-centred, and therefore less cognizant of or concerned with the regions further east. But the Median and Persian lands that sustained these rebels had been the homelands of the Ancient World's greatest empires. Molon's seat, Ecbatana, situated at the foot of Mount Alvand, was one of the celebrated cities of the world. It had been originally the centre of a Median state and then winter capital of the Persian Empire before Alexander arrived. It was always a vital, if much-looted, treasure house, boasting a large population, a citadel with gargantuan defences and an administration that was one of the most complete and efficient in the world. All of this gave the rebels a very secure base when Xenon and Theodotus Hemiolius arrived in the region. They had, it seems, neither great confidence nor any considerable armed force with them. Polybius suggests they were 'terror-struck', but it is more reasonable to propose that the intention from the start was defensive, to hold what could be held against a rampant Molon.

When the Seleucid commanders arrived, they found Molon advanced into Apollonia at the base of the Zagros range to the east of the Tigris. Control of this country gave him plenty of supplies to support the considerable army he had brought out of Media, as well as their many animals herded there as transport or food on the hoof. The soldier-settlers of Media, presumably bolstered by those of Persia, gave him something of a phalanx, and his Iranian subjects provided numbers of the best horsemen. As Molon crossed the Zagros he also recruited the savage tribesmen of these rugged mountains. The

Cossaeans, who had troubled both Alexander and Antigonus the One-eyed in their time, the Corbrenae and the Carchi were some of these. With such martial resources and his enemies handing him the initiative, Molon took the advantage, moving towards the eastern capital of the Seleucid kingdom. But here he found an officer of more resolution and energy in his way. Zeuxis, satrap of Babylonia, seized all the boats on the Tigris so that nobody could cross over from the far side. This activity looked to end the campaigning season, and the Seleucids settled into their camp on the west bank while Molon moved into more permanent quarters on the east bank near Ctesiphon.

Xenoetas had by this time received the baton of supreme command in the Molon War, and he began to exercise it without restraint. He reached Seleucia, the capital of the East, on the west bank of the Tigris and began to assert himself. He called in two key officers from the country still under Seleucid control; Diogenes, the governor of Susiana, the lowlands to the south east, and Pythiades, the ruler of the coastal lands around the Persian Gulf. With these men and their retinues, he approached the river opposite where Molon had established himself. Xenoetas' confidence was now boosted by the reports of deserters claiming that Molon's army was riven with deep-seated disloyalty and would come over at the appearance of legitimist forces in arms. The Seleucid supremo was also not without invention; there was a large island in the Tigris, close by Ctesiphon, where he made a considerable noise of building a bridge in preparations for invading the east bank. He did not intend a frontal assault but, instead, took his best troops, leaving Zeuxis to encourage the enemy to believe the whole army was still there. The expeditionary force marched downstream through the night for about ten miles. There boats had been gathered, and during the night they crossed without opposition and made camp 'the greater part of which was surrounded by the river and the rest protected by pools and marshes.'[1] When news arrived of his enemy's manoeuvre, Molon responded by rushing off his cavalry to crush them. But the action was not carried out well, and Molon's Iranian horse, unfamiliar with the terrain, rode into the marshes, where they could make no progress and not a few were drowned. Xenoetas, still convinced his enemies' troops were ripe for desertion, marched back up the river and led his men into a camp within sight of Molon's army at Ctesiphon. This bellicose stance had an immediate impact, and the rebel army packed up and fled upriver in the direction of Media, under cover of night, apparently leaving most of their heavy baggage in the camp. Xenoetas immediately took over the encampment and brought Zeuxis, the rest of his army, and his own baggage over the river. But it turned out all to be a ploy; Molon had not gone far, but had rested and fed his men and returned in arms to find exactly what he hoped for. Xenoetas' army had looted the camp and found the alcohol that had no doubt been left with this in mind. They indulged with no thought of danger from a foe they considered beaten and far off, their officers could not retain order and any attempt at keeping guard was very negligently carried out. Molon and his men came out of the dawn in organized battalions and found the enemy befuddled and boozed and completely unable to make a defence. Xenoetas could not face the shame of being caught with his pants down; he searched for death in the enemy ranks and quickly found it. The only effort any of the defenders could make was to run the short distance to the river with what baggage they could salvage. But few got over safely. 'So that the picture presented by the stream was indeed tragical and extraordinary, horses, mules, arms and corpses and every kind of baggage being swept down by the current.'[2]

Molon did not allow any chance of his enemy rallying. He crossed the river, took Zeuxis' camp (who had also fled) and then went on to Seleucia and took it too at the first assault. Diomedon, the governor of the capital of the East, and many of the other officers of the province were dead or dispersed and there was little sinew in the remaining defences of the Mesopotamian region. Columns were sent down to the coast and into Babylonia, and Molon himself broke into Susa at the first time of asking.

Aglow with energy, Molon overran Parapotamia all the way up to Dura Europus, a Hellenistic foundation from the end of the fourth century, hundreds of miles up the Euphrates and, more than this, he also pushed up the Tigris into Mesopotamia as far as another important town, also called Dura, near Apollonia. In 312, the first Seleucus had won back a kingdom by just such another surprise attack on another unwary opponent amongst the marshes of the Tigris as he had achieved against Xenoetas, an adventure that led to the foundation of a dynasty. Soon it would become clear if Molon was going to be able to emulate this achievement.

The messenger who brought the news of these awful events to Antiochus was the catalyst for another abrasive council, where once again Hermeias abused Epigenes for sustaining the case that the king should have dealt with Molon himself before and certainly must do so now. But the very obvious danger in the east encouraged other council members to support the old soldier. Hermeias had to accept that he would not win this one, but he was still determined to bring Epigenes down. As the expedition was got under way, amongst the compounds for soldiers and animals at Apamea events fell out that allowed him to move decisively against his rival. Many soldiers had apparently not been paid in some time and now they were being told they must march out to fight another enemy. They were no longer prepared to put up with this contractual trifling and they mutinied, plunging the royal camp into furore. Hermeias, with his hands tight on the purse strings, was the only one in a position to solve the problem, and with the king clearly rattled by this insurrection, in the very heart of his army, he saw his opportunity. He made it a condition of his providing the required funds that Epigenes be forced into retirement. Hermeias' rationale was that he and Epigenes would never be able to effectively work together. Antiochus had to agree, but he was unhappy and had wanted the old soldier at his side when he took on Molon and Alexander. So, if Hermeias had gained one major point in the matter of the confidence of his king, his position had undoubtedly been dented. Epigenes, knowing when to concede defeat, slipped quietly into private life.

With the atmosphere evil and his own hand strong, Hermeias now decided to make permanent his advantage and count a fatal coup on his retired rival. The actual process was devious even by his standards. His agents subverted Epigenes' household and arranged for forged letters, purporting to be from Molon, to be introduced into his house. Alexis, the governor of Apamea, where the general's house was, and crony of Hermeias, made sure he found them and executed the old soldier for treason on the spot.

Now Hermeias was without any competitor, and more than this, the untouchable minister travelled with a clattering escort of heavily-armed soldiers as virtual retainers. This Carian Greek was no doubt unscrupulous enough, but he had won confidence in a few important quarters. He had been left as vizier at Antioch when Seleucus III set off to deal with Attalus, and he must have played a part in arranging the acclamation of Antiochus. Reports on his damning cruelty and malice are convincing; bringing up false charges was just the beginning. But still, his apparent poisonous rivalry with Epigenes may obscure real foreign policy differences. Something of a wild man, at one council, at least, he seems to have completely flown off the handle at his rival. And any devious scheming was reported as definitely up his street.

Whatever the outcome of these machinations, Antiochus determined on heading east against Molon. It was the beginning of 221 and Hermeias was still well entrenched at the head of affairs when the Royal army marched out from Apamea. His strategy of the king not leading in person against the Asian rebels had been overturned, but in recompense, his main rival had been eliminated and his discovery of the money to pay the soldiers arrears had made him man of the moment for this key demographic. If the previous strategy on the eastern front had been essentially defensive, aimed at keeping Molon out of Babylonia, it had failed, and now the principle was to bring into play all the resources required to deal with the rebel in detail. The army marched to Antioch in Mygdonia (Nisibis), deep in Mesopotamia, where they wintered for six weeks prior to opening the main campaign. Then it was on to Libba on the Tigris, where they were required to decide on the strategy they intended to employ against their enemy, who (though he had sent an army up river to try and take the fortress city of Dura) was himself with his main forces, still established further south near Babylon.

The strategic options were a direct march down the right bank of the Tigris, sponsored by Hermeias, or crossing the river into Apollonia to threaten Molon's communications with Media, and so bring him out to battle. The first alternative involved a six-day desert march and fighting across a difficult irrigation canal (King's canal) in the country to the front of Babylon itself, which was defended by the enemy in force. For this reason, even the apparently ascendant Hermeias could not get his way, and it was decided to cross the river into a well-supplied area, where it was also expected that the Hellenic colonists planted there would rally to their rightful king.

Three columns crossed the river and headed for Dura in Apollonia, where they saw off a besieging Molonian detachment before making an eight-day route march over mountain country to Apollonia itself. By now, Molon had reacted as expected to the threat against his lines of communication with Media and the constancy of the inhabitants of the newly occupied provinces of Babylonia and Susiana. He re-crossed the Tigris and was heading north on a collision course with Antiochus in the foothills of the Zagros, where ranges of mountains run parallel with the Tigris north of Seleucia. The rebel had great faith in his Cyrtii slingers and so tried to reach broken terrain to fight a battle where they might show to their best. He seemed to have achieved this, as the initial fighting we hear of consisted of some skirmishing in amongst the rugged mountains of the Apollonia region.

Both sides encamped about five miles from each other after this indecisive entrée. A dénouement, though, certainly seemed in the air. We are told of a planned night attack by Molon that was scuppered by the desertion of a squad of ten men, whose absence convinced him that the surprise must be aborted because these men would have alerted the enemy. The next day the climactic encounter of Apollonia in 220 could not be delayed, and the two armies trooped in serried ranks out from their camps and moved through the dust towards each other. Antiochus' battle line is reasonably attested; on his right he had his lancers under Ardys, then Cretan allies and Gauls. Then came a unit of Greek mercenaries abutting the central phalanx. The left wing was comprised just of the 'Companion' heavy cavalry, and in front of all these were ten elephants, evenly distributed along the front. Hermeias and Zeuxis led on the left, while the king himself held the position of honour on the right. The Seleucid high command also deployed a considerable reserve of both cavalry and infantry; these were kept behind the main battle line with the intention of working round the enemy's flanks.

Molon's men had been disturbed by the fiasco of the night attack, so it was a somewhat jaded army the rebel leader led out through the gates of his own encampment. Their deployment was conventional, with heavy infantry in the centre, 'the *scutati*, the Gauls and in general all his heavy armed troops' and horse on the flanks, but his valued light infantry were placed beyond the cavalry on the extremities of the wings. Molon's brother, Neolaus, commanded on the left and the rebel monarch on the right. He had no elephants; his writ never ran far to the east, where they came from, and he never had any access to the royal herds around Apamea. Still, he did have some scythed chariots (Babylonia had military

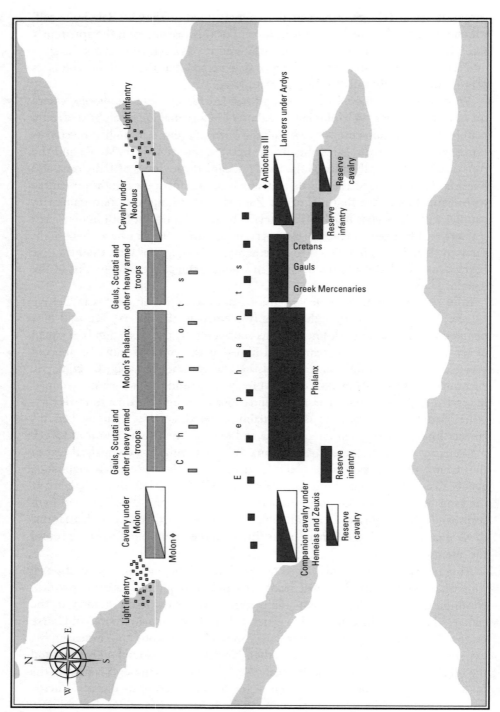

Plan 5: The Battle of Apollonia, 220 BC.

settlers specializing in this weapon form since at least the Achaemenid Empire) that were distributed in front of his lines in the hope that they might cause some disruption amongst an enemy phalanx that was surely larger than his own.

There is a paucity of details for this crucial combat, but what is certain is when the orders to advance came the men under Molon on the right acquitted themselves well and pushed hard against Zeuxis' men on the Seleucid left. But on the other wing it was different story: 'as soon as they closed and came in sight of the king, went over to the enemy, upon which Molon's whole force lost heart, while the confidence of the king's army was redoubled.'[3] Whether this applied just to Molon's left or to his phalanx as well is not clear, but it is reported that his position became untenable when the Seleucids got behind those men who remained loyal and threatened to surround them all. With any line of retreat about to be closed off, the rest of Molon's army laid down its arms.

Molon committed suicide straight after the battle, and the rest of his faction and his family dissolved in a welter of blood. Neolaus, who had fought alongside his brother, took the road to Persia, where Alexander might have fought on. But events seemed to have persuaded them all was over, and Neolaus, Alexander, Molon's wife and children all took their own lives. It was a sanguine solution brought on a by a realization that, after the news of the battle arrived, any local support would dissolve, and that Antiochus was more likely to be cruel rather than merciful in victory. A prescient understanding, if the treatment of Molon's body is anything to go by. It was discovered, crucified and left as an example to other rebels at the foot of the Zagros Mountains. Ambitious Macedonians since Pithon in 318 had tried to use Media as the base to create seats of independent power, but Molon would be the last to make a credible attempt in a region that would, anyway, soon be lost to the expanding power of the Parthians.[4]

Antiochus needed the officers and men of Molon's old army back in Media to sustain his own position in the east, so the settler soldiers and Iranian conscripts were packed off with the gift of pardon and what the young king hoped would be a real commitment to himself and his dynasty. After this, he proceeded back to the eastern capital, his old home of Seleucia on the Tigris, where people had not covered themselves in glory by opening their gates to Molon very easily indeed. This timidity, if not outright treachery, Hermeias was determined to make a source of profit. He settled down to squeeze the locals till the pips squeaked, but then something disconcerting for the vizier came about. The young monarch began to assert himself; he overruled his advisor and himself determined on the final punishment the city fathers would suffer. The population had to find a 150 talent fine for their transgressions, but they were hugely relieved to find at least Hermeias' more brutal depredations were to be curtailed.

Antiochus had done well in this his first real campaign. He had run out winner against a very dangerous enemy. He had led well from the front and his prestige with both military and civilian establishment must have grown by leaps and bounds. So it is no surprise that he began to balk at the controlling presence of his all-powerful vizier. But Hermeias, far from stepping back a bit to allow room for the royal ego, became even more ruthless in his exercise of power. There is a suggestion that Antiochus was actually afraid of him and, of course, he was well aware that his elder brother had been struck down by officers of considerably lower in rank and influence than the great vizier. Rifts began to appear when Antiochus, seeing a vista of eastern conquest before his eyes, considered an expedition against king Artabazanes of Media Atropatene, that northern part of Media, southwest of the Caspian Sea. But Hermeias was concerned over risks to the prince in such an expedition and anyway still had his sights set on gains against Ptolemy in Coele Syria. However, after a son was born to Antiochus, Hermeias came on board about this war to the north, apparently consoling himself that if Antiochus died in action he could then continue to rule through the infant son. But when the invasion began the war was quickly concluded; the defending monarch Artabazanes was an old man and did not have it in him to resist for long.

Tensions in the court of the new conqueror king certainly seemed to be ratcheting up with the passage of time. Polybius tells us about the king's doctor Apollophanes who persuaded Antiochus that Hermeias was intriguing against him. The post of physician to a monarch is one of great potential but also considerable danger. It is always possible that suspicious deaths of the great and powerful can be laid at their door with fatal consequences but, equally, if they gain the confidence of the reigning prince the potential for manipulation is huge. Apollophanes had noticed the growing rift between prince and first minister and saw his chance. He found he was pushing an open door; Antiochus already hated and feared his chief official. But Hermeias' power base was a real difficulty for the king; he feared this spider in the middle of his administrative web with great military clout and money to spend. If his actions in any way seemed to threaten Hermeias' position, it could act as a catalyst for a palace coup.

Yet the young monarch was aching to rule his own roost and determined to be rid of his over-mighty subject; it only remained as to method. This was done by Antiochus feigning an illness, giving the doctor control of those allowed close to him. Then, these confederates lured the minister to attend the king alone on an early morning walk where he was stabbed to death. The key contrivance was to get Hermeias away from the camp, which indicates it was the military that provided his most loyal support and defence. Later events suggest Apollophanes was a little more than just a medic; he certainly took a high place in future councils and in all probability represented a cabal of high-placed opponents. For, without solid backing, it is difficult to imagine anyone having the confidence to approach the king on such a dangerous matter. This palace revolution is reported as being greeted with joy by almost everyone and Hermeias' wife and family were stoned to death by neighbours in their home in Apamea. What always makes an observer a little quizzical about stories of these apparently universally loathed chief ministers, like Hermeias, and the common joy felt at their demise, is that, apart from it being a continual riff played by Polybius, one is bound to ask how such utterly loathed creatures could have sustained themselves in power? Hermeias was a senior figure in at least two reigns and his counterparts Sosibius and Agathocles in Ptolemaic Egypt for far longer. But certainly he was no Philotas, whose father Parmenion and his whole faction must be murdered to ensure against vendetta. We hear of no others eliminated; not even his friends amongst the soldiery seemed to have been so attached that they required purging. The king, after the fall of his chief minister, continued, as usual, to take advice at council, but what is certain is that after Hermeias no man ever stands in the same way at the head in Antiochus' administration. There are high officers, civilian and military, but the king is always the man in charge.

Where geographically this murderous business took place is not clear, but from the site of the minister's homicide the king moved to Antioch, where he dismissed the army for the winter. But if one issue had been dealt with another one simmered; the problem of Achaeus remained. Although in the years of his pomp he had shown steadfast loyalty to the senior Seleucid line, there were still likely to have been the usual abrasions between the two power foci that ensured relations between the courts at Sardis and Antioch were not absolutely smooth as silk. And whatever these underlying agendas and tensions, the whole business came to the boil when Antiochus started his war against Artabazanes. Achaeus concentrated a large army at Sardis and set off east, stopping only at Laodicea in Phrygia to celebrate his own acclamation as monarch. The warlord's intention was then to invade Syria itself. Initially, Achaeus had kept his followers in the dark about his plans, but in Lyaconia, halfway along the road in the middle of Anatolia, the truth leaked out and the army began to murmur against their general. This invasion, and the concomitant civil war it would prompt, was a step too far. It became clear that his men would not carry on, and a frustrated Achaeus only saved the day by persuading them that his real intention was to suppress the Pisidians, always a popular target, and one that provided his soldiers with sufficient booty to cement a fidelity that Achaeus had almost pushed too far.

So, when Antiochus met with his council at Apamea, as so often before, he was faced with difficult choices on which way to jump. Apollophanes, who had helped rid him of his shackles, pressed the cause of his native city, Seleucia in Pieria, just 12 miles from Antioch and held by a Ptolemaic garrison. This hangover from the Laodicean war was clearly of significant strategic importance, and the doctor's arguments met little opposition, as taking the town was clearly crucially important in clearing the lines for an all-out attack on Ptolemy's Levantine holdings. As 219 began, a Diognetus was designated to command a fleet that set off to blockade the town, while the king led the main army against the walls. Theodotus Hemiolius, apparently rehabilitated from his setbacks against Molon, was sent south to block off the routes north from Coele Syria that Ptolemaic troops might try and utilize to send relief to the garrison. Seleucia itself 'descends in a series of broken terraces to the sea and is surrounded on most sides by cliffs and precipitous rocks.'[5] This tough nut Antiochus first tried to crack by subverting those in charge. He could not pay his way straight in, but he apparently made arrangements that if his forces captured the crucial district near the port, the men he had suborned could then persuade their commander to surrender. Diognetus, with his marines from the fleet, and Ardys, who had shown well leading the lancers in the battle of Apollonia, with a task force, made for there, while two other groups made a great show of it, attacking other parts of the city. Soon ladders were in place and assault groups got onto the walls of the port quarter. The other attacks meant no reinforcements were available to counter the Seleucids established under Ardys, and soon Antiochus' contacts within the walls showed their worth. They browbeat Leontius, the garrison commander, that all was lost and that weak vessel sent out emissaries to arrange a surrender. The total lack of Ptolemaic effort to equip a relief force must have been uppermost in that officer's thinking when he decided his position was untenable, and the reason for this apathy was soon to become very clear.

The campaign had started at a gallop, but it got even better. Theodotus, the Aetolian, Ptolemy's commander in Coele Syria, offered to sell the pass. He had done good service in the past, but his star was obviously not in the ascendant with the new crew at Alexandria, despite his exemplary work in blocking the Seleucid invasion of two years before. Once he decided to swap sides, he put himself in a good position by setting himself up in Ptolemais (modern Acre) and putting his cohort Panaetolus in Tyre, while he opened discussions with Antiochus. This was news that definitely decided against any Antiochid move against the rebel Achaeus; he could wait as Antiochus acted swiftly to exploit this new opportunity. He crossed the desert, as he had two years previously, entered the Marsyas valley again and passed down to near Gerrha, where his army had been stopped before. Here news arrived that the Ptolemaic administration had reacted promptly to Theodotus' treachery. Nicolaus, another Aetolian, now given command, had penned the traitor in at Ptolemais and was besieging the place. The Seleucid king left his heavy troops to lay siege to Gerrha and Brochi, towns that commanded the passage south, whilst he led his light troops to rescue his new friend. Nicolaus, hearing Antiochus was on his way, withdrew from his siege lines and sent most of his men under Lagoras, the Cretan, and Dorymenes, yet another Aetolian, to occupy the coastal pass near

Berytus (modern Beirut), which Antiochus would need to traverse. The king barrelled through these defences and camped to wait for his heavy troops. The Lagids, for the moment, had had enough, and the rest of the journey to link up with Theodotus and Panaetolus was a cake walk. And it was not just these crucial strongpoints that Antiochus acquired; there were also trapped in the harbours 'forty ships, twenty of them decked vessels admirably equipped, none with less than four banks of oars, and the remainder triremes, biremes and pinnaces'.[6]

Much had been achieved with bribery and intrigue, but the Seleucids had not had to face their enemy's main forces. But now this looked set to change, as messengers came in with news that Ptolemy and the royal army had moved to Pelusium and were putting that fortress into good shape for defence. Further progress was going to be more testing, and if Antiochus had really thought of attacking Pelusium and even Egypt beyond, he abandoned the project and contented himself with snapping up smaller places on the coast. The better-defended towns, aware that Ptolemy looked as if he was coming to take care of his own, dug in behind their walls. Antiochus tried his luck even against these, but no names are mentioned except another Dura, a city south of Ptolemais on the coast, where the Seleucids were still bogged down when winter came. Such stuttering in Seleucid progress encouraged a positive response to peace feelers put out by Sosibius and Agathocles. With Rhodians, Byzantines, Cyzicuns and Aetolians greasing the diplomatic wheels, at the turn of 219/18 both sides were content to sign to a four-month truce.

Chapter 5

Raphia

In 222, a Spartan king stepped off a boat into exile in Egypt. There he found his mother and children, who had been sent there as hostages when he began receiving subsidies from the Ptolemies. After the battle of Sellasia, Cleomenes had gone directly back to Sparta, and apparently not even pausing to strip off his armour, he set sail, only collecting his thoughts on the heaving deck of the ship he found to carry him. These ruminations led him to steer towards Cyrene and throw himself on the mercy of the government at Alexandria. On reaching that city, Ptolemy III soon learned to love Cleomenes' laconic charm, to the extent of twenty-four talents, an annual stipend sufficient to keep him and his friends in some style.[1] But unfortunately, this king, whose good graces Cleomenes had earned, did not last long after his arrival; by 221 at the latest he was dead, and his son, Ptolemy IV, reigned in his stead.

It was a new world, where an apparently debauched monarch was ruled by his ministers Sosibius and Agathocles; the latter, the brother of the king's mistress Agathoclea. Poisonous faction rivalry was the order of the day, and all three, though close to the king, apparently walked on eggshells for fear of other powerful groupings. There was a royal uncle, called Lysimachus, with a powerbase down the Nile, the dowager Queen Berenice, and the king's brother, Magas, who had considerable pull with the Alexandrine army. In this dynamic, Cleomenes cut a figure of some importance, because 3,000 of the guardsmen quartered in the palace were in origin Peloponnesians or Cretans, who were as attached to him as either Magas or indeed the king who paid their wages. Sosibius was an Alexandrine political fixer who had consolidated his position when Ptolemy IV became king, and he it was who spoke through the young monarch's mouth. He convinced Cleomenes to keep the guards onside as a cull of competitors was realized; Magas was despatched in his bath and Berenice poisoned.

But if Cleomenes had stood on the sidelines during this bloodletting, it did not win the support that might boost him back to power in Sparta, where his heart still lay. The dénouement of the story of this frustrated man of action starts when a Messenian, Nicagoras, arrived in Alexandria to trade. There was bad blood between them, and he determined to do the exile some harm. During their conversations, Cleomenes had made disparaging remarks about the king preferring musicians and catamites to warhorses, and Nicagoras reported all this to Sosibius and his king. Hearing it, they put Cleomenes under house arrest, although Ptolemy still showed ambivalence, claiming all the while that he was Cleomenes' friend and supporter. But soon the exile was persuaded that there would never be any help from the quarter of the royal palace. Irascible and slightly irrational by now, when the court and most of the royal army left town for Canopus, eighteen miles to the east, near Abukir bay, Cleomenes and his friends decided on insurrection. It had to be triggered early, but fortuitously the guards round his house had been drinking and were already incapacitated by noon. The thirteen revolutionaries slipped past them and took to the streets, an extraordinary tableau of armed men stalking down, in the shadows of the Great Library of Alexandria. But the people did not respond to Cleomenes' offer to depose the ruling faction, and the only real satisfaction for the incendiaries was in managing to set about the city guard commander. As they left him dead, Cleomenes and his followers headed for the citadel, killed some gendarmes and tried to free the prisoners who they hoped to recruit to the cause. But the rest of the jailers barricaded themselves in the prison and even this long shot was a flop. Wandering the city, with the people fleeing at the sight of their bloody swords as they hurried down the wide streets with no sign of local espousal, Cleomenes decided self-destruction was the only way out. Most of the thirteen stabbed themselves, while Panteus, a close friend of the king, stayed alive to ensure that all were dead before committing suicide himself. The Spartan king's family followed suit or were murdered by Ptolemy when he returned to Alexandria.

So, in 219, a Spartan king's life had concluded in ignominy. An existence that, perhaps, should better have ended a few years earlier on the battlefield of Sellasia. The world where his tragic end was encompassed was one where two great Hellenistic kingdoms contended on a much grander stage than he ever had in the south of Greece. Yet his dramatic end reveals something about the stability and vigour of the kingdom he had found himself in. Egypt, on this occasion, resembles some banana republic with a few men of violence in the streets almost able to destabilize the whole polity, and this only a generation after Egypt's rulers achieved one of the great, if indifferently recorded, achievements of the ancient world. From 246–241 Ptolemy III Euergetes fought a hugely successful campaign against the Seleucids, whose familial antics not only allowed his intervention but ensured its success.

In 246, Ptolemy marched north to Antioch and an extraordinary achievement that is recorded in several places. An inscription at Adulis claims he conquered, or at least took vassalage, all the way to Bactria, including the countries in-between, and mentions the return of the precious things that the Persian

Cambyses had looted from Egypt centuries before.[2] The question of how real were Ptolemy's achievements in this blitzkrieg war is open to debate, but even the most optimistic estimates of the range of these conquests do not propose that control went much beyond the great imperial cities on the western edge of the Iranian plateau.

The most dramatic events of the war occurred on two main fronts. The conquering thrust into the heart of the Seleucid realm and a major naval offensive around the shores of Anatolia and the Levant. This second hangs on gossamer evidence too, but it is still compelling.

The Ptolemaic marine had already had some solid achievements; it dominated the coasts of Phoenicia, Lycia, Caria and the islands of Cyprus, although the Cyclades may have mainly been lost after a sea battle at Andros that is a mystery in terms of both date, result and opponents.[3] But now, against the Seleucids, the Egyptian marine prospered, establishing hegemony over the great city of Ephesus and much of Cilicia, and even constructing a foothold in Thrace, where the Seleucids had previously ruled. As the Seleucids had become the most fractured and fragile of dynasties, it ought to have seemed that a much rosier future was in store for the great conqueror of the 240s. On his return from the east, Ptolemy must have anticipated the good news would keep on coming. His main enemy was deeply wounded, rent with fratricidal strife, and his own administration controlled, apart from the African heartland, a necklace of strongholds around the Eastern Mediterranean. A Ptolemaic garrison was well dug in at Seleucia in Pieria, a mere 12 miles from the Seleucid capital itself. And he had left 'a particular friend, Antiochus' established in Cilicia, that crucial region thrust between the Seleucid centres of power in Syria and Anatolia, and also a trusted officer called Xanthippus to rule in the east. All a bit stitched together, but it was still impressive in a world where any community that was not a single city state could look equally as jumbled in composition.

Domestically, Alexandria remained Queen City of the Hellenistic World; in terms of both commerce and culture, a great new polyglot centre. The head of government, the home of money, and the centre of intellectual endeavour, 130 miles northwest of Cairo; it was so different from those citizen polities that had held the stage before. If Pella had been a boom town on the back of Persian loot, the Egyptian city was more than that. It did not just suck in, but it created wealth too. The port and shopping bazaars bustled with crowds that included the poorest slave to the super-rich merchants and office holders. A powerhouse of cultural and scientific advancement, it remained a great place in a way that was miles away from the mothballed intellectualism of the likes of Athens. Yet despite all this golden glow, the picture of Ptolemaic power faded very soon indeed. Ptolemy III is only glimpsed through the mists in the last twenty years of his tenure. Little seems to have been achieved or even attempted, and by the time the sources shine again on the riverine kingdom, its government is a sink of intrigue, its army a shell, needing complete overhaul, and its policies mere responses to the threats of more active neighbours. The causes for this are hinted at. Indigenous unrest had probably been the cause of Ptolemy III's return from his eastern conquest in the 240s, and perhaps it was this development that meant this active and talented monarch never significantly strode the world stage again. There is no other reason given for this quiet middle age for a monarch who in his young manhood had rivalled Alexander himself. And if he had to struggle to maintain internal security, how much more tenuous would be the position of his successors, who had neither his talent nor his reputation to bolster what for most people outside of Alexandria was still an interloper ascendancy. Indeed, evidence of unrest was never absent for long in Egypt under foreign rule, whether it was Assyrian, Persian or Macedonian. By 207/6 things were thoroughly unstable, with local kings called Haronnophris and Chaonnophris at Thebes, mentioned as established against all Ptolemaic attempts to suppress them.

So, until the war that led to a bloody encounter at the hinge where Africa meets Asia, virtually nothing is known, only that Ptolemy III's heir looked like a real dip in the Ptolemaic bloodline from the start. The sources have him dominated by the duo we know from Cleomenes' story. Sosibius, the political operator, whose pedigree goes back to the mid-230s, when he was the priest of the Brother and Sister Gods, and of the Benefactor Gods at Alexandria, a 'cunning and world-practised old scoundrel'. Agathocles, the handsome debaucher of Ptolemy IV and his unsavoury mother and sister, kicked off the kind of bloody, treacherous, incestuous and cowardly conduct that would make this dynasty, for the rest of their long tenure, the epitome of eastern Greek depravity that the Romans loved to deride. We should not believe all we hear but, still, it is not unreasonable to assume some pretty strong stuff was underway by the lake of Mareotis in the centuries to come. But, for the moment, it was Sosibius and Agathocles with their hands on the tiller, although these now show in a very different light indeed from the dire press they usually get. The next sequence of events at the end of 219 shows them as good organizers, intelligent planners, and sagacious delegators, and possessed of an Odyssean cunning that made a real chump of the Seleucid administration. They opened diplomatic channels, not only sending envoys of their own but orchestrating ambassadorial missions from friends at Rhodes, Byzantium, Cyzicus and Aetolia, and with these toing and froing in the gilded halls of Antioch and Memphis, they entrammelled a seemingly unstoppable Antiochus in time-consuming negotiations.

Brilliantly, Sosibius kept the envoys from Antiochus constantly attending the court at Memphis, so they would not notice the hive of military activity in progress at Alexandria. They really pulled the wool over the Seleucids' eyes to keep the intensive military training quiet and unreported. Antiochus appears very complacent at this time and seemingly fully expecting to win the balance of Lagid Levantine holdings by diplomacy alone. When he received the Ptolemaic ambassadors at Seleucia in Pieria, he apparently felt all he had to do was outline the ancient history of what had happened after the battle of Ipsus in 301 and the agreement that the Seleucids were due all of Coele Syria. Sosibius' well-drilled envoys argued long and hard on the opposite tack and raised the more recent issues of Antiochus' unwarranted invasion; all the while their army was growing in strength and practising its skills in the camps around Alexandria. Antiochus had not made matching preparations. He may have been intending to next turn his attention to Achaeus, perhaps expecting to extend the four-month truce to a permanent peace that would allow him to concentrate on crushing that rebel. All these exchanges wearied out the winter, but with spring Antiochus snapped out of his torpor and made some decisions. If talking would not round out his Levantine possessions, then it would have to come to swords again.

As this chin-wagging had begun, Nicolaus, Ptolemy's current Aetolian supremo, had kept the Antiochids occupied at the siege of Dura. Now the hiatus was over, this Ptolemaic man on the ground had been well boosted at his base at Gaza; supplies, troops and ships had all been sent. We are not told how many, but certainly the marine force under Perigenes was considerable, with thirty heavy warships and more than 400 transports mentioned. Nicolaus now showed some real defensive nous in disposing of his men. The pass at Platanus was garrisoned while he ranged everyone else near the town Porphyrion, with his sea flank protected by the navy. Now known as Jieh, it is fifteen or so miles south of Beirut and has miles of sandy beach along a coast that is for the most part quite rocky.

Antiochus now stirred, came down to Aradus (modern Arwad) thirty miles north of Tripolis, and once significant enough to be part of a federation with Tyre and Sidon, defended by massive walls and possessing a history that went back at least to Thutmose III in the fifteenth century BC. He soon reached the River Damuras on the coast, and the fleet under Diognetus kept him company to protect his seaward flank. Coming on the enemy defences, he reconnoitred first with his light troops before deciding on a plan of attack. 'At this part of the coast it is reduced by the slopes of the Libanus to a small and narrow zone.'[4] This was just right for defence, and here Nicolaus had utilized a cliff that ran almost down to the sea; they also guarded the inland slopes of the Libanus Mountain. In places they erected artificial defences as well.

The Seleucid high command split their army into three task forces, consisting mainly of lighter troops (this mountain country was no place for phalangites), each with a different job. Theodotus Hemiolius was to force the line at the foot of the hills, the furthest inland thrust. Then a Menedemus was intended to push through further west by a spur of land. The last, under Diocles, was to attack along the seashore. Antiochus, his guard and the phalanx, took up a central position, well placed to see how all his forces were doing. The ships were to support and throw back the Ptolemaic navy, which was posted to defend the seaward flank of Nicolaus' position. The Seleucid fleet, under Diognetus, attacked in tandem with the army, but the Ptolemaic ships did well against what was an equally-matched force. But it was not just to be a naval contest.

At sea, the fight went back and forth, but the real decision took place on land. Firstly, the Lagids, well dug in, held their own, but Theodotus, furthest inland, led his force up from the base of the mountain until he had taken the high ground. That gave the crucial advantage, and Nicolaus' men could not sustain themselves when they saw the enemy up above them. When Theodotus reordered his men and charged, it was all over, resistance crumbled and Ptolemy's troops fled. Nearly 2,000 were cut down, 2,000 were captured, while the remainder scrambled down the roads leading to Sidon. At this point, the Ptolemaic ships, cognizant of what had happened on land, pulled back to the port city to ensure that communications might be kept open with home.

Nicolaus had lost 4,000 men, but he still he had very effectively prepared the defences of the ancient Phoenician city of Sidon, and his navy, little depleted by the fight, joined him there. Antiochus could make little headway when he arrived, and after an aborted attempt at assault, he turned to probe another route south. While the navy, no longer needed, returned to Tyre, the army headed inland to Philoteria at the very southern end of the sea of Galilee in the Jordan valley. The place was on the shore of the lake where the Jordan joins it, before it wends into the plain of Scythopolis and the Jezreel joins the river. Here were a considerable number of Hellenic communities well worth gaining control of: 'the territory subject to them was easily capable of supplying his whole army with food.'[5] Philoteria and Scythopolis both came to terms and were garrisoned, as the invaders passed on almost due west across some hills to Atabyrium, a town situated on the top of Mount Tabor, 2,000 feet up. Antiochus tricked the garrison into coming out to fight and got his own men to flee down the hill. Sucked in by the stratagem, the garrison found the attackers had then turned round and that there were also other men lying in ambush; they were taken in the front and flank. They panicked, and fleeing back to the town walls, allowed the Seleucids to get through the gate on their heels. Antiochus now began to reap the benefits of his success. Enemy officers came over to him, including a Thessalian commander of 400 cavalry. And, more than this, he easily took the towns of Pella, Camus and Gephrus. Abila, up in the hills east of Galilee, for a moment became a centre of resistance, but it soon succumbed, and even the most important place in the region, Gadara, showed little resistance, its garrison overawed by just the sight of Antiochus' siege train.

The Ptolemaic army was not totally out for the count, and it took up position at Philadelphia, and from there they pillaged the local Arabs who had committed themselves to Antiochus' side. These robust but militarily insignificant people were in deep danger of getting crushed between two superpower contestants. But Antiochus valued their support and moved to eliminate the enemy presence. He marched the whole army south to the hill where the town was situated on what is now the citadel hill of Amman. The Antiochid engineers noticed only two places where they could set up their paraphernalia. The siege train had been brought down and it was now deployed at these two sites under the supervision of Nicarchus and Theodotus Hemiolius. These officers were motivated by a considerable rivalry and were soon in competition to throw down the parts of the wall in front of them. When the walls came down, assault groups were led forward over the broken masonry. But all this brutal heave and shove over ditch and shattered stonework achieved little until a prisoner showed the attackers a water pipe upon which the garrison depended. When this was blocked up with rock and earth, thirst finally drove the defenders to surrender.

The campaigning season was now drawing to an end, but this time Antiochus was determined to avoid the mistakes of the previous year when he had allowed the Ptolemies to seep back north and regain control of the passes leading between the Lebanon Mountains and the sea. Apart from the garrisons he had already planted on the east bank of the Jordan, he left 5,000 foot soldiers in Samaria on the west bank. Antiochus was now really making hay; he determined to capture what cities he could before Ptolemy organized any kind of response, and Gaza particularly was important enough to hurry for. It had been a key Egyptian fortress since the early Bronze Age, then an important Philistine stronghold, and more recently such a dominating strongpoint on the road to Egypt that Alexander had been prepared to delay his invasion for five months to get control of the place. And after Gaza's capture, one task force must have been sent even further south, as by next year it is clear Antiochus' forces controlled the coast down as far as Raphia.

Much had meanwhile been on hand in Alexandria, activities that make some sense of what had seemed pretty feeble efforts by the Ptolemaic military in the years gone by. Their martial endeavours, like the diplomatic equivalents before, had been all about buying time, and this time had not been wasted. A team of professionals had been brought to Egypt to create an army that could get payback for Seleucid aggression of the past few years. Their effort produced what must have been the greatest armed force that the Ptolemies ever committed to the field. The force that Ptolemy III led up the Levant and into Babylonia in the 240s is not recorded in terms of strength, but surely it would not have been as large as this one, and the biggest army the first Ptolemy ever led in the Diadochi Wars was well under half the size of the one got ready by 217. The army that Agathocles and Sosibius had inherited had clearly declined greatly since the days of the Laodicean War conquests, while the activity of

Antiochus showed that it now faced a test for which it would need to be at the top of its game. While they span their diplomatic web from Memphis, an army camp was raised at Alexandria, and the stockpiling of huge magazines was ordered, with either Sosibius or Agathocles frequently coming themselves to the seaside capital to oversee matters.

The officers who were recruited have names that will crop up frequently during the coming campaign. They were not just drill sergeants but field officers as well. Most came from Greece. Echecrates was a Thessalian, whose role was to train the Greek and mercenary cavalry. Phoxidas was an Achaean, and had 8,000 mercenaries under his command; and there was a Boeotian named Socrates, who would command the peltasts. Another who also arrived from Greece was to take a leading role; this was Polycrates of Argos, a man with distinguished pedigree, whose father Mnesiades had been a famous athlete. He was in charge of much of the rest of the cavalry training, both the 700 horse of the king's guard and also Libyan and Egyptian troopers who together amounted to 3,000 men. Others hailed from the Greek towns of Anatolia, like Andromachus of Aspendus, who was of a similar stature and reputation as Polycrates. He both trained and led the Macedonian phalanx. Eurylochus came from Magnesia and would command the infantry called the Royal guard. All these were veterans who had previously seen service under the Macedonian kings Demetrius II and Antigonus Doson.

From Thrace came Dionysius, leading 2,000 recently raised Thracians to join the 4,000 Thracian and Galatian settler warriors mobilized from their farms in Fayum and elsewhere. We know what these would have looked like from tombstones.[6] Cnopias of Allaria led 3,000 Cretans, and 1,000 Neocretans were led by Philo of Cnossos in Crete.[7] Ammonius of Barce, a town in Cyrenaica, had recruited a force of 3,000 Libyans from near his home town and armed them with *sarissa* and *pelte* (a small round shield) in the Macedonian fashion. But what is always noticed as a real break point in military tradition, which boded much for the future, is the recruitment of a large native phalanx armed in the same style. Certainly, the Macedonian rulers of Egypt had been very chary of arming locals in the past, and with good reason, as it is widely assumed that in recruiting them as front rank warriors, for pretty much the first time, the Lagids encouraged a military confidence that would generate national resistance sufficient to effectively hamstring any Ptolemaic expansionist ambitions in years to come.[8] Interestingly, Sosibius took personal command of these 20,000 native Egyptian soldiers, not much fewer than the 25,000 Macedonian and Greek phalangites under Andromachus of Aspendus. A real new model army was created, paying no heed to the way many of the old regiments had been organized and accoutred before, now they were frequently pooled together. Old pay grades and organizations were dissolved and most of the recruits and veterans were retrained as phalangites, giving the army a real advantage in this crucial arm. Not that all were treated the same; some were retained as light infantry and others, particularly the most recently recruited, like the Thracians and the Gauls, were kept as warriors of their own particular fighting type.

Warfare in this region where Africa met Asia followed well-trodden paths. The refurbished army, 75,000 strong, left Alexandria in June 217 to force-march to the fighting front under a blistering sun. Ptolemy, like his great forebear more than ninety years earlier, before the battle of Gaza in 312, established a springboard at Pelusium. Rations were distributed at this advanced base, then they struggled through the marshes of Barathra and endured a further three-day desert trudge before fetching up just more than five miles from Raphia, an important border town 'which is the first city of Coele-Syria on the Egyptian side after Rhinocolura.'[9] The latter is now called El-Arish and boasts blue water, a sandy coast, marinas and tourist hot spots. Rhinocolura, however, meant 'cut off noses' in Greek, and according to Strabo was where invading Ethiopians (date unknown) were settled after suffering this punishment. Diodorus Siculus gives a slightly different account, saying it was founded by the Ethiopian king Actisanes (again date unknown) as a place of exile for those found guilty of robbery, whom he punished by cutting off their noses.

Antiochus, meanwhile, had stayed for the winter at Ptolemais, on the coast south of Tyre and Sidon, so there could be no mistaking his priority for the next year would be Egypt. As the campaigning season opened, Antiochus' officers called together all available troops, the guard and settler infantry, thousands of mercenaries, levies and allies from the east. His Arab friends, 10,000 strong under Zabdibelus, their leader still appreciative of Antiochus' aid the year before, presumably rendezvoused with the main army as it travelled south, and when they joined, the whole reached 68,000 of all arms and 102 elephants. They rested when they reached Gaza but soon set out again, cautiously moving past the town of Raphia, and when scouts brought word that the main Ptolemaic military force was not far distant, they camped about a mile and a half away from the enemy.

The two armies now waited; it seemed they had rushed to meet but were now having second thoughts. For some days they havered, a long time to prepare for a climax that had been brewing through several years. Then Antiochus nudged nearer with his camp, to within half a mile of where the enemy were clearly visible through the clear sea air. He was determined to bring on the fight. It also may be that Antiochus, realizing he was outnumbered in phalangites and only equal in horsemen, had no desire to fight on too wide a battlefield, so moved forward to where dunes and sand hillocks restricted the plain.[10] Cheek by jowl, now skirmishing became commonplace, and with considerable numbers of troops moving about between the camps, one of Antiochus' commanders hazarded a gambler's coup. Theodotus, the Aetolian, still bitter at his old master and familiar with Ptolemaic guard routines, attempted an assassination of

Ptolemy himself. He and two others bravos penetrated right into the headquarters tent, killing a court doctor but failing to find the king himself, before insouciantly sliding back the way they had come. Whether this attempt at a crude killing stirred up the Ptolemaic high command we don't know, but at the next opportunity, on 22 June 217, they led out the whole army to fight, and once one side began the cotillion, the other was apparently eager to join in.

We know a lot about the numbers and arrangement of the armies in this colossal battle; the greatest combat in the Hellenistic World for nearly 100 years. Such manpower had not been seen since Ipsus in 301 and, indeed, it had been 100 years since the battles between Antigonus and Eumenes, where elephants were first used on both sides as an important part of the array. Now these beasts were well known, and the sophisticated deployment of them was an important component in the armoury of any commander. In the Egyptian camp, if we totally accept the orthodoxy of Ptolemy as cipher-king, it must be presumed that he mainly listened as the great ministers and generals discussed how to deal with the huge invasion force poised on the very margins of the Egyptian heartland. Certainly, the roll call of experienced warriors that had been brought together to create and lead this, the greatest Ptolemaic army of that or any other period, was extremely impressive, and they showed by their deployment that they were men of flexibility and intelligence, not shackled by tradition. To lead from the right wing, the place of honour, was in most of the armies of the ancient world the norm. This was the unshielded side, and so that of greatest peril, where the brave leader would need to stand to ensure that the weaker links did not slip away from the face of danger. But the Ptolemaic high command decided they had to face fire with fire. Expecting the enemy right wing to be the strongest, they determined to put their king and their best troops on their left to face the threat.

It is likely that the encounter took place around what is now the Sabot and Raphia junction, more than six miles along the Pelusium road past Raphia itself, where a wide, flat area spreads between the sea dunes and drifting sand hills on the inland flank. In this broad, but not unbounded, arena the armies drew up. On the extreme left flank of the Ptolemaic force was Polycrates, placed with 3,000 cavalry, 700 of which were Ptolemy's royal guard. Between them and the central phalanx were a number of other units. Polybius details first the Cretans, who he claims are in line with the cavalry, but it seems likely that these light troops would have been in part, if not all, used as guards for the elephants. Then came a royal infantry guard of 3,000 men under Eurylochus of Magnesia, followed by 2,000 Peltasts led by Socrates, and lastly the 3,000 Libyans under Ammonius of Barce. All of these were armed and trained as phalangites. Then came 25,000 Macedonian phalangites, the biggest half of the phalanx proper, and on their right a further 20,000 pikemen, the native Egyptian recruits all facing their first taste of battle, and probably arrayed thirty-two men deep. The

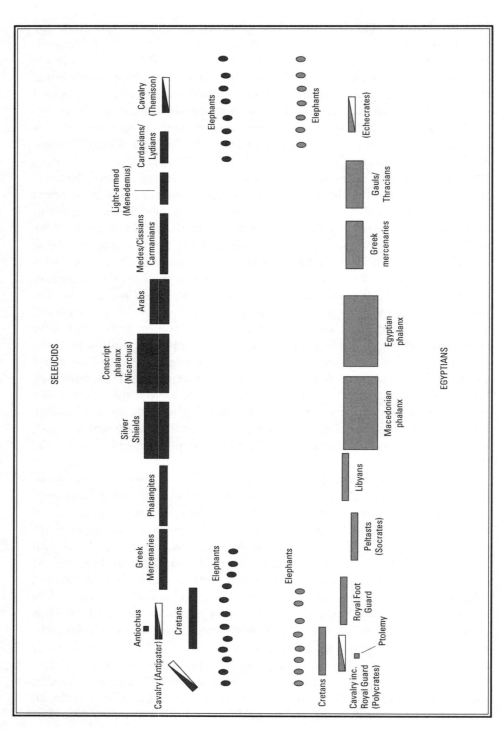

Plan 6: The Battle of Raphia, 217 BC, initial dispositions.

right was held by Echecrates, the Thessalian, and his 2,000 horsemen, Greeks and mercenaries. Here again, a mixed bunch of infantry made the link between the troopers and the centre. To the immediate right of the phalanx was Phoxidas with 8,000 Greek mercenaries, accoutred as phalangites, and after them came Gauls and Thracians to the number of 6,000, still outfitted according to their national tradition, sword and shield men or medium infantry using javelin and sword. The smaller African elephants, with their towers and two-man fighting crew, were distributed in front of each wing, forty on the left and thirty-three on the right.

Dust from the parched earth must have been thrown up in an extraordinary manner as these huge mobs of men and herds of animals manoeuvred into their proper positions. Antiochus would still have been taking stock of the fact that his enemy could bring such numbers into contention; Sosibius and his administration had done a good job of hiding their preparations. The Seleucid king would have had much to brood over the night before; this was the biggest army he had ever commanded and it represented the whole military might of his kingdom. Yet, his spies had reported that Ptolemy's phalanx strongly outnumbered his own, and even in cavalry, where he might have hoped to have an edge, he now heard that he only had parity. The terrain offered little in terms of opportunity, and many of his men were not of a quality that promised much. There were Arabs, Carmanians, Cadusians, Dahae, and Cilicians in his array, and he did not know how they would perform. In weaponry, most of these were at a disadvantage against the heavy infantry phalangites, where the Lagids were strong. They were good in the skirmish, fine in a hillside ambuscade, but how these lightly protected javelineers, bowmen and slingers would function in the coming day was very much open to question.

The fundamentals of Antiochus' battle plan was based on an infantry phalanx and a tradition that went back to the fights of Classical Greece, but it was also influenced by developments in the more recent affrays of the great Macedonian kings. He would exploit what he still considered his more gifted mounted arsenal of both horsemen and elephants. His big beasts were taller and bulkier than the African elephants, and they supported an extra soldier in their turrets in contrast to the two their opponents carried. He could expect them to overcome their counterparts, and then with his heavy companions and bodyguard horsemen, he intended to make his right flank the place of decision. This would be a classic encounter reminiscent of Paraetacene, Gabene and Ipsus, but what no one knew beforehand was what tactics, accidents and subtle ploys might make the decisive difference in this epic encounter.

On both sides, accompanying these mixed hoards, there were interpreters and priests who catered to the different gods of diverse nations. Religious ritual would have been undertaken by both the young kings in preparation for this set piece, where no elements would be missed that might make a difference to the outcome. Each side doled out words of encouragement, but our source specifies that, as both kings were too inexperienced to mention their own achievements, they concentrated on those of their antecedents and the prospects of rewards for bravery. The deployment of great blocks of pikemen and long lines of cavalry would have taken a good part of the fighting day, and it would have been many hours after dawn that the ranks finally established themselves into the array that the high commands had decided upon. Before the officers settled at the head of the files of phalangites, orders given by flag and trumpet ensured that as far as possible the subdivisions of the armies knew what their roles were.

Much happened as the Seleucids had planned. On their extreme right flank were deployed 4,000 cavalry in two groups, the inner group under Antipater, the nephew of Antiochus, and the second placed 'at an angle with them'. Then, between them and the main phalanx came first the Greek mercenaries, then 5,000 others armed as Macedonians commanded by Byttacus, the Macedonian, and all of these were armed as phalangites. In front of these, opposite their Ptolemaic counterparts, were sixty of the larger Asian elephants under Philip, a 'foster' brother of the king. Next came the phalanx, divided in two. The right side was comprised of the Silver Shields, 10,000 strong, and then 20,000 conscripted settler soldiers, presumably some of whom had been fighting in recent years, but also some straight off the farm. On their left were 10,000 Arab soldiers, then Medes, Cissians and Carmanians, then 3,000 light-armed troops under Menedemus, then the Cardacians and Lydian javelineers, who linked with the left-wing cavalry, 2,000 horse under Themison. And in front of this wing were the remaining elephants, forty-two in number, under a young blueblood called Myiscus.

It was the right wing that was the first to advance, and when the elephants stepped forward they impacted powerfully on their African cousins.

> A few of Ptolemy's elephants ventured to close with those of the enemy, and now the men in the towers on the backs of the beasts made a gallant fight of it, striking with their pikes at close quarters and wounding each other, while the elephants themselves fought still better, putting forth their whole strength and meeting forehead to forehead... Most of Ptolemy's elephants, however, declined the combat ...[11]

This started the kind of domino effect common enough when elephants got out of control; the Africans, pushed back in panic, alarmed both the guards' infantry and Socrates' peltasts, who were deployed behind them, breaking their ranks and ensuring they were in little mood for resistance when Hippolochus' Greek mercenaries went for them.[12] With this forward movement of the right wing infantry came a headlong charge by Antiochus and his cavalry, passing the flank of the elephant line towards Polycrates' horse, where Ptolemy and his guard

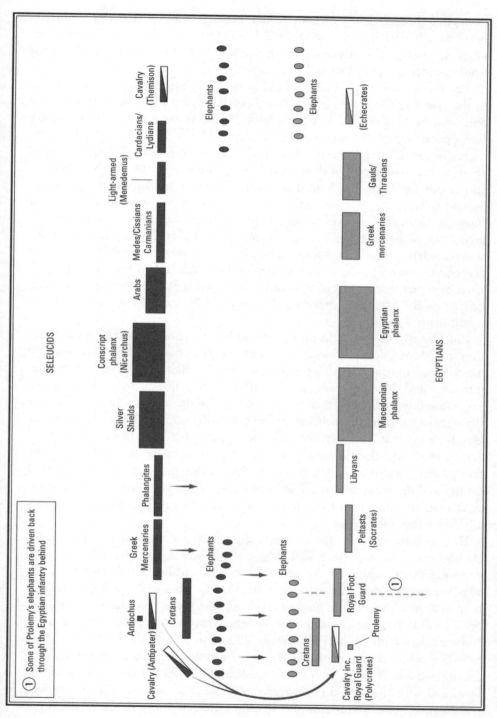

Plan 7: The Battle of Raphia, 217 BC, phase 1.

troopers were placed, all of whom braced themselves for impact. The Ptolemaic horse were bowled over and soon the Seleucid king was looking for his opposite number, hoping, like Alexander with Darius, to overthrow the head, which would render the body lost and impotent.

The pursuit was typical of that kind of occasion; blood was up and dust was in the eyes and throat, Ptolemy's heavy cavalry trying to break away from the Seleucids hacking at their retreating backs. Most would just have been looking for personal safety, but amongst the officers and guardsmen close to Ptolemy, more corporate responsibilities held sway. Horses, men and elephants swayed about in the great cloud of dust kicked up by the tens of thousands of hooves, and in this fog Antiochus looked for his royal opponent. Antiochus was young but far from a tyro; he had only recently overseen his army carolling down through Coele Syria, overturning long-emplaced defences, and of course, before that he had crushed the pretender Molon. This had given him a buoyant self-confidence that he would never lose. He was not foolish, and the explanation for his failure to turn against the exposed flank of his enemy's centre must be either that he lost control of his men in this pursuit or that he felt that getting to and killing or capturing Ptolemy would make up for anything that might happen elsewhere.

But Ptolemy and the tight group around him had not simply run off as far as they could. Whatever Ptolemy's failings, he kept his nerve here, his group moving out of the onrush of defeated men in flight and their triumphant pursuers and working back to the infantry phalanx at the centre of the Ptolemaic line. Many hearts of both lowest and highest born must have risen at the sight of the magnificently apparelled but dusty monarch riding out from the bloody chaos that had been the left side of the battle line. It was not just his cavalry that had failed him; the Seleucid Greek mercenaries had carved into the foot guards, peltasts and Libyans who had filled the space between the left wing cavalry and the main phalanx. They had been disrupted by their own elephants in retreat, and they could not stand against the Seleucid veteran mercenaries advancing into the havoc.

But, despite all this, the decision was made in the centre with 45,000 Ptolemaic *sarissae* matching 30,000 Seleucid. The king and his officers yelled encouragement, while the highest officers, like Sosibius and Andromachus, were present, making sure every man, however far back in the ranks, knew their monarch was present to observe their conduct and reward or punish as necessary. It is even claimed that Ptolemy's presence caused consternation amongst the enemy phalanx, but this is difficult to credit; either most would not have been able see him or would not have been discouraged if they could. But for his own men, it was a very much needed fillip as they stood in the blistering heat, and with this added boost to morale, the great mass of pikemen moved ponderously forward towards the sparkling line of spear heads in the murk

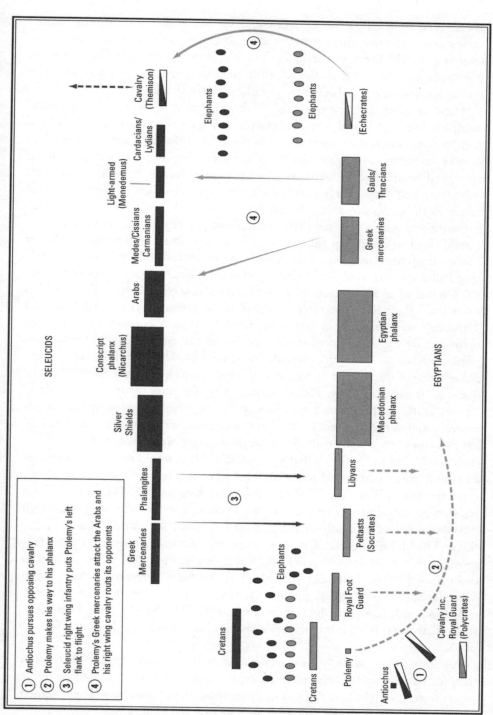

Plan 8: The Battle of Raphia, 217 BC, phase 2.

The following labels appear within the figure:

① Antiochus pursues opposing cavalry

② Ptolemy makes his way to his phalanx

③ Seleucid right wing infantry puts Ptolemy's left flank to flight

④ Ptolemy's Greek mercenaries attack the Arabs and his right wing cavalry routs its opponents

SELEUCIDS

Cavalry (Themison)
Cardacians/Lydians
Elephants
Light-armed (Menedemus)
Medes/Cissians Carmanians
Arabs
Conscript phalanx (Nicarchus)
Silver Shields
Phalangites
Greek Mercenaries
Elephants
Cretans
Cretans
Antiochus

EGYPTIANS

Elephants
(Echecrates)
Gauls/Thracians
Greek mercenaries
Egyptian phalanx
Macedonian phalanx
Libyans
Peltasts (Socrates)
Royal Foot Guard
Ptolemy
Cavalry inc. Royal Guard (Polycrates)

ahead. The Ptolemaic commanders could see the wreck of their left, but the saving grace was that there was as yet no sign that the victorious enemy were swerving to take them in the flank. The centre of their battle line was more numerous and deeper than the bristling phalanx opposite, and now the only option left was to try and see if they could still win the day.

Their training had clearly paid high dividends; it was with measured discipline that the brand new phalangites and their comrades moved forward with *sarissae* couched or upright as the position in the file dictated. They had greater numbers and were deployed deeper. This banner-mottled tide of armoured men came forward; not many were veterans, but they were still confident, and they charged with ferocious war cries, just as they had been taught in the camp grounds at Alexandria.

On the opposite side of the battle-plain, bellies were full and heads clear, after a good night in camp, but the tens of thousands of men holding their pikes in sixteen-deep files knew they were heavily outnumbered and could see that their king had gone way over the horizon, giving no indication of returning to their aid. On the other wing, meanwhile, their comrades seemed to be in flight, which must leave their left vulnerable to attack if the enemy cavalry, Galatians and Thracians were capable of mounting one. In these circumstances, it is no surprise that the Seleucid phalanx approached the coming push of pike with some trepidation. When the two sides met, we are told that Nicarchus' men on the left side of the Seleucid phalanx just turned and fled but the Silver Shields, like their namesakes under Eumenes of Cardia 100 years before, were made of sterner stuff. In the great scrum, few could see what was happening; sounds reverberated in their helmets, but what it meant was a mystery. Just to clench in hands dripping with sweat the long handle of their weapon, bunch up behind their shield and push was all that was possible. Most would not have come near an enemy spear point, and those that did were the veterans who peopled the front few ranks. They fought it out, but there were only 10,000 of them, and resistance could not last forever. It was draining combat as tossing masses of warriors prodded violently at the nearest enemies they could reach. But the Silver Shields had been deserted by their comrades; these men on their left, recently mobilized from the reserve, had failed at the crisis. Nicarchus, who commanded them, could not keep them at the fight as the huge numbers of Macedonian settlers and Egyptian pikemen, a great sweeping tide in flood, rolled forward. Now, left fighting on alone, the Silver Shields needed succour from their king, but he was far off chasing chimeras in the dust of a blasted plain.

It is interesting that Polybius specifies that an older officer apparently tried to turn Antiochus back to help his infantry; no doubt the young bluebloods in his escort were as caught up as he was in the exhilaration of the chase. They seemed to be doing damage to the foe; Ptolemy's loss of 700 cavalry must have mainly

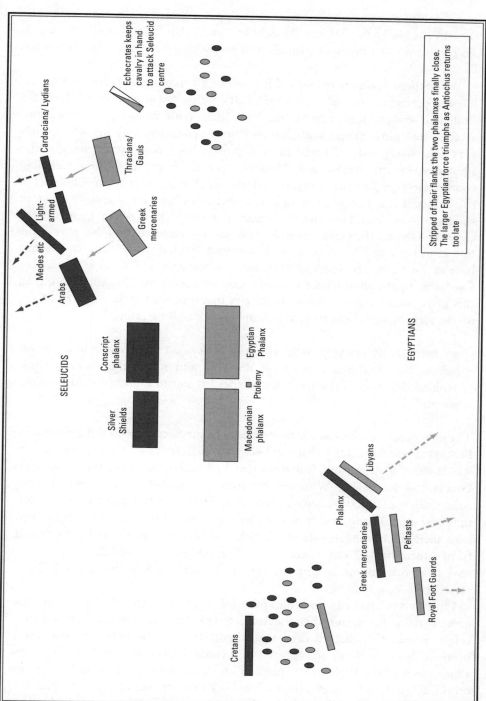

SELEUCIDS

Cardacians/Lydians

Echecrates keeps cavalry in hand to attack Seleucid centre

Thracians/Gauls

Light-armed

Greek mercenaries

Medes etc

Arabs

Conscript phalanx

Silver Shields

Egyptian Phalanx

Macedonian phalanx

Ptolemy

EGYPTIANS

Stripped of their flanks the two phalanxes finally close. The larger Egyptian force triumphs as Antiochus returns too late

Libyans

Phalanx

Greek mercenaries

Peltasts

Royal Foot Guards

Cretans

Plan 9: The Battle of Raphia, 217 BC, phase 3.

come during this pursuit. But they were to pay a great penalty for taking their eyes off the big picture. It was the sight of a great cloud of dust moving towards his own camp that eventually caught the young king's attention, but it was too late.

While these dramatic matters of life and death were being played out on the left and centre; on the right side of the battle much had also occurred. Here the Ptolemaic commander Echecrates, with little faith in his puny elephants, avoided committing them at all, but took up the challenge with his other troops very offensively indeed. First, he had thrown his Greek mercenaries, under Phoxidas, at the Arabs and Medes opposite them; like their Seleucid counterparts on the other wing, they drove off all in front of them. This part of the Seleucid line consisted of light opponents without body armour or stout shields who just could not face the brazen men swarming down on them. On the right the Greeks, the Galatians and Thracians also attacked, and that part of the line soon became a heaving mass of ferocious combat, with many swordsmen bare to the waist, hacking with their long swords against Lydian javelineers or Cardacian lights, all of whom were ill protected against such assaults. But, if all this was a good start, it was still the cavalry that represented the real strike force on the right wing. These troops' movements are well described:

> while he [Echecrates] himself with his cavalry and the division immediately behind the elephants moving off the field and round the enemy's flank, avoided the onset of the animals and speedily put to flight the cavalry of the enemy.[13]

The only confusion here is which was the division directly behind the elephants. Perhaps it was the cavalry that were not part of Echecrates' own squadrons. Or was it the Thracians and Galatians that had been posted between Phoxidas' Greeks and the cavalry? Whoever they were, the upshot of all this was that the Seleucid left of 2,000 horsemen under Themison was attacked with great élan in the front and flank, and their resistance evaporated in a very short time. And with them gone, the left side of the Seleucid phalanx was no longer protected from a teeming and victorious enemy. The threatened attack did not, in fact, have to be carried out, as with its flank 'in the air' the Seleucid centre had not stayed very long to fight.

Ptolemy's officers had done him proud, Echecrates, particularly, had kept his cavalry well in hand, and when the Antiochid phalanx collapsed he pursued with relish; it was this that ensured that almost half of the enemy phalanx was brought down in blood or captured in a country that now seemed alive with Ptolemaic soldiers. Ptolemy and most of his exhausted pikemen could not get in on the act, only able to drag themselves back to camp, cupidity and respect for the fallen left to the following day. We are not told but can assume that the cavalry that had fled on the Ptolemaic left, if they had not fallen, would have come in later when word was spread that it was finally their side that had ended up taking the palm of victory. They would have experienced considerable relief as well; if the battle had not been won, it would have been a long flight through the desert to reach any sort of safety or comfort of home.

History concentrates on kings and generals, and it seems that on this occasion it is to some degree warranted. Although the whole picture paints Antiochus as an active Alexander-like figure, if finally flawed, and Ptolemy as a pathetic sybarite, addicted to male prostitutes and lute girls under the thumb of his great ministers, the story of this encounter renders a very different judgement. The former had left the field of combat, leaving the responsibility of leadership to others, while the latter had to dig in with his battalions at the heart of things and fought it out to victory. But perhaps Ptolemy was returning to type when he failed to press his pursuit with great purpose, or maybe the fight was a harder-fought matter for his phalanx than Polybius suggests. Whatever, it was the ritual that Ptolemy now concentrated on, and no doubt his followers demanded that fallen comrades were buried and opportunity allowed for looting the enemy dead.

So it was not until the following day that the victorious army packed up camp and marched on to Raphia itself. On arrival, they saw the tail of the defeated Seleucid multitude trailing north on the road to Gaza. Antiochus, having returned from chasing phantoms and seeing his phalanx shattered, had had no option but to ride away from the battlefield and try to pick up his remnants in and around Raphia, where most had run in desperation to avoid pursuit. The Seleucids moved north, but it was a much-bloodied force that tramped towards Gaza. Fourteen thousand infantry had been lost, either dead or as prisoners. The cavalry, more able to escape their tormentors, had suffered much less, with only 300 casualties, indeed 400 less than the victor had sustained. But in infantry it was far more decisive; Ptolemy's army only incurred 1,500 casualties.

The comments about the elephants are mysterious. For the Seleucids, it is reported that three died in battle and a further two of wounds, whereas sixteen of Ptolemy's beasts died and most of the rest were captured. It seems a strange result, considering that they were on the winning side. And whilst it is possible that sixteen died in battle, and they clearly suffered at the hands of their bigger cousins, the loss of the rest is unlikely. Perhaps there is mistake in the source, as any capturing that went on must surely have gone the other way, as the Antiochid forces routed away.[14] Whatever the exact calculations here, the reality of defeat was clear enough, and when he reached Gaza and was able to draw breath, Antiochus sent to Ptolemy to ask for the traditional truce to bury his own dead.

What is very noticeable at Raphia is that there was no cull of leadership, no generals in gorgeous cloaks and gilded armour falling in combat, which is perhaps surprising when clearly many of them fought deep in the ranks of the cavalry or infantry. But, if it had been mainly the common man who had paid the blood price, as was not unusual in all ages, the sacrifices they made dramatically affected the strategic picture almost overnight. Coele Syria fell like a ripe peach into Ptolemy's commanders' hands, with the communities there tumbling over themselves to be friends with the victor in a territory where it was conveniently claimed, anyway, that the local people always preferred Ptolemaic rule to that of the Seleucids.

Sometime during this excursion, Antipater, the king's nephew, and Theodotus Hemiolius were discovered on the road with offers of peace from Antiochus, who was suddenly feeling very vulnerable with a victorious enemy to the south and just beyond the Taurus his cousin, Achaeus, still very much not dealt with. An armistice was concocted, and Sosibius packed his bags ready to head to a peace conference convening at Antioch, while his king left for the delights of Alexandria. The matter of Coele Syria was, for the time being, decided, but it was still clear to many at the Seleucid court that it was just shelved, and the young king would return to the matter later. Indeed, this great battle did not turn out to be decisive at all. Despite the fact of a very clear defeat, there was no testing of Antiochus' authority as a result of what was clearly a very considerable blow to his prestige and reputation.

Chapter 6

Antiochus Achieves Greatness

Anatolia had always been central to the post-Alexander Macedonian world. Wealthy, populous and anciently civilized, its draw for the great power brokers was always there, even if often our sources fail us in detail about what was taking place. As the Social War rumbled in Greece and Antiochus and Ptolemy faced off near Africa, another player stirred the waters in that particular pond. Achaeus, in Sardis, was a more powerful figure than any of his local rivals, whether the dynasts of Pergamum and Bithynia or the great west Anatolian Greek *metropoleis,* and he remained ambitious, as was shown by the direction his eyes looked in the summer of 218.

Pisidia is a very rugged region, north of the central southern coast of Anatolia, very defensible and with some important cities speckling the mountains. Here a war was begun by the Selgians, a considerable city state in Pamphylia, who had called up their citizen militia and marched over a couple of very steep ranges to take a swipe at their neighbours at Pednelissus. The causes are unknown, but doubtless concern some centuries-deep bigotry that gave, at least, cover to what was a spat about local dominance. The people being attacked probably already had a relationship with Achaeus and reasonably hoped he might help them, so they sent off messages begging for assistance, as they settled down to defend their ramparts. The Anatolian warlord was only too willing to fish in these troubled waters. He sent his man, Garsyeris, with a strong force of 6,000 foot and 500 cavalry into the area. Some local places also came on board. Apparently, 8,000 hoplites joined from the Etennes who lived in Pisidia, above Side, and 4,000 more came from Aspendus. Garsyeris arrived at the besieged city and encamped the relieving army nearby. Despite the newcomers' large numbers, the Selgians outside Pednelissus made a hard fight of it. They poured out of their siege works and attacked Garsyeris' camp, but their failure to observe the enemy cavalry, who slipped out and came in behind them, meant that the Selgians went down in defeat. Garsyeris pushed on after the routed enemy, apparently 10,000 of whom were killed before they reached the shelter of their homes. This was desperate blood-letting, and as Garsyeris advanced towards Selge, the people decided to not risk battle in the open but to shout defiance from behind their city walls.

Selge itself lies where the Eurymedon River descends from the Taurus Mountains and widens into a fertile valley that reaches down to the coast. It is high up, cradled by peaks, snow-covered for much of the year, and very difficult of access. Also, as the city is neared, it seems that at each turn of the road that anybody approaching is confronted by massive defensive walls. In fact, these are rock faces weathered to look almost like Cyclopean ramparts, but for any enemy drawing near they would be deeply unnerving. And this even before reaching the difficulties posed by the real man-made defences that crowned a very inaccessible site. So, if the Selgians had been bested in open country, they felt secure enough in their eyrie, so it was not unreasonable for them to believe one of their leaders, Logbasis, when he suggested he could try and talk their way out of the trouble their actions had brought on their heads. But his intention was really to turn the place over to the enemy. There is no explanation of his motives, but perhaps this man, who had previously been a friend of Antiochus the Hawk, was just inclined to whoever ruled at Sardis. On this occasion, he both tried to play out negotiations until Achaeus, who was on his way, could arrive to lead the attackers, and under the cover of a truce, Logbasis apparently hid more and more soldiers of the besieging force in his own house ready for the final coup.

The attempt, when it was made, was well planned. Achaeus, with half of his army, approached the city walls while Garsyeris, with the other half, was positioned to assault the citadel, where a temple to Zeus dominated. But both the movements of Logbasis' interlopers and the troops outside the city were noticed by a goatherd, spelling the end for the traitor. The citizens quickly manned the walls and the citadel, before putting to the sword Logbasis, his sons and all the soldiers secreted in his house. With the ploy a busted flush, Achaeus tried a frontal assault on the city gates. This was a fight to the finish, as shown by the report that the defenders freed their slaves, as reward for aiding the defence. Achaeus sent his Mysian troops in first and they suffered to the tune of 700 when the Selgians sallied out and drove them off. It was becoming very frustrating for the Seleucid warlord, cut off in the boom docks, with no immediate sign of a successful conclusion to his campaign. But he was lucky; the defenders realized that in the long run they were bound to succumb to numbers and sent out emissaries bearing attractive terms. They offered 700 talents in instalments as tribute to Achaeus and also the return of the prisoners they had taken from his Pednelissian allies. This was enough for victory to be claimed with some credibility, so the invaders turned away to deal with other matters that had arisen while they had been fixed in the backwaters of Pisidia.

While Achaeus' back was turned, Attalus of Pergamum had been active. He approached a Galatian tribe called the Aegosagae, who were at this time still in Europe, and with his military beefed up, he marched off to put pressure on those Aetolian cities who adhered to Achaeus. It seems Cyme, Smyrna, Phocaea, Aegae, Teian, Colophonia and Temnus all came over, either because of real affection for Attalus or more probably at the sight of his burly barbarians. These places had formally been Pergamum adherents, but fractured times and a powerful enemy at Sardis meant he required hostages to be handed over to ensure their future good behaviour. Then he marched east, on Mysia, where not only Carseae city and Didymateiche came over, but Achaeus' general in the region, Themistocles, changed sides as well. Meanwhile, the Galatians became unruly at this time, apparently alarmed by an eclipse of the moon, but maybe to pressure Attalus to give them land, as we know they had brought their women and children with them. Attalus decided he had achieved enough and allowed the Galatians to depart *en route* for Europe, and he returned to the Hellespont to hearten his supporters there before returning home.

There is nothing to tell us exactly what Achaeus did when he returned to find Attalus had been making hay in his absence. We only know he put pressure on Prusias, of Bithynia, to ensure this local potentate was not tempted to side with Attalus. But this apparent quiescence in the face of Pergamene aggression may well be because little time was available to achieve anything before another took a hand in this quarrelsome western Anatolian patchwork.

Antiochus, with an offensive south ruled out by his peace with Ptolemy, now began to make plans against the incumbent in what had before been proper Seleucid country. Achaeus' taking of the diadem and threat to invade in 219 had more than erased for the young king any latent gratitude he felt for the man's role in putting him on the throne. So he mobilized the whole royal army and pushed, just like his older brother had years before, through the Cilician Gates. But, unlike Seleucus III, his efforts rapidly paid dividends. That king had been cut down by his own officers before he could get at his enemy, but this latest Seleucid leader to venture into Anatolia headed a state and army more secure and loyal than his predecessor. Attalus, this time, who on the previous occasion of an invasion by a Seleucid king had been the main enemy, may have sided with Antiochus, and there was also much residual loyalty amongst both the Greek communities and native peoples of the region. It took a three-year war (216–213) for Antiochus to fight out Achaeus from along the royal road in Anatolia, but eventually he had him on the run and bottled up in Sardis itself. Battling around this city was hotly conducted for more than a year before the conflict moved to a climax that would have more to do with trickery, intrigue and betrayal than stand-up shield-to-shield fighting.

Antiochus had clearly not been fazed by his reverse at Raphia, and he was showing determination and confidence exceptional in a still young man. But Sardis, the old capital of Lydia, was very defensible, with a steep spur of land where the citadel was positioned, and it soon began to look as if starvation would be the only way in, when a Cretan officer called Lagoras came forward with a cunning plan. There was a piece of land between the city and citadel called the 'saw', comprising a narrow ridge with precipices either side, where the garrison would throw corpses of men and horse outside to try and preclude the spread of disease. The behaviour of the vultures who feasted there convinced the Cretan that this place was not guarded at all, and he suggested an escalade, personally reconnoitring the route before he brought the plan to the military council. With his plan approved, Lagoras was given some high quality troops to do his work, commanded by Theodotus, the Aetolian, and Dionysius, captain of the royal bodyguard.

Waiting for a moonless night, the plan was put into effect; fifteen men brought up the ladders and got into the town. This was Aratus-like behaviour, but this time no dogs delayed them; these stalwarts found their way over the wall and to the nearest gate. Outside this entrance, many others had waited and now attacked the hinges of the gate from the outside, while the intruders dealt with the bars and bolt pins from the inside. Two thousand Aetolian troops, who had previously been hiding outside, barged through the now open entrance and established themselves inside the defences on the commanding heights of a nearby theatre. All this activity was supposed to be seconded by a ruse, whereby information was passed to the defenders that these same Aetolians were somewhere else, intending an attack through a ravine against a completely different part of the city walls. The Seleucids had also been aided by the fact that, though they could see clearly what was happening with their comrades, a rock overhang hid their activities from Achaeus and his men. And, as a final component to keep the garrison occupied, Antiochus made a feint attack at what was known as the Persian Gate.

In fact, apart from the initial success in capturing the theatre the commandos seem to have achieved little, and it was Antiochus' feint attack that actually took the town. Aribazus, Achaeus' commander, first sent his men to oppose the Aetolians in the theatre and then tried to bring some of the troops fighting Antiochus outside the Persian Gate to reinforce them. When the gate was opened to let Achaeus' men pass, Antiochus' attackers charged, following them in. These Seleucids then secured other gates and the whole besieging army poured in. Aribazus, completely overwhelmed, had no option but to flee with his leader for the citadel.

The citadel of Sardis was exceedingly formidable, and although caught like a rat in a trap, Achaeus looked, at least, to have secured his safety for some time to come. Nor was he without friends outside. The Ptolemaic court had retained a very considerable interest in Anatolian affairs and the very last thing they wanted was for their arch enemy, Antiochus, who had so recently tried to invade their country, to overcome another who had largely been their friend.

A cabal of Cretans now emerged to move things along. One was Cambylus, a senior officer commanding Cretan mercenaries in the siege works round the citadel. He had a compatriot and kinsman, Bolis, in the Alexandrine administration, and they had been in touch. Bolis and Cambylus were promised money in advance from Sosibius, the key man at Alexandria, to secrete the caged Achaeus away from the stronghold of Sardis so he might raise more armies to oppose Antiochus. Bolis enlisted Achaeus' friend Nicomachus, who was on Rhodes at the time, and a man called Melancomas, a long-term agent of Achaeus, who was then living at Ephesus. Moving from town to town, Bolis acquired associates who would give good *bona fides* to reassure Achaeus when they met. Then Bolis gathered with Cambylus outside Sardis to get the plot in hand. 'With this before them they discussed the matter from a thoroughly Cretan point of view.'[1] The upshot was that they split the ten talents, already handed over by Sosibius, and reported the intrigue to Antiochus, promising to deliver him Achaeus for further reward. Antiochus bit Cambylus' hand off in agreement.

Cambylus took Bolis to Antiochus to confirm their bargain and then Bolis ascended to Sardis citadel with Arianus, who had been taking messages to the trapped king. Achaeus was not too convinced by his putative saviour and suggested three or four friends be sent out first, but he then consulted his wife, Laodice, who was beside herself about the dangers involved. In the end, however, after calming her down, he came out in a shabby disguise. It was dark and confusing as he and his companions scrambled down to meet Bolis, and the track they used was difficult and precipitous. On their way Cambylus was waiting in ambush. The conspirators were worried Achaeus might kill himself when he realized he was betrayed, but they stayed close enough to pin him down when the trap was sprung. The fugitive was brought straight to Antiochus. A council that was set up to decide on the fate of a man who had kept them tied down for nearly two years did not hesitate. He was brutally mutilated and killed before his body was crucified. The troops still loyal to the dead man in the citadel held on to espouse the cause of Laodice, despite the end of her husband. But, with hope pretty much gone, the high command sundered, with Laodice and the general Aribazus falling out. Soon these two began to fear each other more even than Antiochus and a capitulation was agreed.

Antiochus, with his Anatolian flank secure, began that look to the east, which would define his reign before the Romans came to interfere in the world of the Hellenes. The regiments that had spent many months around the walls of Sardis, and the mercenaries, who had done little in the way of activity for their pay, now were paraded together in preparation for another enterprise. A dominant king took advice from his great officers, but it was he who decided on Armenia as a suitable target, and once the decision was made, all fell in behind. Xerxes, the king there, commanded a considerable country and his capital of Arsamosata between the Euphrates and Tigris was another very strong fortress.

But, when Antiochus and the pack closed in, the fox fled the set, and the invaders sat down and began a regular siege. It was enough; the Armenian armed forces were absolutely no match against the full panoply of Seleucid might, and more than this, the loss of his capital might mean the complete extinction of the royal line. Xerxes, from his bolt-hole, sent emissaries to propose a personal meeting, but when this took place many of Antiochus' wilder elements suggested they should seize the king and give the country to Antiochus' nephew Mithridates.

However, Antiochus settled on a more conciliatory policy, and negotiating with Xerxes' son and heir, reinstated the old regime once more as a Seleucid tributary.

> Receiving from him a present payment of three hundred talents, a thousand horses, and a thousand mules with their trappings, he restored all his dominions to him and by giving his sister Antiochis in marriage conciliated and attached to himself all the inhabitants of the district, who considered that he had acted in a truly royal and magnanimous manner.[2]

Media Atropatene (Azerbaijan), to the east of Armenia, was presumably still secure since Seleucid intervention years before. So now, in theory, Antiochus was the king of kings from Sardis to Ecbatana, and so it was in the upper satrapies themselves that action was needed. What the extent of Seleucid control was in large parts of the east is unknown. Antiochus' itinerary is far from completely clear; nor do we fully understand what his intentions were. There is no record of an agenda; only an ability to guess at what a ruler of his time and with his resources might reasonably have contemplated. Antiochus knew there were rebels and intruders in many of these lands that had once given tribute to the Seleucid throne, and he was determined to re-establish hegemony over them. Antiochus was far from a fool. He had campaigned and travelled over Mesopotamia, Levant, Anatolia, Armenia and Media Atropatene since he clambered onto the throne on the back of Achaeus. He knew the country and he knew the limitations of control of any administration. A loyal governor of a week before could become a rebellious satrap, once the royal court and its armed support were over the horizon. Antiochus knew the legitimacy of 100 years was something, but not everything; Greek colonists might cleave to him in self interest, but only as long as he had the power to help them. But if another protector was more at hand, why should they stay loyal to a power whose interests often seemed to be far more centred on the waters of the eastern Mediterranean than those of the Caspian Sea or Persian Gulf.

What did Antiochus want? Tribute, certainly, but this might not do much more than the pay the costs of the expedition. Further economic motives would not be completely absent; there was gold in the hills of Siberia and India to which control of the upper satrapies gave him access. What he really craved was the fame and glory that went with the title of conqueror. He must have known that what he built could crumble unless he kept returning to shore it up, and how practical that might be would depend on matters in other parts of his realm. Unfortunately, the resultant *anabasis* of Antiochus is described in only a few pages of our sources; even so, it is a few pages more than we have for any other Seleucid ruler who went east.

The first Seleucid called Nicator, we really can only make assumptions about after he crossed the Zagros mountains, on the basis that his efforts were regarded by contemporaries as a great triumph. There are a few hints on his dealings with Chandragupta, the new ruler in northern India, but this episode is really so opaque that the debate is still open as to whether he achieved a victory or suffered a decisive defeat at this time. We have almost no facts at all regarding what occurred when Seleucus II went to fight the Parthians, apart from Justin, who merely tells us he was defeated.[3] At least with the adventures of Antiochus we have something that makes sense, not only in terms of a general picture, but also several military encounters are recounted in some sort of fashion.

The years 211–210 were about preparation; Antiochus descended the Euphrates, which suggests he had returned from Armenia to Antioch to make military and administrative arrangements that would have needed to be extensive and comprehensive. That the force he mobilized for the push east initially went by boat shows it was probably the full royal military panoply with all his heavy baggage, and no doubt a siege train. Antiochus had been able to mobilize a very great army in 217, and this one for the defining enterprise of his life would have been of a similar magnitude. He did not face many great threats at that time, so the defences he had to leave in place at home could be fairly scanty. The expedition followed the royal road to Ecbatana and was in Media in the summer of 209, a place that was still firmly managed by Diogenes, who had been established there since the defeat of Molon more than ten years before. The treasures of Ecbatana had been plundered by Alexander the Great and Seleucus II in the past, but precious metals from the temples still provided enough for Antiochus III to coin almost 4,000 talents in specie with his own features on. And this was badly needed so that, at this advanced base, he could equip and pay the troops in preparation for what lay ahead.

The great caravan now progressed to Rhagai, near Rey, just outside modern Tehran. Then on to the Caspian Gates and into a desert terrain that led in the direction of passes that gave access to the country around the Caspian Sea. An army of many tens of thousands of combatants and non-combatants could only normally carry sufficient food for a few days, before they had to re-provision, and making sure they had sufficient water was an even greater problem. Essentially, they must travel in regions where water was easily accessible from rivers or springs, and to campaign in desert or near-desert country was extraordinarily difficult. Antiochus' next target, after Media, thought this was their ace in the hole. They were a people, called the Parni, of Saka stock, who had been leaders of the Dahae confederation. In 238, they overran Astavene and established a seat of power in northeast Iran, near the modern Turkmenistan border, an intrusion made easier by the revolt of the local Seleucid governor, Andragoras, in 245. The Parni leader, Arsaces I, took advantage of the confusion to take over the country and apparently also killed this local secessionist. A little later, in 235, Tiridates, who succeeded his brother in Astavene, moved his people into the satrapy of Parthia proper, a displacement probably encouraged by pressure from the ruler of Bactria. These incumbents did not think Antiochus would risk the route east 'chiefly owing to the scarcity of water'. When Arsaces II, their king since 211, realized the invaders were not to be put off, he decided to destroy or poison the watercourse and would have succeeded if Antiochus had not taken immediate action. He sent Nicomedes of Cos, with an advance guard of a thousand horse, and drove off the Parthians, allowing the main army to slake its thirst in the chase across the desert to Hecatompylos (the 'Many Gated' or '100 Gated').

Alexander had stopped there after he had caught up with the corpse of Darius, and had first let it be known to his paraded army that he intended to continue east to conquer all that the Persians had owned. Hecatompylos, on Sahr e Qumis plain, capital of Parthia, was re-founded by Seleucus but had been inhabited for many centuries before. It was situated to the south of the Elburz Mountains, which acted as a barrier between the great desert in the centre of Iran and the Caspian Sea country.

Here at Hecatompylos, a meeting place of many roads, the army rested, resupplied and prepared for an encounter with the Parthian army. This was flat country, perfect for their horse archers, but it soon became clear that Arsaces had no intention of risking a stand-up fight even to defend his heartland. This left Antiochus with some directional choices to make, and the road he decided upon was north to Hyrcania over the mountains. The officers and men of the Seleucid royal army now saw the massive Elburz Mountains rising in front of them, craggy deciduous tree-covered country. Reaching more than 18,000 feet in places, oaks and chestnuts grew where eagles, wolves, leopards and even tigers were said to abound. First, they traversed the foothills, which were more generally juniper scrubland descending down into the desert itself. Then the route became more difficult; the road began to follow a riverbed with beetling cliffs along its course, ideal for the local Tapurians to put up barricades of trees and giant rocks. This made life very difficult for Antiochus, who took the whole army over just one pass.

The Seleucid king split his men into several groups to overcome the inventive obstructions of his opponents. Diogenes, satrap of Media, led light-armed men, slingers, archers, and what are described as mountaineers 'expert in throwing javelins and stones'. These were sent up to gain the higher ground. Then came Polyxenidas, a Rhodian exile, leading 2,000 Cretans, who are described as armed

Theatre at Sicyon built at the end of the fourth century AD and a well known haunt of Aratus. Assemblies of the Achaean League would have met there. (Authors' own photograph)

Acrocorinth in the distance behind a temple at Nemea, showing what a dominant feature this fortress was. (Authors' own photograph)

Medieval defences atop the Acrocorinth, clearly showing what a feat it was for Aratus to capture this place in the way he did in 243 BC. (Authors' own photograph)

Coin depicting Philip V.
(courtesy www. mlahanas.de)

The Menelaion, a shrine on a steep hill just across the river Eurotas from Sparta that Lycurgus occupied but was driven off by Philip V's peltasts and Illyrians. (Authors' own photograph)

Cleomenes' Isthmus of Corinth defensive line against the advance of Antigonus Doson; the Acrocorinth can be seen on the left and mount Oneion on the right. (Authors' own photograph)

Portrait head of Ptolemy III found at Vlacholias House, Sparta. Sparta Archaeological Museum. (Authors' own photograph)

Ptolemy IV 244-204 BC, the victor of Raphia, who allowed his government to be run by Agathocles and Sosibius. British Museum. (Authors' own photograph)

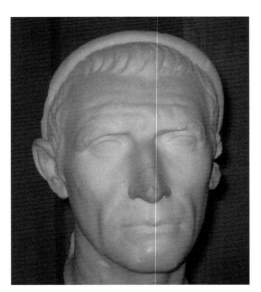

Bust of Antiochus III looking suspiciously Roman. In the Louvre Museum Paris. (Authors' own photograph)

Sculpture of the torso of a Hellenistic general in full armour, Museum at Corinth. (Authors' own photograph)

Frieze showing typical Hellenistic armour, helmets, corselets and swords from the Archaeological Museum at Side in Turkey. (Authors' own photograph)

The theatre at Selge, showing the mountains ringing the city that made it so defensible when Achaeus attacked it. (Authors' own photograph)

Mount Ithome, Citadel of Messene city where Philip V took the advice of Aratus not to take over the place by force, against the urging of Demetrius of Pharos. (Authors' own photograph)

Walls at Messene, the best preserved defences of any place in the Peloponnese. (Authors' own photograph)

Above: A 19th century representation of Philopoemen (detail). Sculpted by the French artist David d'Angers (1788–1856). In the Louvre Museum Paris. (Authors' own photograph)

Left: Frieze showing heavy cavalryman from Pergamum. Attalus would have brought a good number of these troopers with him when he intervened in the war against Philip V. Like most cavalrymen by this time, apart from cataphracts, he carries a shield. From the Archaeological Museum, Istanbul, Turkey. (Authors' own photograph)

View from the north of Mantinea. The far end of the hill on the left was the left end of Philopoemen's line at the battle of 207 BC, the line of the walls of the city can be seen running almost in a half circle below. (Authors' own photograph)

The subterranean Treasury House at Messene where Philopoemen was reputedly imprisoned at the end of his life and invited to drink poison. (Authors' own photograph)

Stele of an infantryman from the necropolis at Sidon from about 200 BC. Typical of many Hellenistic warriors in this period with body armour, helmet, *thureophoroi* shield and spear From the Archaeological Museum, Istanbul, Turkey. (Authors' own photograph)

Relief of the stern of a *trihemiolia* from Lindos, Rhodes, of the type used in the Battle of Chios. (Authors' own photograph)

with bucklers. The Cretans most famously were bowmen, but the island also produced effective mercenaries of most types. They were followed by light infantry, though armed with breastplate and shield, under Nicomedes of Cos and Nicolaus, the Aetolian. These were trailed by the engineers, who built up a road that was usable for the heavy troops and the baggage. Eight days of battling took place; it was hard going but the army was well handled, and the defenders withdrew each time the attackers got around and above them. After these staged defences, when Antiochus' men finally reached the pass at Mount Labus, the very summit of the range, the locals decided to make a stand at this, the most advantageous post. They were no longer skirmishing, but formed all their soldiers together in a dense mass, and this last battle was head to head. It seems that initially the defenders actually managed to hold against the Seleucid phalanx. But the Seleucid lights were in the groove of outflanking their enemies, and after a long detour, got in behind the defenders. Panicked by the sight of men in their rear, the Tapurians took to their heels, and the king's only problem was to stop his men from chasing pell-mell in pursuit and exposing themselves to a counterattack. But Antiochus' officers had called back their men from pursuit using buglers, showing what a well-disciplined force they had in hand, and in the end the invaders descended into Hyrcania in pukka order.

This invasion of Hyrcania probably took up much of 209–208, and certainly a number of cities were taken. Tambrax, which had a Parthian palace but was un-walled, certainly fell, while nearby the defenders hunkered down in Sirynx, capital of the province. Antiochus delayed to besiege the city, despite it being very well protected by what are described as three moats and double palisades. Whether these were concentric or not is unclear, but certainly they were at least sixty feet wide and thirty feet deep, and there was a very strong defensive wall as well. This proved to be a digging war, with much use of mantlets to protect the sappers as they filled in the ditches and even deep mining to get under them. All was accompanied by furious fighting about the earthworks above and below ground, to such an extent, that, on occasions, dead and wounded could not be evacuated for treatment or the rites of the dead. Eventually, Antiochus' determination and his engineers' skill accomplished the filling in of the moats and the undermining of the walls. With defeat imminent, tensions grew in the town. Whether the defenders were Parthians or Tapurians, or both, they clearly did not trust the Greek settlers within, and equally coveted their goods. But their cupidity was punished as they tried to escape after killing the Greeks and taking their valuables. They were thrown back by Antiochid mercenaries under Hyperbas, who, leading his peltasts in after them, took the surrender of the town.

Dysfunctional family affairs were not restricted to the western Seleucid kingdoms. According to a venerable but far from uncontested historian, difficult queens had as significant an impact east of the Zagros as they had at Antioch and

Sardis.[4] Seleucus II's sister (whose name is unknown) had years before married Diodotus I of Bactria, who had established himself in an independent kingdom in about 250. However, she clearly did not become so attached to her new family that she forgot her old one. When Diodotus II, the son of Diodotus I, made an alliance with the Parthians, she, still a powerful dowager, took a hand to revenge herself on a man who was prepared to befriend a people who were the most significant threat to Seleucid power in Iran. She married her daughter to Euthydemus of Magnesia, an officer of Diodotus II, who she later persuaded to kill his commander-in-chief and take over the Bactrian kingdom. Despite this Seleucid connection, this was the prize Antiochus was aiming for.[5]

The aim was to re-establish control of Bactria and Sogdia; rich territories, where irrigation from rivers like the Oxus and Jaxartes sustained agriculture in an almost Babylonian fashion. Later records by Greeks, Romans and Chinese may be suspect in detail, but all highlight the number of considerable population centres in these regions. Bactria of 1,000 cities may be a touch over the top, but certainly well-ordered and considerable centres of population were plentiful in these lands, which now cover much of Afghanistan and parts of Turkmenistan, Uzbekistan and Tajikistan. And, there was more than riches; it was necessity. These provinces were the 'limes' of central Asia, the defences against the constant threat of nomad bands eager to purloin the goods of their settled neighbours. Defences were of the essence, whether the great ramparts of Balkh or Samarkand, or much simpler affairs at what were hardly more than walled villages. The influence of the Greek settlers also had a major impact in establishing communities with real sinews, and not just in the Alexandrias that we know of. However, their example must have encouraged the development of neighbouring towns, who after a century's rule by Hellenes, no doubt adopted the usages of their masters as the open sesame to advancement of all kinds.

The extent of Hellenization in many of the communities of the upper satrapies is debatable. We know that there were Greek cleruchs at Susa, but whether this was the norm is unclear. For those that were significantly Hellenized, the relationship with the Seleucid monarchy was a kind of symmachy or alliance, but this was a reality that had much to do with what the citizens needed from the king, how near he was and how able to provide it. Hellenized places existed far to the east at Bactra, and even at Pushkalavati in Gandhara they put down deep roots. But how widespread the settlement was in the far east is unsure. Alexander left 13,000 men to garrison Bactria and Sogdia, but Pithon killed thousands of settler soldiers in the Diadochi Wars after the Babylonian settlement. Twelve cities/colonies were founded in Alexander's time, but they would have been a very small proportion of Justin's Bactria of 1,000 cities. But his comment presumably indicates that urban communities were common enough, and many must have included more soldiers who had come to the area in the first 100 years of the Seleucid era, not just Macedonians and Greeks but Thracians, Anatolians and others.

So it was a populous and important country that Antiochus aimed for, with mineral wealth to boot. Lapis lazuli, found nearby, brought in a considerable income from trade, and though it was over a century before the direct silk route took off in the region, still east–west trade towards China, and south to India offered opportunities for advancement to many. Gold also passed this way from Siberia, particularly in Achaemenid times, and stories still lingered of eastern treasure troves, myths that sometimes, as much as hard reality, had peaked the sensitivities of invaders down through the ages. Eldorado was not an invention that just appealed to hard men from Estremadura.

Now again for Antiochus, it was choices about which road to take. His objective was Bactria and Sogdia, but there were two routes. It was a Hellenistic kingdom that he was approaching, but still this was a land barely known to most of the people in the Seleucid army. They were again involved in that fragile dependence on locals to give them information, in an age before maps, and the intentions of the peasants or nomads or local aristocracy they interrogated could only be guessed at. The most direct route led northeast towards the great oasis of Merv and on to Bactria itself.

But another, longer route existed, southeast through Seistan and up the Helmand valley to the Hindu Kush. Alexander had taken this southern route to outflank Bessus and also to crush satraps, like those of Seistan, before they could join the new Great King. It was an indirect approach, but one that had the great advantage of surprise. Their arrival from that direction would be unexpected. Antiochus did not face the same problems, and for him, the shortest and most direct approach made much more sense for a large army, one that had already come a very long way.

Euthydemus and his government must have established decent relations with the local barons, because when he sent round his agents to call these men to arms, 10,000 well-accoutred Bactrian cavalry answered. Ten thousand is an impressive number, considering that Bessus could only mobilise 8,000 when he raised the eastern satrapies against Alexander. In Euthydemus' muster we hear of no European-style infantry, heavy or light, so it is possible that he made no attempt to call up the Greek settler troops, aware as he was of what happened to Molon, when their equivalents in that rebel army deserted in battle when faced with the legitimist array.

These 10,000 first-class troopers were deployed to guard the crossing of the Aria River and when Antiochus got news of this he decided to pounce. The river was three days away from his camp, and after a couple of marches of moderate pace on the night before the third day, he himself pushed quickly ahead with the cavalry, light-armed infantry and 10,000 peltasts. The rest, presumably the phalangites and baggage, kept to the old pace and only began to march at dawn.

All to surprise the enemy guards, who, scouts had learned, had taken to the habit of retiring to a town more than two miles away from the river at night. Antiochus' celerity was rewarded, and in this flat country with easy crossing points, he got most of his advanced guard over the river before the Bactrians could respond. Despite this initial success, he still had to bear the brunt of his enemies' ferocious attack with only his own guard of 2,000 horse, while the rest got themselves into order, after the inevitable disruption caused in crossing the river. The young king was inspirational as the two sides clashed. 'In this affair it seems that Antiochus himself fought more brilliantly than any of those with him.'[6]

The best Bactrian warriors were Cataphracts, whose horses and persons were fully protected by cuirasses or padded suits with small metal plates sown in and protective bands round arms and legs; these were in the first group to engage. With their long barge pole lances, they no doubt outreached the companions of Antiochus, who still carried their shorter spear, in use since Philip and Alexander's time. It was a very bloody affair, and only the king's example kept the Seleucid mounted guards to their task. 'In this battle Antiochus's horse was transfixed and killed and he himself received a wound in the mouth and lost several of his teeth.'[7] Fortunately for the invader, the second and third line of enemy horse was either of poorer quality or much less well led: 'they were in difficulties and had the worst of it'. Now Panaetolus arrived with what must have been the rest of the advanced guard, if not the main body of the heavy infantry. Panaetolus, last heard of holding Tyre for Theodotus, the Aetolian, when he sold out from Ptolemy to Antiochus, clearly had made good headway in his new attachment. These men he brought forward not only ended the main fight but also saw off some of the first Bactrian wave, who had been pursuing groups of guardsmen who had fled at the initial onset. Casualties were heavy in the pursuit by the royal cavalry, and when the Seleucid army settled into camp on the other bank of the river, it was a wrecked Bactrian cavalcade that rejoined their king Euthydemus.

It was a long way from the battle site to the Bactrian capital Balkh. The river the Hellenes knew as the Aria flows from the Hindu Kush not far from Herat, and is now part of the border of modern Afghanistan and Iran. Then in Turkmenistan it becomes the Tejen, before it peters out in the Karakum black sand waste. It is hundreds of miles to the west of Balkh, with several rivers between the two that might have been utilized for holding up Antiochus. But Euthydemus seems to have completely lost confidence. Indeed, Polybius claims he was 'terror-stricken', as we are not told of any further attempt to make a stand in the long trek back to Balkh.

Balkh was as ancient as the world, a political and religious hub, and a great place long before the Persians arrived. Nearly fifty miles south of the Oxus, on a tributary that irrigates the land around, contrasting with the gravel desert elsewhere. It had been Alexander's headquarters in one of his most difficult campaigns and a place where he commenced in earnest one of the most central and dramatic processes of his life. Here Alexander put down crucial Mediaising markers. He instituted the training of 30,000 native boys in the Macedonian way of war, much to the resentment of his followers. Here, Hephaistion was made Chiliarch, a distinctly Persian conception, and here began the first real steps towards him slipping on the persona of Great King with the attempted introduction of *proskynesis*, which saw Callisthenes, Aristotle's nephew, first lose his king's favour and then his life.

Balkh was massively defended, and the Bactrians had clearly stockpiled all the stores and munitions they needed. It appears Antiochus actually failed to take the place in a two-year siege, but this investment is a most famous event. Unfortunately, the descriptions of this encounter that was so well known to contemporaries have not survived. It must have had the kind of dramatic resonance as great epics like Demetrius the Besieger's assault on Rhodes or Alexander's attack on Tyre. It might have been far away, but Antiochus' efforts, despite not being completely successful, brought his name even further into the limelight for many contemporaries.[8] After he had thrown everything he had at the defenders for twenty-four months, Antiochus decided he would have to see what a little diplomacy might achieve. Euthydemus, who had fought so well once backed into a corner, now showed no less enterprise in arguing his case than in defending his city. The Bactrian ruler began negotiations with Antiochus through a fellow Magnesian called Teleas. Via this man, he claimed innocence of any crimes against Antiochus' line as in coming to power he had only overthrown a man who was clearly a rebel against the Seleucid empire. He also stressed the practical; that if he was deposed then the resultant chaos would open a door to the nomads that his dynasty had always been a bulwark against. In putting the case, Euthydemus found he was preaching to the converted. Antiochus had no desire to be bogged down, like virtually everyone else who came into this part of the world before or since. Limited aims were the order of the day, and when Euthydemus' son Demetrius arrived the agreement was both to be ratified and guaranteed by his proposed marriage with one of Antiochus' daughters. The new axis was cemented. On top of a written treaty that allowed Euthydemus the title of king, he swore allegiance to Antiochus, made presents of corn for the Seleucid army, and organized the handover of what elephants he had in his own compounds. This was *real politick*; Antiochus could not be turned back, but nor could he stay indefinitely, so some such arrangement was inevitable. Still, the details left no doubt as to the clearly subservient position of Euthydemus as the ruler at Balkh.

The whole adventure of the east was topped off by an excursion over the Hindu Kush to India, where Antiochus renewed his alliance with King Sophagasenus, to such an extent that he replenished the Antigonid elephant corps to 150 beasts, and an officer had to be left behind to organize the treasure this generous king had promised. Whether this was some sort of tribute or a gift is unclear. In fact, the relationship of Antiochus with this ruler in India is almost as opaque as that of Seleucus I when he encountered Chandragupta almost 100 years before. Antiochus then led them back through Arachosia and then crossed over the River Erymanthus into Drangene and on to Carmania, where the army was allowed to winter. They had traversed what is now southern Afghanistan, and made camp near the modern border of Iran. Even after this, it was a long way back home, but there is little to tell us the route or of events along the way; except that Antiochus was still looking to recoup control wherever his dynasty had had some claim, however tenuous, before. He took the trouble to re-establish hegemony over the waters of the Persian Gulf and the lands that bordered them. He cruised these waters in a navy intended to overawe the Arab peoples of this region, who serviced very rich trade routes. What exactly he achieved here we do not know either; only that he visited Tylus, near modern Bahrain, and received a very considerable tribute in treasure and spices from a place called Gerrha, an Arab kingdom, on the west side of the Persian Gulf. It was these years of activity in the east that gained Antiochus his reputation right across the Hellenistic World.

> In a word he put his kingdom in a position of safety, overawing all subject to him by his courage and industry. It was this expedition, in fact, which made him appear worthy of his throne not only to the inhabitants of Asia, but those of Europe likewise.[9]

In 204, Antiochus was still just short of 40, and had not yet achieved twenty years on the throne, but his reputation was already immense. Since Raphia, he had been undefeated in numerous campaigns and had planted his flag in vast stretches of the known world.

Chapter 7

Balkans in Turmoil

In the year 219, as the Macedonians returned from the invasion of Aetolia, Philip encountered a single galley in the Gulf of Ambracia. On board was a man who had already had a peripheral part to play in events but now would move to the centre. This was Demetrius of Pharos, a prince on the run from the Romans. He had been around for many years; some would have remembered him for leading a corps of Illyrian warriors at Sellasia and others as a freebooter who infested the Adriatic sea lanes. In fact, his regional significance for some decades had been even more considerable than this.

Demetrius' exact antecedents are unknown, but the Greeks had penetrated Illyria by the early part of the sixth century. They planted cities on the coast as they spread up the Adriatic to Epidamnus; after that they did not linger on the mainland but, keeping to their boats, they established communities on three islands further north at Hvar, Issa and Melaina Korkyra. Demetrius' power base was the Greek colony of Pharos, founded in the fourth century, where the town of Stari Grad stands on the island of Hvar; a typical Croatian island with pine on the lower slopes, scrub further up and a large fertile coastal plain. Forty-two miles long, it was ideal for a putative sea lord to use as a base, positioned as it was to control trade routes across and up and down the Adriatic. How Demetrius came to power is unclear, whether inheriting a family position or making himself tyrant by dint of talent, determination and ruthlessness. Whichever, from his stronghold, he appeared to have made himself indispensible in a number of camps. He prospered under the umbrella of King Agron of the Ardiae, a people renowned as big drinkers who battled their neighbours over salt rights and then took to piracy with a will when the Autariatae forced them to relocate down to the coast. On Agron's death, his wife, Teuta, took over, while Demetrius slipped effortlessly into the good books of the new regime, and his regional clout was enhanced when she put him in command at Corfu. But when the first Roman Illyrian war opened in 229, Demetrius is described as in disgrace with Teuta and turned his coat, throwing his lot in with the invaders and handing Corfu over to them. Queen Teuta fled to Rhizon and the Romans installed Demetrius in her place, as regent for the young king of Illyria ruling most of the coastal area.

But, as was now becoming habitual, Demetrius bit the hand that fed him; he had spat in Teuta's face after she raised him up and now he did the same to the Romans. He sent fleets south of Lissus, absolutely against his agreement with them and, by winter 219, word was getting through to Rome that he was seizing places in Illyria that were allied to them. Our main source may describe his activities as that of a temerarious ingrate, but this is perhaps blinkered. Demetrius was a local potentate who for years had been aiming to expand his principality on the Dalmatian coast. This was natural enough behaviour, but it was very far from the Roman vision of how things should be. And when they took notice and intervened, Demetrius' allies deserted him, and he found himself reduced to his home base of Pharos. When the Romans decided on a night attack there, a battle on the beach sucked in all the defenders, and when they were defeated they had no choice but to run. The Greek prince got away on some boats that he had had drawn up nearby, while the invaders levelled Pharos town.

This was the despoiled and fugitive prince picked up by Philip, and for a few years he would figure as an 'eminence grise' vying with Aratus for the soul of the king. He would get the blame for the desecration at Thermus, specifically, and more generally be held responsible for the king's fall from grace as a 'Hellenic epitome'. In a way, he almost fitted the vacated shoes of Apelles; like him, his was a direct rule programme, caring little for Philip's liberal reputation amongst the Greek allies. It was garrisons, not alliances, that he promoted as the way forward. But the question of how this runaway became so influential is difficult to answer; he no longer led soldiers or disposed of wealth or ships. He may have had charisma, but would this have won him the position that is suggested, or is there exaggeration here to construct a satisfying balance of good and bad surrounding Philip? Polybius, certainly, likes to indulge in the age–old proclivity that blames the advisor, not the monarch, so Demetrius is a convenient hook for those with an interest in airbrushing history and who are not happy with piling blame on royalty itself.

By July 217, Demetrius had been around the court for some time, whispering in the royal ear, and what he had seeded there chimed with the prevailing mood. Agelaus of Naupactus, a man central to the peace negotiations that ended the Social War, prophesied that the winner between Rome and Carthage would soon be looking greedily across the Adriatic and beyond. And that if the Greek states had any sense they would make peace in order to face this terrible threat in a spirit of unity. The Peace was duly ratified, but the second part of the advice was less well followed. No one yet believed in the danger, and instead looked to short-term advantage. Philip decided the immediate troubles faced by Rome would give him the space to increase his influence in Illyria, and the one who is recorded as persuading him of this was the prince from Pharos. There is an improbable assumption that Demetrius' motive was a desire for revenge against the Italians who had despoiled him of his principality, but this comes from people who can only see things as being centred on Rome. Certainly, he had been at work pressing for Philip to intervene again in Illyria, and his background made him a capable and convincing advocate. And anyway, to persuade the Macedonian leadership to move north was not an arduous task, with the behaviour of another local firebrand demanding a reaction.

King Philip after the conclusion of peace returned by sea to Macedonia, where he found that Scerdilaidas... had now pillaged a town in Pelagonia called Pissaeum, had got into his hands by menaces or by promises several cities of the Dassaretae, namely Antipatreia, Chrysondyon, and Gertus, and had made extensive inroads on the neighbouring parts of Macedonia.[1]

Philip was bound to try and recover his position in this crucial border country round Lake Ohrid. Many of these places had been willing partners in the Macedonian project before Scerdilaidas arrived, and they needed to be rescued and those who revolted brought back in line. This is enough of a motive. We don't need to countenance it as a preliminary to an invasion of Italy, a strategy put in the king's mind by silver-tongued Demetrius. But, whatever the exact ruminations, the Macedonian military made short work of the interlopers. Scerdilaidas had made headway in Pelagonia and in the lands of the Dassaretae north and south of the lake country of Ohrid and Prespa, but now he was swiftly pressed back close to that part of Illyria where Roman writ claimed to run. Control of the valleys of the Apsus and the Genusus had been the main cause of this fighting, running as they do from Macedonia to the Illyrian coast.

After such good work, Philip was able to dismiss his men for a winter break after long years of campaigning. But if the men rested, Philip and his administration did not; the off season for them was full of planning. They intended to construct a very considerable navy. The boats laid down were designed on the Illyrian model: *lembi*, not built to fight sea battles but ideal for quickly transporting armies from one place to another. A hundred were built at Demetrias in a very short time, each of them carrying about fifty men, and by the summer of 216, Philip was ready to make his move. From the arsenal at Demetrias, the mint new navy was launched, reaching the Adriatic via Euripus and Cape Maleas to Cephalonia and Leucas. The presence of a Roman fleet at Lilybaeum on the west end of Sicily apparently made Philip nervous, but he still determined to sail on towards Apollonia. Near the island of Sasona at the entrance to the bay of Aulon, a sheltered place to beach his fleet, news reached Philip that Roman quinqueremes were not far off. He panicked and ordered the fleet back the way they had come, reaching Cephalonia after sailing two nights straight. In fact, it was wind and smoke; Scerdilaidas had asked Rome for help, but only ten ships came anywhere near, and if they had attacked, Philip would have outnumbered them ten to one.

In summer 215, after this embarrassment, Philip formalized an alliance with Hannibal. The form of the agreement is recorded but the timing and what the Macedonian's exact ambitions are still open to debate. But one thing is clear, that Demetrius was seen by Philip as crucial. It was actually mentioned in the treaty that after victory the Romans will be kept out of 'Corcyra, Apollonia, Epidamnus, Pharos, Dimale, Parthini, or Atitania: and that they shall return to Demetrius of Pharos all his friends who are in the dominions of Rome.'[2] Yet, straight after the treaty, when Illyria seemed top of the agenda, Philip turned in a different direction. It was to that perennial tinder box, Messene, that he inclined. The Aetolian-Elian syndicate had been plaguing the Messenians for years, and a divided Messene was so attractive for predatory rivals that Philip needed to act swiftly in the autumn of 215 if he was to ensure no one could, by expanding there, turn into a dangerously powerful rival in the peninsula.

The occasion of turmoil was, predictably enough, an outbreak of class war. Instability wracked the city, where the richer citizens had been sent packing and their land redistributed. The democrats had made something of a social revolution and the moneybags didn't like it: 'those of the old citizens who remained found it difficult to brook the equality which these men had assumed.'[3] Philip, no doubt egged on by Demetrius, hurried to the city to exploit the party strife and proceeded to incite the factions against each other:

> In private he asked the generals of the Messenians if they had not laws to enforce against the common people, and again in private he asked the leaders of the common people if they had not hands to lift against the tyrants.[4]

It fell out that the popular party had an unexpected triumph when the aristocrats tried to arrest their leaders, but they turned the tables and killed 200 officials and their blue-blooded friends. A result not unpleasing to Philip and Demetrius, who sought to exploit it to their own ends. Aratus, who may have been deliberately excluded from the original descent on Messene, now heard what was happening, and disliking even this partial dawdling with extreme democrats, rushed with his son, only a day behind, to the centre of the maelstrom. They briskly took the king to task for stoking the disorder and bloodshed that had occurred. Philip was clearly taken aback by the vehemence of the Achaeans when they arrived. There also seems to have been a personal dimension, as it is suggested that Aratus' son was a lover of Philip, and the king was worried that his behaviour had made him unlovable to the young man. Philip, angry, but concerned for a reputation for moderation, accepted the rebuke, and showing his faith in Aratus, gave him his hand and walked with him from the theatre. The king still apparently had much regard for the Achaeans.

Now the drama moved to the temple of Zeus at the citadel on Mount Ithome. The king convinced the city fathers to let him process up to the acropolis to make a sacrifice. With a great mob of attendants, and declaring an intent to sightsee and make a religious offering, he took the steep path to the fortified hill, which completely dominated the town. It was a place described as so defensible and well-walled as to be easily held with any sort of garrison, and even today the walls, extant and high, are almost unique in the region. In the temple, a seer brought the entrails of an ox just sacrificed, and Philip proffered them so that both Demetrius and Aratus could view the remains and decide whether he should take over Ithome. He apparently first asked Aratus, but Demetrius butted in and vociferously posited:

'If you have the mind of a diviner, it bids you withdraw at once, but if you have the mind of a vigorous king it tells you to keep it, so that you may not after losing this opportunity see hand in vain for another more favourable one. For it is only by holding both his horns that you can keep the ox under,' meaning by the horns Mount Ithome and the Acrocorinthus and by the ox the Peloponnese.[5]

Demetrius was in no quandary; for him, the king should stick to this piece of real estate with all his might and main. Aratus, when pressed for his opinion, appealed to the king's pride. He was not eager to see more Macedonian troops in the Peloponnese, and knew the young man he was dealing with still clung to the importance of his reputation. So he suggested that in taking the place by treachery his allies would cease to be able to trust him. Telling him that only bandits based their power on control of 'cliffs and crags' and that a king's strength was not in a defensible lair, but in the gratitude of subjects and friends. Philip's resolve, already affected by the scolding earlier, handed back the entrails, and leaving arm in arm, showed clearly that Aratus had won the argument. High on this hill, the Achaean's advice won out, and the king and his entourage descended and withdrew from the town.

If this was a setback, by 214, Philip, to Demetrius' satisfaction, felt sufficiently confident to initiate an enterprise in the Adriatic again. In August, the king embarked about 6,000 men on 120 *lembi* and sailed again to the bay of Aulon, landing at the town of Oricus. He took it by assault and then moved north against the great city of Apollonia, a really ambitious target. The king's pilot took the shallow-draft ships up the Aous River (Vjose) and disembarked the army to open the siege lines around the city. But the Macedonians were not to be left unmolested; a Roman officer, alerted by refugees from Oricus, moved quickly from Brundisium to intervene. Arriving in two days, he drove out the few men Philip had left at Oricus. The Apollonians, hearing of their proximity, appealed for help, and 2,000 picked soldiers apparently slipped up river by ship before entering unobserved through the besiegers' lines.

Their Roman leader, seeing that the attackers were ill-prepared, decided on a sortie. At the darkest time of night, he led his men into the besiegers' camp. Apparently, more than 1,000 men had entered before the alarm was raised, and it was only because they stopped to kill every sleeping enemy that they were delayed in getting to the king's tent. Panic ruled; Macedonians and monarch ran for it in their underclothes, only reaching safety with the ships at the river. Less than 3,000 were killed or captured, but they had lost their siege equipment and baggage. Morale was rock bottom, with the enemy ships blocking the river mouth and their troops controlling Oricus. Philip dragged his ships onto the river bank and burnt them, and determined to avoid further calamity, he marched up river and back to Macedonia, safe enough but still humiliated.

No wonder that when we next hear of Philip in that year it is way away from Illyria, in Messene, where in the past he had experienced little except success. No explanation is given as to exactly why this much-abused polity again demanded his attention, but he 'with more passion than reason' started taking the place apart. Demetrius was still with his sponsor, despite the Macedonian effort having moved away from an Illyrian dimension, and although he was not young, he was still vigorous, and pushed himself forward as the ideal military executive in this new enterprise. The prince from Pharos took an elite force and tried a decisive coup; the men he led inside the walls of Messene looked set to get full control. But the townsfolk recovered their wits and courage, and realizing that they were strong enough to deal with the numbers that had entered, they armed themselves with spear and shield and in a united body drove the attackers out again. In this desperate melée, Demetrius himself was cut down in a pointless skirmish in a country far from where his interests lay.

If one half of the duo who had buzzed about Philip's head for years was gone, the other did not have long to go. In recent times, Aratus had made his disapproval of the Messenian policy very evident; an independent Achaea had no interest in encouraging the Macedonians to take up a permanent, increased military presence so near. There may also have been a personal dimension, as the king is reported to have seduced Aratus' son's wife at about this time, creating tension as an old mentor and a now grown-up apprentice tried to keep the shreds of their old relationship together. It is suggestive that when Philip pressed hard for the Achaean to join him on his Illyrian campaigns, the invitation was spurned. In 213, the man who had virtually stood for Achaea for at least three decades began to sicken at an alarming rate, and the divisive ambience between these two inevitably led to some rumours of foul play. The story was that Philip, through the agency of Taurion, ordered the poisoning of Aratus. His downfall was cunningly arranged:

Taurion made an intimate companion of Aratus, and gave him poison, not of a sharp and violent sort, but one of those which first induce gentle heats in the body, and a dull cough, and then little by little bring on consumption.[6]

The truth of this is very much open to question, as is the suggestion that Aratus knew what was happening, but only told his manservant: 'Such, my dear Cephalo,' said Aratus, 'are the wages of royal friendship.'[7]

A dramatic ending, fitting the *topos* of the ungrateful prince, but not likely; Philip had no interest in an unstable Achaea. Even if he had asked some difficult questions of Philip in the recent past, Aratus remained useful, and it is difficult to imagine Philip would have wanted him eliminated. In addition, if there had been anything in it, the whole world surely would have talked about the murder of this great man by the King of Macedonia. Whatever the exact circumstances, the long-time (sixteen or seventeen times) *strategos* of the Achaean League was dead. As befitted such a seminal figure, he was given hero's rites and by special permission of the oracle at Delphi was the first person to be buried inside Sicyon's city walls as 'founder and saviour of the city'.

Aratus' demise was certainly linked with the final brake coming off in Philip's metamorphosis from beloved young prince, imbued with Hellenism to his fingertips, to impious despot richly deserving of downfall. He was a young ruler who came to power with a reservoir of affection amongst his subjects, and with a reputation that allowed even the archetypically disputative Cretans to perceive him as a potential arbitrator and leader. But he then changed, disregarded honourable friends, followed the advice of villains and made errors that brought calamity down on both his own house and on many Greek states as well.

Since these deaths close to Philip, much had transpired across the whole world of Hellenistic kings. Antiochus was building a reputation based on what looked like permanent achievements that must have been reported in detail to fellow monarchs and to lesser powers over the years. But now the conduits of news were buzzing with the interesting tidings that he was on the way to the semi-detached satrapies at the eastern end of his massive empire.

But, while Antiochus' column of conquest snaked off east into the dust of Asia, the Balkans were again thrown into turmoil. This Greek world was geographically dominated by mountains. It was difficult, defensible, problematic to dominate, inevitably divided, and now these factors were as evident as ever in the coming conflict, as was that other constant, the sea; by far the easiest means of communication and intervention.

This region, after hardly five years respite, in 211, saw something very like a 'second round' of the Social War get underway. If earlier in the century there had been a labile quality in the matter of who allied with whom, now things had firmed up; the sides that lined up did so in a very similar way, with just a few new contestants to spice up the play. A king from Anatolia would muddy the waters, which meant the pattern of activity would be different in this second great test of the Macedonian king and his Symmachy. But before this outbreak flared up, the Macedonians had kept themselves busy. The Illyrian imperative had always been strong in the decision-making councils at Pella. There were riches to be had there and a hardy population who could be turned into steady soldiers, but it was a difficult land to pacify; in a later age, it was the last coastal region of the '*mare nostrum*' that the Romans properly pacified. Augustus still had to go toe to toe with battling Illyrian tribes, long after the coasts of Africa, Spain, Gaul, Greece and the Levant had succumbed to the charms of Latin political emasculation.

In 213 and 212, Philip was making a statement of intent. Campaigns were in progress that are difficult to understand, but which are still clearly central to the ambitions of a ruler who had previously spent so much time in the Peloponnese, Aetolia and Thessaly. His commanders subdued the Atintanians, the Dassaretae and the Parthini, a swathe of territory a couple of hundred miles from north to south. But this expansion was all terrestrially bound, showing perhaps how shaken the Macedonian military had been by the bloody noses they had taken when they had adventured on Adriatic waters before. But to acquire real hegemony, Philip needed to get a foothold on the western coast and Lissus seemed an ideal place to start. He had been long convinced of the importance of the city and its very defensible acropolis, so he decided to act. He had prepared well and a strongly founded force took only two days to cross the mountain pass to the east of Lissus. Still, it was gruelling enough, and by the time they emerged on the banks of the Ardaxanus River the Macedonians needed rest. While they recuperated, the king took his engineers forward to check the approaches to the city. The lower town was well defended down to the sea, as was much of the landward side, and the citadel sitting on top of an extraordinary high hill promised to be extremely difficult to scale. But Philip determined to exploit an area of open ground that lay between the town itself and the citadel. Here he planned an ambush, hiding light troops 'in some thickly wooded ravines' close to the open space but hidden from the defenders. He then marched round 'with his peltasts and the rest of his light-armed' making a play of looking for a weak spot to assault, and when he came to the open space again, he halted for all the world as if he had just hit upon an ideal place to make an attack.

Just as intended, the defenders, with their confidence boosted by reinforcements from neighbouring communities, decided on a sortie. They probably thought Philip had only a portion of his army with him, the peltasts and some light infantry. The king now ordered the latter to attack uphill against the men sortieing out of the town, while the peltasts held their position. The Lissians and their allies were able, by dint of numbers and advantage of ground, to push back the Macedonian lights, who fell back on the peltasts drawn up on the level ground. Philip now made as if to withdraw, and the defenders were suckered in, unable to resist, 'owing to their confidence in the strength of the place, and then abandoning Acrolissus in small bodies poured down by bye-paths to the level ground, thinking there would be a thorough rout of the enemy and a chance of some booty.'[8]

Now the trap was sprung; the hiding light troops ran out from the gulleys they were concealed in, while the peltasts turned and charged. The ambushing lights got between the garrison and the citadel, while the other defenders were driven back behind the city walls. The citadel fell and put the attackers on the front foot, and the successful ploy must have been a kick in the guts for many of the defenders. Still, they fought hard the next day, and only desperate and bloody assaults brought the fall of the city itself. This success, against such a defensible place, gave pause to the people in less well-protected towns around, and the Macedonians soon found representatives from the surrounding Illyrian communities offering to accept their 'protection'.

Whilst Philip was a happy man for a while with his Illyrian success, it was not long before events occurred that shook him to the core. Old foes were gathering; the Aetolians had strong expectations that old anti-Macedonian cohorts like Elis, Sparta and even Messene would back them again. And the Romans, who had twenty-five quinqueremes available now, offered support to the Aetolians to reopen the war with the Symmachy. In the agreement, the Aetolians were to get any real estate acquired, while the Italians took the movables and slaves. Also, moves were made to recruit not only old Peloponnesian friends, but also the likes of the Illyrian Scerdilaidas and his son, Pleuratus, to join in this treasure hunt for the property of the Macedonians and their friends. The reasons for the Aetolians striking at this time are difficult to understand. They had not been unremittingly belligerent in the last few years; in fact, they showed no signs of taking advantage when Philip had earlier got his two bloody noses in Illyria. It was unlikely to have been just the encouragement of the Romans; after all they had long been involved in a desultory war with Philip. The new factor may have been Attalus of Pergamum committing his hand; he had been involved in the region before, but at last seemed prepared to put 100 per cent into despoiling the Symmachy.

That the old warhorse of previous hostilities, Scopas, was to start with an advance into Thessaly was no surprise, while the other component of the offensive was a Roman fleet that allowed an effective allied assault on Zacynthus, an island off the west of the Peloponnese. After this, a joint force took Oeniadae, the very place Philip had captured as his first major prize of the Social War, and presumably had returned to the Acarnanians, as these were the people evicted in this latest attack. And, to round things off, the nearby island of Nasus was taken over by this acquisitive coalition.

About August 211, news of this activated association reached Pella; it inevitably dragged Philip away from the Illyrian front. For all that he would have liked to deepen his hegemony there, he would need to respond to these emerging menaces. In particular the Anatolian princeling, Attalus, who although no super power, had a formidable navy, and as he was no longer entangled up with Achaeus, who was dead, or Antiochus who was off in the east, he might very well be able to have a significant impact in tandem with Philip's other adversaries. Philip and his commanders' first response, though, was to get in some rough work on his perennially troublesome neighbours to keep them cowed while he attended to events elsewhere. He shored up his northwestern border by attacking Oricus and Apollonia, friends of Rome. After this blood-letting around the mouth of Aous River, he attacked the Dardanians and took the town of Sintia to block off one of their usual invasion routes south. Then he marched south through Pelagonia, Lycestis and Bottiaea in West Macedonia, to show the flag in highland regions that were always bothered by residual separatist tenancies, to get down to the Vale of Tempe and face off the Aetolians themselves. But instead of trying to force these ever-slippery enemies into battle, he left 4,000 men to occupy them. Having covered this danger, the Macedonian army chased off to hit the Thracians before they could hit them. This was lightening stuff, pouncing on the Maedi and besieging Iamphorynna, their capital.

Now, Scopas and his Aetolians, frustrated by Philip's swift response in Thessaly, decided on an attack on Acarnania. These neighbours and bitter enemies prepared to sell their lives dearly. With extirpation well on the cards, the Acarnanians got serious, sending the old folks, women and children into the protection of Epirus while they mobilized all the rest, and with the most awful curses, determined to win or die, even demanding of their Epirote friends to give no help to any Acarnanians who came back defeated but alive, and to ensure funeral rites were arranged for all who died in defence of the fatherland; 'having aroused their spirits by these means, they pitched camp facing the enemy at their very frontier.'[9] But it was not just a council of despair; they also sent to ask Philip for help. These appeals brought the Macedonians hurrying down from the north so quickly that the Aetolians backed off and went home. This even before Philip got to Dium, which allowed him to take his men home and demob them for the winter.

In the following fighting season, one of the most significant actors was to be Attalus I, King of Pergamum. He was well in his sixties now, but like so many of the successor kings, he remained belligerent and aggressive well into advanced age. Apparently a paragon of domestic virtue, he made up for it by the energy he expended to make trouble for the rest of the world. He had a defensible home base, Pergamum city, set 1,100 feet above the fertile Caicos valley in ancient Mysia, a solid income, an effective army and access to lots of bloodthirsty mercenaries – the very Galatians he claimed great credit for having tamed. And something of a navy as well, founded on those coastal Greek cities of Asia Minor he had come to control in the thirty odd years since his reign began. He had involved himself in the Greek peninsula before, but now it was something different. In the autumn of 210, the Aetolians elected him general in chief of their League, an important honorific, and another piece was put in place when Sulpicius Galba sailed the Roman squadron round the Peloponnese and captured Aegina in the Saronic Gulf, which the Aetolians then sold to Attalus for thirty talents, no doubt as part of the agreement that brought that king into the war. It was his threat that ensured the next year's fighting would centre along the eastern road that Philip had taken a great interest in at the end of the Social War.

The Aetolians, with these new friends in the wings, had started very energetically; the old war party was clearly up and running. They believed that with more allies on board the imbalance of power in the earlier struggle could be rectified, and they had their eyes on getting back the places they had lost in Acarnania and south Thessaly. They still had faith in the power of Sparta on the Peloponnesian front, who they expected also to be eager to upset the Symmachy cart. Elis and Messene had to thrash details out too, for the axis to have real sinew and purpose and we can be sure Aetolian representatives travelled the roads of west Peloponnese frequently in these months. The Aetolians, led again by Scopas, realizing that Philip was up and active, first tried a pre-emptive strike to distract him. An allied attack on Phocian Anticyra on the Gulf of Corinth overcame resistance, and while the Aetolians garrisoned the defences, the Romans enslaved the people. If this brutalizing of communities under his protection was intended to distract Philip, it failed; he pressed on with his own agenda, looking for action, and he found it at Echinus, where a lone tower now stands overlooking the strait between Euboea and the mainland. It was a well-protected settlement and the Aetolians were determined to try and hold Philip there, so it demanded all the tricks of Hellenistic siege craft to encompass its downfall. In the gap between two towers along the city wall, where the Macedonian engineers determined to attack, a covered way to protect the sappers was built, and sheds were made ready to protect the men who would fill in the moat and the rams constructed to batter down the walls.

Siege towers were built with rams below and water kept on the second level to drench any incendiary devices dropped by the defenders. The third storey was made level with the city walls to protect against the defenders there attacking the men and engines on the highest storey of the tower. More than this, three batteries of stone throwers were set up, some throwing stones of a talent's weight, and some of even two and a half talents (a talent was approximately 60 lb). Trenches were dug from the covered way towards the walls to bring up assault troops and to protect them from the defenders' missiles as they moved forward. Philip knew that Aetolians, Attalus, and even some Romans might arrive at any time, so he built defensive lines to protect his siege works and camp from outside attack. It was a timely endeavour as the Aetolian war leader, Dorimachus, supported by Sulpicius, arrived on their ships and tried to raise the siege with a force of both foot and horse. But their attack on Philip's lines of contravallation failed, and a further careless attempt to put pressure on the besiegers did not even stop Philip getting supplies by sea, a fact that brought the Echinaean defenders to despair and surrender.

But, if clearing the eastern road was going well, elsewhere, Symmachy members were getting jittery. The Achaeans called for help because of threats from Machanidas of Sparta and the Aetolians who had crossed the Gulf of Corinth at Rhium. The Spartans were apparently hovering on the borders of Argos, when Achaean envoys were able to bring their worries to Philip's court at Demetrias. The Boeotians and Euboeans also felt themselves under threat, with Attalus' navy now a real danger to their long coastlines. The Acarnanians and Epirotes were there as well, urging the king to actively take up the gauge against this new and alarming axis. As head of the Symmachy, he needed to respond and chose to move south to buttress friends in central Greece and take on the main enemy in the Peloponnese. Meanwhile, the Aetolians had spies out and were anxiously eying the coast road from Echinus, down which the Macedonians clearly intended to travel. They prepared a defence force under Pyrrhias, who we know from the Social War and who had been a bit of a damp squib when it came to an invasion of Messene. He was in command of Aetolians, Pergamenes and reportedly a 1,000 Italian sailors, and almost immediately after starting out near Lamia, Philip found himself face to face with this army. He attacked straight away, and again Pyrrhias did not show well. Two separate battles were fought, and the veteran Macedonians had great success against what must have been a fairly motley coalition force. At each encounter the Aetolians and their allies lost 1,000 men; these were bloody setbacks and a good result for Philip, which took his enemy off the map as they cowered behind the walls of Lamia. The Macedonians also succeeded in taking Phalara, the port of that region with a good harbour and 'well protected roadsteads'. When the Macedonian army briefly took breath at this place, representatives from Ptolemy, Athens and Rhodes arrived to try and broker a peace.

These peacemakers would be hovering around during much of this period of belligerence, which was both bad for trade and blocked important recruiting grounds for the likes of the Ptolemaic military. On this occasion, they certainly achieved something, introducing Amynander, King of the Athamanians, as spokesman for the Aetolians, and a thirty-day truce was arranged to allow peace proposals to be taken to the Achaean council. Philip then marched out of Phalara, through Thessaly and Boeotia to Chalcis. Despite the truce, there were still enemies in the field, so Philip buffed up the regional defensive arrangements. He took particular pains at Chalcis, which was the key fortress in the area that he knew would be a target for any Attalid intervention. Livy certainly suggests he left most of the army behind, only travelling on south with 'a few horsemen and light-armed.'[10]

The Macedonians arrived in the Argolid in summer 209, where Philip was booked to attend the Nemean Games. At Argos, he orchestrated a real public relations coup to bolster connections with Peloponnesian friends that he had not seen for some years. He 'laid aside his diadem and purple robe, wishing to produce the impression that he was on a level with the others and a lenient and popular prince.'[11] This sounds a genuine attempt to garner goodwill by the common touch, despite the fact that it is presented as a backdrop for Philip as grand debauchee, who seduced high-status virgins, caroused round the town revelling and threatening any who got in his way. Indeed, it is claimed that this was the occasion he took Aratus the younger's wife, Polycratia, back to Macedonia. In fact, it is difficult to believe much of this, as Philip needed to cement relations with his Achaean allies, and to have behaved so would have alienated the very men he wanted on-side as he tried to contain a many-tentacled enemy, whose components might come at him and his Symmachy allies from almost any point of the compass.

The discussions at the Achaean assembly that the thirty-day truce meant to allow came to nothing; the Aetolians were pitching their peace demands high, wanting Pylos given back to Messene, the Atintanians returned to Roman control, and the Ardiaei to Scerdilaidas. That they did not want anything for themselves is extraordinary, but anyway, it was all far too much for Philip, who so far had had a decent war and was cooking up a strike of his own. He had high hopes that a number of Carthaginian ships would arrive, together with the five ships the Achaeans had provided in return for 4,000 troops he left to help them, and another squadron was due in from Prusias of Bithynia, who was already allied to the Macedonians. No party was really ready to talk yet.

There is confusion in the sequence of these events, but soon enough there was action that made any talk of peace irrelevant. Philip was enjoying the Games with his friends when news arrived that Sulpicius Galba was in the Gulf of Corinth and based at Naupactus. And, more than this, he had actually landed men from his ships between Sicyon and Corinth and was laying waste to the country. All this was very visible to Philip's men on top of the Acrocorinth – a great eye in the sky in this whole region. Probably the commander at Sicyon, too, was rushing to warn about this activity, which would be the ruin of local farms, even if the defensible town itself was not likely to be taken. Whoever told Philip, they found the king relaxed but not lax. He apparently leapt to horse and spurred off with just the cavalry he had with him, straight for the raiders, ordering the foot soldiers to follow as soon as they could be mobilized. The Italian troops were not in battle order but looking for loot when the Macedonians arrived, and they were herded like cattle as they dropped what they had pilfered and legged it back to their ships.

Whatever his alleged bad behaviour at Nemea, it did not seem to slow Philip and the alliance down. It is reported that they decided to take a hefty swipe that might neutralize a troublesome local enemy. The Eleans were at it again, urging successfully that the Aetolians send an army to join them, which would threaten the Macedonian garrisons at Heraea, Alipheira and Triphylia that guarded western Achaea and Arcadia. The Achaean *strategos* for 210/9, Cycliadas, marched to Dyme, where the Macedonians were concentrating too. There, both decided on a direct strategy of heading straight for Elis city despite it being held by a considerable garrison. They regrouped at Dyme before reaching the boundary, the River Larisus, where the land opens out from the mountains that cramp in the north coast of Achaea. There the Eleans, with Aetolians in support, came out to meet them.

Among the senior commanders of Cycliadas' army was the 'hero' of Sellasia. Philopoemen was hipparch in command of the Achaean cavalry, and the troops he led were very much his own creation. Only just returned from ten years of mercenary service in Crete, but with his military credentials and important family connections, he was straight away elected for the year 210/09 to the second-highest military command in the League hierarchy. He was an Arcadian blueblood from Megalopolis who as a child had been taught by a follower of the Megalopolitan philosophers Ecdemus and Demophanes. The former of these had years before helped Aratus to break the power of the Tyrant of Sicyon at the commencement of his career. What Philopoemen learned in his years of mercenary service he was not long in applying in reorganizing the army in a systematic and orderly fashion. It made sense to start with the cavalry; he was very familiar with the Achaean mounted arm from before going to Crete, and they were particularly neglected. Many previous hipparchs saw the post only as a stepping stone to being *strategos*, and so invested little in it. The veteran condottiere took the young aristocrats, who provided his recruits, in hand to create a cavalry model that was still regarded highly in Polybius' day, ensuring a hands-on style for the commander to keep each trooper up to scratch. First individually, then in formation, he worked them. Practising wheeling, deploying, throwing out columns from line of march and, most importantly, practising keeping his squadrons in hand and organized when they entered battle. Finally, after travelling to the individual cities to organize training, he arranged a day of manoeuvres for the whole corps in the spring of 209.

Dyme was the first test of these cavalry units, reformed over the winter, and in the fight that followed, Philopoemen's troopers acquitted themselves very well, and their commander, himself, saw off the enemy cavalry general, Damophantus, in a personal duel. After the skirmish, the Eleans backed off, while the invaders plundered the country outside the walls of Elis itself. But now the Romans showed up, 4,000 men under Sulpicius on fifteen ships crossing from Naupactus to Cyllene, disembarking and slipping into the town at night to bolster their allies in this mounting contest.

'Consequently the surprise inspired great alarm, when they had recognized Roman standards and arms among the Aetolians and Eleans.[12] So when Philip, his Macedonians and the Achaeans gathered under the walls to provoke another battle, they found that the enemy they had trounced before had been reinforced in considerable numbers by these foreign allies, whose appearance and dispositions came as something of a surprise. The king and his officers decided to pull out of battle. He tried to recall those of his men who had gone into the fight, but his Illyrians were already deeply involved in battle with the Aetolians.[13] In the light of this, he decided he had to commit. So, perhaps decked in another of the horned helmets we know he wore before, he charged at the head of his Companion cavalry against a Roman cohort that was supporting the Aetolians. It was a bitter melée, with the Macedonians hacking and prodding at the infantry below them. The king's horse was transfixed by a javelin, which caused it to throw its rider. On his feet, he was the centre of the Romans' attention, and his guardsmen needed to be very alert to save their master. He fought like a champion on foot amongst the swirling horsemen. Eventually, another mount was brought for him. 'Then, when the combat was now one-sided and many were falling and being wounded around him, he was seized by his men, was lifted upon another horse, and fled.'[14]

The order was given to fall back to a defensive position at a fort called Pyrgus. But, trudging slowly back five miles from Elis to their defended camp, Philip's column of deflated warriors had had a stroke of luck; they found and scooped up lots of locals who had also gone to the fort with their herds for protection. This windfall included 20,000 cattle and 4,000 prisoners; clearly, this loot and the rest they had garnered in the campaign meant the whole enterprise had ended pretty positively, despite Livy's desperate attempts to paint the Elean project as a disaster for the Symmachy.

But, as the well-remunerated allies retraced their steps back to Achaea, news arrived that the north was blowing up. Messengers were buzzing down the roads of Greece to let the king of Macedonia know that his home was in awful peril. Whether this was part of the plan hatched when the Aetolians began the war is not known, but certainly some of those involved were characters mentioned at that time. The details are not precise, but we are told: 'Scerdilaidas and Pleuratus were again active and that Thracian tribes, especially the Maedi, were prepared to invade Macedon.'[15]

An Illyrian called Aeropus had bribed the Macedonian in command at Lychnidus, by modern Ochrida at the northeast end of the lake of the same name, on the main road from the Adriatic to Thessalonica. These interlopers also occupied the country south of the lake, where the Dassaretae, an important Illyrian tribe, lived. More than this, Aeropus had stirred up the old Macedonian bugbear, the Dardani, who came from far north of the lake and now attacked and occupied Orestis, in upper Macedonia, and had war bands down on the Argestaean plain. The homeland was in turmoil, and it was common talk on Macedonia's borders that Philip was dead from an accident, when chasing off the Roman raiders near Sicyon earlier in the year. He had crashed into a tree, chasing the marauders around the country, and broke off one of the horns on his helmet, and an Aetolian who found it assumed the king had been killed. This news travelled like wildfire, finding at least one ready believer in Scerdilaidas. All this meant that important parts of Macedonia were either occupied or under threat by historic enemies who could be expected to do a great deal of damage, particularly as Philip had given many of them a precautionary drubbing only the year before.

Leaving Dyme, Philip rushed his army out of Achaea overland through Boeotia, across to the island of Euboea and in ten days was at Demetrias. Not that this removal of Philip to the north stopped action on the Peloponnesian front. The Achaean general, Cycliadas, took the army, supported by the 2,500 Macedonians left by Philip, and on the road to Messene met and defeated the joint forces of Aetolia and Elis. As for Philip, when he reached Demetrias, he heard that the danger from the north had largely evaporated, the effect of the incursions and the numbers involved had been exaggerated and no specific action is mentioned as being necessary to restore order on the home front. He settled the army at Larissa, while he and his officers planned their next moves from the corridors of the palace of Demetrias.

Spring of 208 began a year of two assemblies. The Aetolians had become greatly encouraged by the arrival of King Attalus, and their ambitions inflated as the accretion of the Anatolian warlord would make them significantly more dominant at sea. In addition, Sulpicius Galba had sailed round from the Adriatic and joined Attalus and wintered the year 209/8 at Aegina. The Symmachy elite understood that they now faced the imminent prospect of a powerful seaborne threat from the Aegean and were unnerved by it; each with their own agenda, they were soon badgering Philip and his commanders at a Symmachy assembly in Demetrias. A cacophony of voices delineated the threat these Pergamenes and their Italian auxiliaries represented, a real ratcheting up of a danger from a new direction, and the coastal allies in Boeotia and Euboea were wringing their hands in despair at the menace to their property. Achaean delegates also entreated his help against both the Aetolians and Machanidas, the Spartan, who had taken Tegea and was encamped with his army on the frontier of Argos.

For reasons that are obscure, Attalus and Sulpicius Galba had at the beginning of the season upped anchor and cruised briefly off to Lemnos in the north Aegean, but after this, these two, with an awe-inspiring fleet of thirty-five Attalid and twenty-five Roman quinqueremes, were soon confirmed to have been sighted in the sea roads off Peparethus and disembarked soldiers to gain this island, which lay just east of the Pelion peninsula and offered an ideal launching pad for invasion. Philip, responding, left the phalanx at its base at Scotussa, while the guard and light-armed troops were moved to Demetrias, and boosting vulnerable sectors, he despatched a garrison to Peparethus town. An officer called Polyphantus was sent with a troop into Phocis and Boeotia, and Menippus with 100 peltasts and 500 Agrianes to Chalcis in Euboea. As well as these concerns, Philip's own long-matured plans to open the eastern road down through central Greece were clearly being very seriously contested by the Aetolians. He received news that they were heavily fortifying the pass at Thermopylae with well-garrisoned stockades and trenches to throw an insurmountable barrier across his road south. His success at Echinus and outside Lamia would be cancelled out altogether if the Aetolians could make the 'hot gates' impregnable.

While panicked politicians infested the halls of Demetrias, and Philip did his best to reassure them, the Aetolian block arranged an assembly at Heraclea Trachinia to thrash out a direction for their war effort. The anti-Macedonian alliance thought coordination was the way forward, now Attalus was on hand with his navy, as opposed to the scrappy stuff of the last years. Much was anticipated as he sailed with his handsome war galleys into the port of Nicaea and contacted the Aetolians at Heraclea, informing them that he would soon be amongst them. In regal panoply, he took the short road to Heraclea to confer with his new friends. On arrival, he found there were also delegates from Egypt and Rhodes offering mediation for the warring parties but, at this stage, nobody was interested, and all they got was the brush off for their troubles and the brusque proposal that they go and proffer their wares to Philip. This conference was a major event and was inevitably reported to the Macedonians by their agents or passing travellers. Sitting in Demetrias, this collection of adversaries within striking distance offered an irresistible target. Only too glad of an excuse for action, the king mobilized his army and force marched down to catch them napping. But they were too late; when the Macedonians arrived all the parties had departed, warned of the danger they faced. Philip ravaged the region anyway, if only to emphasize how hard he could hit when he wanted to. But ultimately, despite the satisfaction of scaring his enemies, and plundering and destroying the crops in late summer, nothing significant had been achieved. Soon the army marched back to Scotussa.

He would not have wanted to stay away long due to the constant concern about the threat offered by Attalus' forces against his eastern flank. The importance to Philip of being on his guard from this direction is shown by the investment he now made in a system of fire signals built at this time to keep him up to date with what might be coming from the Aegean. Polybius goes into great detail about how this arrangement of signal towers could detail happenings at

Peparethus or on the island of Euboea, and how all the news was collated at Mount Tisaeum in Thessaly, the centre of the whole operation.[16]

For Philip, this preparedness was a real requisite; his enemies were soon on the move, going after as their first target Oreus city on the northern tip of Euboea, commanding the northern entrance to the Euripus. It had always been strategically key, and battles had been fought there back in Cassander's time when a different generation of long-dead warlords were clashing over the same real estate. The intruders began a well-ordered siege of this town, which was so well defended that it possessed two citadels: one on the heights and one down by the seashore. And more than this, on the waterfront was a 'very remarkable five-storied tower' well stocked with plenty of artillery. The allies agreed that Attalus would lead the assault on land while Sulpicius would attack from the sea, but it was at the tower that the fighting became concentrated when the town commander, Plator, pondering tergiversation, made a decisive impact. He had been put in charge of the defences by Philip V, but immediately after the enemy arrived, he got in touch with them. His price was high, and it took four days to negotiate it, but in the end it was agreed, and it only waited a time to arrange his treachery. When the combat was intense around the tower, Plator let the attackers into the citadel down by the shore, and more than just letting the enemy in, the turncoat had placed men to stop Macedonian loyalists being able to get to the other citadel to continue resistance. The Macedonian garrison, itself, was allowed honours of war and shipped back to their king at Demetrias. Whether Plator remained in command or not under a new master is not known, but with Oreus secure, Attalus headed to that other great fortress on the island, Chalcis, which commanded the narrowest crossing place over the Euripus channel. This was not only well fortified, but the commandant was firm in his fealty to Philip's cause. The impossibility of taking the place soon became clear to Attalus and his allies, as did the dangerous nature of the anchorage thereabouts, so they shipped across to the mainland to Cynus, the port of the Locrian town of Opus.

Philip was getting sick of receiving news from his fire signal stations that these interlopers were bustling about where he had been used to holding sway. At sea he might be outgunned, but on land his enemies still did not have the resources to face him in the open. He had information from his agents that the Aetolians had become lax at Thermopylae, or if Frontinus is to be believed, he duped the defenders by pretending peace feelers.[17] So he decided to abandon any attempt to retake Oreus; he did not have the ships to make a safe crossing anyway. Instead, he marched from Demetrias to Scotussa. From here, he force marched for 60 miles in a single day and night, brushing aside the Aetolian defenders at Thermopylae. He first headed to Chalcis to secure it from attack, but hearing the enemy had left, he paused at Elatea, in Phocis, to decide on his next move. There he learned that Attalus was not far to the east, squeezing the locals for funds. Philip almost caught him napping at Cynus. Here he was apparently enjoying himself, counting his plunder, while his allies had returned over the water to Oreus. The king of Pergamum would have been caught and captured but for bit of luck. Some Cretans from his army were foraging on the road to Elatea, when they saw the dust of Philip's army on the horizon. Realizing this meant danger, they headed back to warn their employer. Attalus acted quickly enough; he rushed to his ships, launched as many as he could into the water and just got away as Philip's advanced guard arrived to bag the boats and crews that had not got off in time. This had looked like a real gift but the pounce failed. The Macedonian king was deeply exasperated at this failure to knock a major foe out of the game. But, at least while he was there, he could shore up his defences at Opus, which was a crucial staging post on the road south as long as the Aetolians controlled egress and access to Thermopylae and Epicnemidian Locris.

The discomforted Attalus managed to make his way back to Oreus. How substantial his losses had been is unknown, but probably they were considerable, because he seems really spooked by his close call and decided to withdraw from the struggle. It had been a while since an Anatolian power had tried to extend their influence into mainland Greece, and he realized he had overplayed what, considering Pergamum's limited resources, was not a great hand. There were also troubles at home; officers sailed in carrying the very unwelcome news that an old rival Prusias, the king of Bithynia, had apparently been just too tempted by the absence of his rival from the Anatolian arena. This powerful potentate, stirred up by Macedonian agents, and who was anyway related by marriage to Philip, raised an army and invaded his neighbour's kingdom, and when Attalus heard, he packed up his soldiers and navy and returned home at double quick speed. His tyro kingdom just did not have the armed forces to fight a war on two fronts. What he told his Aetolian allies and Roman auxiliaries is unrecorded, but this ambitious old monarch was for the moment cancelled out of the cauldron of south Balkan power politics.

Philip, meanwhile, vented his bile on the people of Opus, who he considered had far too easily succumbed to an enemy who had but to arrive at their doorstep for them to surrender. But he was far from just satisfied to hunker down and preen over recent successes, particularly as Attalus' removal now left him noticeably less fettered. Determined to shore things up, he marched his army to Thronium, between Opus and Thermopylae, a town which interestingly had been the destination of many of the refugees from Phthiotic Thebes when he had destroyed that place in the last year of the Social War. These people knew better than to resist, and from there he consolidated his position in north Phocis; he had clearly come to stay, contesting the route south that had been in Aetolian hands for years. Not that all was success; he could not hold Lilaea, which he had besieged and taken. Pausanias tells of a local named Patron who mobilized the young men and retook it from the Macedonians. But, in general, he could feel he had made progress when he brought his men into camp near Elatea. There this active monarch found envoys from Ptolemy and the Rhodians waiting for him, but any talks were aborted when he heard news from the Peloponnese that Machanidas was moving against the Eleans while they were preparing for the Olympic Games.

Why he did this is something of a mystery, as this people have so far entered our narrative only as fast friends of the anti-Symmachy alliance. It is possible that the Achaean League had taken over the Olympic Games or that Machanidas, dissatisfied with Elis' work against Achaea, intended to use Elis itself as a base to attack his enemies down the easier routes from that country.[18]

Now, instead of talking to the peace envoys from Egypt and Rhodes, Philip marched in light order south, down past Megara and on to Corinth to impose his own blueprint on the mess that had broken out since he had ceased to keep this place close under his eye. Light shod, Philip was soon again crossing the heart of the Peloponnese through Arcadia to Heraea, a town that was not that far east of Olympia itself. There, he found the Spartans had slipped away at word of his coming, so he returned to be hosted by his Achaean allies at their summer assembly.

It is also generally mentioned as part of his motivation for this move to the Peloponnese that he hoped a Carthaginian fleet would show up, which might correct his long-standing weakness at sea. The Carthaginian admiral Bomilcar was supposed to come down to the Oxeae islands just off Oeniadae, and Philip had dragged his seven quinqueremes and twenty *lembi* across the isthmus to rendezvous in the Gulf of Corinth. But this Punic weak link, hearing that the Roman fleet had left Euboea and was coming west, worried he would be bottled up in the gulf, if he entered it, so slunk away.

Frustrated, this did not prevent Philip from trying to motivate his Achaean allies into action. He made every effort to convince them that the enemy were weak and afraid of facing his army, and to give him his due, the martial procession that was the rest of that year's campaigning definitely suggested there was no rival around interested in putting their case to the test of battle. First, with the Achaean *strategos*, Nicias, he did some raiding across the gulf, scooping up herds of cattle and hitting the Aetolian centre of Erythrae; few men were taken, but plunder aplenty, although no towns were captured. He let his allies keep most of the booty before deciding to cross back over the isthmus and risk his navy, although not the army that marched via Boeotia, in a sail round Attica and Sunium, and as the Roman fleet did not appear to block him, his earlier confident words seemed to have even more veracity. These had been optimistic times; he had restructured things in the Peloponnese, even offering to remove his garrisons from Heraea, Alipheira and Triphylia, and handing them over to the Achaeans or Megalopolitans, and on the way home, re-established full control at Chalcis and Oreus before reaching the comfort of his palace at Demetrias.

For the Aetolians, June/July 208 was a worrying time. The king of Macedonia was full of vigour and seemed determined to pin them back around the Malian Gulf and in Phocis, and was also now having things all his own way in the Peloponnese. The bitter truth was that Attalus had turned out a broken vessel, but the Macedonian king was made of real steel and looked set to come down hard on them. The Romans might be a great power in the west, but they were still mired with Hannibal, and at the most, as their contribution, they could give Philip difficulties at sea. And in the years 207/206, the Romans did nothing except leave a bloody calling card by brutally sacking and enslaving the people of Dyme.

Yet, something else was to happen in this year that really had the Aetolian commitment to the anti-Symmachy war rocking – a blow not even struck by Philip, but by their own poisonous rivals, the Achaean League. Two men were to be at the centre of an epic encounter. One was Machanidas, the so called tyrant of Sparta. His background is obscure; indeed, he may not even have been a Spartan, possibly having come to the city as a leader of Tarentine mercenary cavalry. Whatever the case, he probably became regent for Lycurgus' son Pelops and assumed power and, as we have seen, began to rough up his neighbours at the first opportunity, taking Tegea, threatening Argos and invading Arcadia and Achaea.

The other was Philopoemen, the cavalry commander who had so ably seconded Philip around Dyme in 209. Now, at the end of 208, he was elected *strategos* and set about reforming the infantry, as he had the cavalry before. Electoral success had been easy for a man away so long; it is possible Philip had been his patron in Crete and brought him back for the purpose of boosting Achaean leadership now that Aratus was no more. Since his death, there seems to have been something of a vacuum at the head of the League; *strategoi* came and went, but no one individual dominated.

As hipparch, he had been backed by the *strategos* who was elected at the same time, Cycliadas, a pro-Macedonian, who would suffer for his allegiance in later years when Rome became more involved. The new military approach instigated by these men was at odds with previous Achaean tradition. Defeats were at least as common as triumphs in the pages of Achaean military endeavour, and they had seldom achieved much without the support of powerful allies. The new man would change everything, and he would be seen as something of a dying breed, the last of the Greeks. And, although chronologically he does span the period of Roman involvement that saw the end of an independent Greece, he was, in most ways, quite a typical example of the sort of dynamic aristocrat who had peopled the history of Greece over the last few centuries. He would have probably felt at home with Alcibiades, if perhaps critical of some of his personal lifestyle choices, and would have had plenty to discuss with the likes of Agesilaus about exploring the wider world as a mercenary leader.

The next year, Nicias was *strategos*, but then at the end of 208 the veteran of the Cretan wars was elected to the position. When he achieved the promotion, he set about organizing the local infantry levies of the different Achaean towns, ensuring the officers and men were well prepared for the warfare to come. Philopoemen was pretty frugal in his own behaviour, but he demanded a commitment to war of a very different kind from his recruits. He wanted them to look splendid in burnished armour and to lavish on their war gear what they had previously on their street clothes, to develop morale and commitment to the cause they were fighting for. It was dandies out and warriors in he wanted, and to achieve it he travelled the land reorganizing the levy. He drilled and trained so effectively that in eight months it was possible for the Achaeans' reconstituted army to face the Spartans in battle. He also changed the tactical arrangements, turning the Achaean infantry from hoplites or peltasts (they are described by Plutarch as effective at distance but not close up, carrying javelins or short spears and small, light *thureos* shields) into phalangites on the Macedonian pattern, wielding the *sarissa*. He knew that to face the Spartan phalanx he required just the same kind of warriors if he were to stand a chance of carrying off the prize.

The cities of Tegea and Mantinea had been rivals in their Peloponnesian plain for centuries. The former place to the south had habitually been in cahoots with Sparta, while the latter took the side of her enemies. And now was no different. Machanidas was 'extremely happy' at the prospect of a fight and that his enemy had come down to towards Laconia and well within reach at Mantinea. Plutarch, though, suggests it was the Spartan invasion of Mantinea that kick-started the Achaean reaction. The army was mobilized, the mercenaries paid up if possible, and all picked up at daybreak and marched north out over the mountainous boundary and down to the flat country round Tegea. Allies were collected up and then it was a clear, well-travelled road to confront a rival that had been a constant now for long decades, but one who was now led by a skilled and dynamic principal.

This vital local encounter is fascinating, not just because we have considerable detail as to what happened, but because we can be sure as to its exact geographical location, not something that could be said for all confrontations in this period. The fighting took place south of the city by a considerable hill, above a temple to Poseidon, a building seen by Pausanias in the second century AD, and which he claims as the requisite seven stades (about a mile) southeast of the city walls, fitting with the account of the battle. Just above it are the slopes of a hill called Alesion, which runs east of the city. The Spartan army approached on the Tegea road, and their line of march is described in some detail, with Machanidas riding at the head of the right wing of the phalanx, and the mercenaries following along in two parallel columns, either side of the van and the wagons with engines and missiles that came behind. This sound defensive formation was for the road, and the Achaeans knew they would soon deploy to besiege the city or prepare for battle.

Philopoemen's first move when the dust of the enemy column was noticed was to make sure of the eminence above the temple of Poseidon. He got his light-armed men, javelineers, bowmen and slingers under arms, and ordered them up the hill themselves, before the enemy could secure this ground, which would have served as an ideal base to press the siege of Mantinea. Philopoemen, in fact, had no intention of allowing himself to be beleaguered, and determined to come out and fight in open battle. He had already drawn up his men behind the southern city gates, and now in three divisions moved them out of the town. The Illyrians, Tarentines and 'men with body armour' were marched out of the gate that led out to the temple, and with them tramped his mercenaries and more light infantry. Then, through the next gate west, came the main phalanx itself, and debouching from the exit after that came the Achaean cavalry, men Philopoemen had schooled and fought with from way back. It was effectively in this formation that they deployed for the fight to come. By the temple itself, the Tarentines were arranged, most likely with the mercenaries and some light infantry. Then south of the hill were situated the 'body armour men' and the Illyrians, then behind this left flank of the Achaean line 'the whole of the foreign contingent, drawn up in lines one behind the other.'[19] The Achaean supremo took his place in command of these men.

On their right in the centre of the line was the phalanx itself, with gaps between companies. And finally, to the west, the Achaean cavalry under Aristaenetus of Dyme were positioned, forming for Philopoemen the far right of his battle line. Crucially important, in front of the whole was a dyke that started just short of the temple of Poseidon and led across the whole plain of Mantinea.

Now we imagine a classic example of pre-battle exhortation as the commander-in-chief carolled along the front of his phalanx. Few probably heard amongst all the noise of shouting, tramping troops, but apparently he touched on the usual guff about how they were fighting for freedom, while the other side were a bunch of tyrant's lackeys fighting for servitude. Something of an irony, in that if progressive politics had emanated from anywhere over the last decades, it had been Sparta. Anyway, this was the usual stuff that most sides in most wars have trotted out, and if the confidence of Philopoemen's followers was as great as is reported, it probably had far more to do with the effectiveness of their training, rather than any words used at that time.

The Spartan commander was in aggressive mood and intended as soon as he could to engage the Achaean army, and he deployed his army 'by the right' into line. By this manoeuvre he ensured that his own right wing was just opposite

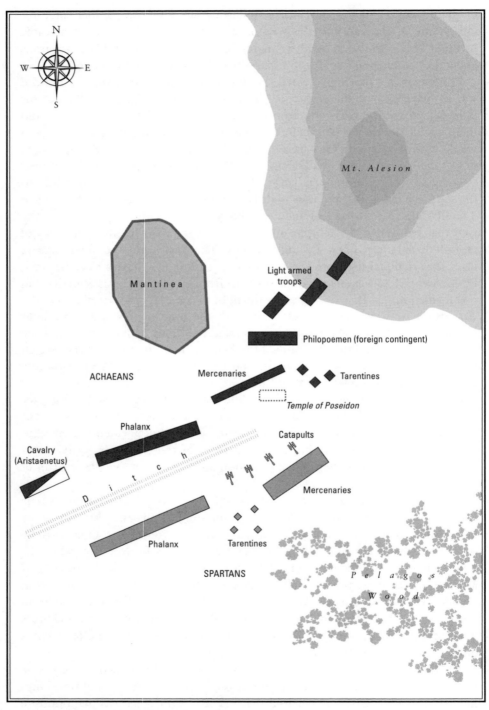

Plan 10: The Battle of Mantinea, 207 BC.

and covered the same frontage as the Achaean. Then, in an interesting tactical innovation, he placed catapults as field artillery spread along the front of his right side. The intention was by 'shooting at the divisions of the phalanx' to break up and disrupt the Achaean pikemen facing them in serried ranks opposite. But Philopoemen was unfazed by this bizarre tactic, and before the machines could do any damage, he gave orders to shut this missile assault down. He had his Tarentine cavalry drawn up near the Temple of Poseidon, and these he felt were the men for the job. The ground around was flat enough, and he sent these professional troopers in. But this, as so often in ancient battles, drew more actors onto the stage like a vortex. The first to respond were Machanidas' own Tarentines. Fighting fire with fire, they were ordered to take on the horsemen riding towards the line of catapults. As these mounted men manoeuvred, more units were sucked in. Light-armed infantry arrived to support the horseman, who were themselves really skirmishers, so this combat was not a great scrimmage, but a scene of roving javelineers on horse or foot moving and throwing and sometimes coming to hand-to-hand blows. 'In quite a short time, the mercenaries on both sides were mixed up.'[20]

So now Tarentines, light infantry and most of the mercenaries, many of them thureophoroi/peltasts, were involved. Sometimes in close order and sometimes in pairs, loosely duelling, thousands of men must now have been caught up from both sides. Nothing decisive it seemed was happening, while the phalanxes just looked on at their comrades battling in the dust. Nobody gave ground for a long time, but Machanidas' mercenaries were seasoned men, veteran and determined, and this eventually gave them the edge. The explanation given for this is that mercenaries fighting for democracies were less eager, because if they won out, all their employers would do would be to discharge them, while those fighting for tyrants would be kept on to sustain their paymaster in power! Yet these effective hirelings had more work to do; there were Illyrians and 'men with body armour' held in reserve behind the Achaeans. But Machanidas' mercenaries pushed these back as well, and with this the Achaean formations broke and fled back towards the walls of Mantinea.

Machanidas now provided yet another example of how, in battle, the skill or lack of it, of the commander-in-chief could make all the difference. The Achaean forces on the left had disintegrated, and it was open to the Spartans to take the main body of their enemy in the flank while attacking in the front with his own phalanx. But 'with childish lack of self-control rushed forward to join his own mercenaries and fall upon the fugitives'[21] who were anyway completely panicked and could have been swept up later. But the sight of their retreating backs was too much, and Machanidas could not resist running them down, and in so doing, left the initiative he had done so much to win in another's hands.

Philopoemen, horrified by the disintegration, forced his way into the fray. Standing in the path of his fleeing mercenaries, he tried to get their officers' attention, but these men he had drunk with at camp council did not hear or were not taking notice. They and their men surged past avoiding their general's gaze, and it seems they were 'hopelessly beaten'. The Spartans were on their heels, but Philopoemen did not get caught up in the rout, and instead galloped off to find protection in the very heavy infantry phalanx he had been so instrumental in constructing. From their protection, he was able to look back and see the enemy rushing past over the ground he had himself just vacated. Here, at the heart of things, he took control and issued orders to the phalanx captains that their files of men should wheel to the left, but not break ranks. By this manoeuvre, done at the double, he was able to put the full phalanx exactly upon the location his defeated mercenaries and light infantry had occupied. This planted them between the enemy pursuing his mercenaries and the rest of the Spartan army. It was not an easy position to hold, but it was one with possibilities, situated between two parts of his enemies' forces. His reconstructed army might be willing, but now he needed experience. He delegated one of his professionals, with Illyrians, mercenaries and 'body armour men' who had not been caught up in the rout, to stand steady and create a protective front to face the rear and defend against any return of Machanidas and the pursuers.

Now the key encounter developed; pike to pike would decide, in a world where the Macedonian phalanx had dominated since the age of Philip and Alexander. The Spartans had lost their commander, for a time, but they were good soldiers with high morale who considered they had the beating of anything the Achaeans could throw at them. The early success of Machanidas, and no doubt the imminent expectation of his return, kept their confidence high. These descendants of Leonidas' 300 had been using the long *sarissa* for well over a decade since Cleomenes' reforms and were ready to cut to the chase. But, with overall command fractured, unintelligent decisions were made. The regimental commanders in charge called for an advance without sufficiently reconnoitring the ground. The great Spartan phalanx steamrollered forward but soon found itself at the edge of the dyke. The drop was not severe and there were no obstacles in the trench, so they did not stop but pushed straight on. But these ponderous phalanxes did not need much to disrupt their ranks.

The Spartan advance had not gone unnoticed by Philopoemen and his officers; feeling the crisis of the battle had arrived, they ordered the Achaean phalanx as best they could and, trusting to training and morale, deployed the front ranks to bring the new fangled long spears to the level position and prepare to meet the enemy attack. Philopoemen had judged his opponents well and reckoned they would push forward despite the obstacle in front of them. The Achaeans were resolute and showed it by wild cheering as they took the Lacedaemonians at a charge, just as they came out from the ditch they were traversing. *Sarissae* crossed, men fell, and officers exhorted soldiers who a minute before were full of confidence, but who now, face-to-face with their enemies, felt fear. A push of pike was an awful scrum of armoured violence that, on this occasion, did not last long. The Spartans were good soldiers, whether veterans or young men who had recently gone through the re-established *agoge*, but disorganized by crossing the dyke, they could not hold. In the ditch, they were squashed together with little room to stand and grasp their long spears; falling over each other they could not be effective and were trampled if they fell. They 'lost courage as they mounted the bank to meet the enemy above their heads and took to flight.'[22] But this was a death sentence, as so many were cut down with their backs turned, defenceless in the trench itself.

With the battle seemingly won, the Achaean general began to look round to ensure he completed the triumph by eliminating Machanidas, determining to prevent his escape to fight again. Philopoemen ordered his general, Alexidamus, to guard the trench against any attempt to escape, particularly at the section where there was a bridge across it. This was now a very confused battlefield, with Machanidas, under the walls of the city, still enjoying his triumph when news arrived that what he thought he had won might well have really been lost. Peering through the dust of battle, he saw that his main army was in flight, with the Achaeans chasing them over the trench and cutting them down in droves as they tried to escape. Perhaps he now regretted his own precipitous pursuit, or perhaps he just responded unreflectively with what men he had to hand. Whatever, the Spartan ruler drew together the mercenaries that were near him and determined to escape and rally his army. The Achaeans were like any victorious force, themselves disordered, so he had some hope that he could get away unscathed. But when he and his mercenary guard got back to the trench, they realized that Philopoemen had been thinking ahead of them. An Achaean force had blocked the bridge that was the easiest way across and now the Spartan ruler's men lost heart. It was each for himself, and everybody, including Machanidas, was riding the length of the edge looking for an unguarded way to traverse the trench. Attended by two officers, Polyaenus and Simias, Philopoemen rode along the far side to cover the way Machanidas might come. In this chaos, Philopoemen recognized Machanidas by his purple cloak and the trappings of his horse. Now the two generals rode along on opposite sides of the dyke, one trying to escape and one determined to stop him. The Spartan had apparently only two followers when the crisis came, Arexidamus and one of the mercenaries, these three looking for a place to cross. Two of them found it, driving their horses down into the ditch and up the other side. 'Philopoemen turned to meet him. Giving him a mortal wound with his spear and adding yet another thrust with the lower end of it, he slew the tyrant hand to hand.'[23] The officers with Philopoemen brought down Arexidamus, while the mercenary officer did not even try to cross, but fled in another direction. Plutarch as usual is more florid:

The spectacle was not that of two commanders fighting, but that of a powerful hunter attacking a wild beast that has been forced to turn at bay and Philopoemen was the hunter. And now the tyrant's horse, which was vigorous and high-spirited and felt the bloody spurs in his sides, essayed to make the leap across, and striking against the edge of the ditch with his breast, was struggling with his fore-feet to extricate himself.

At this point Simias and Polyaenus, who had always been at Philopoemen's side when he was fighting and protected him with their shields, rode up both at the same time and levelled their spears at the horse. But Philopoemen was before them in attacking Machanidas, and seeing that the tyrant's horse was lifting its head up in front of its rider's body, he gave his own horse a little swerve to one side, and then, clasping his spear firmly in the middle, pushed it home with all his weight and overturned his enemy.[24]

Simias now stripped the dead bodies and took Machanidas' head as trophy and rode off to show it to the soldiers so that they could be sure of their victory. This was the last straw; the phalanx was broken, the commander-in-chief dead, the whole army was now a wreck looking only for escape; no steady withdrawal for Sparta's finest, despite centuries of military tradition.

The Spartans were chased back to where they started, and in the rush of fleeing soldiers, Tegea itself was taken by assault by the Achaeans. Four thousand combatants of Machanidas' army apparently fell in the battle of Mantinea and its aftermath, a bloodletting unparalleled since Sellasia. And more than this, many more of Machanidas' followers ended as prisoners and virtually the whole of his baggage and weapons store fell into Achaean hands. From Tegea, the victors pushed on into the valley of the Eurotas itself, the very homeland of the Spartans, and encamped there. No attempt seems to have been made to take the city itself, but perhaps the Achaeans were not present in sufficient strength to occupy a whole enemy country in the face of a hostile people, and presumably left in the hope that the bloodletting would keep them quiet for a time.

But extraordinarily, they were to be rapidly disabused; this second brutal culling of the Lacedaemonian polity in a generation still could not keep them down. This was no decisive suppression of regional military ambitions, and soon enough, Nabis would emerge. Sparta was amazing; knocked down, like a Morean Messi, it got straight back up again. Just what made the place tick? How, after such another battering could she so soon embark with such eagerness on the next round of fighting?

The new city boss, Nabis, was a middle-aged man, born in about 250, who had a connection with the Eurypontid line and took control first as another regent for Lycurgus' son Pelops, and then as king in his own right. The Laconian elite had for some time seemed content and eager to be fodder for hard men. It had been about ten years since *ephors* or the *gerousia* had been heard from as significant players. In no time, the old place showed it was far from spent yet. Despite the peace elsewhere, border conflicts in the south showed Spartan vigour. In 206/5, Megara rejoined the Achaean League, now an expanding polity; yet still defeated Sparta could offer it a threat. In 204, we hear of Nabis with an army of Cretan mercenaries attacking from the south, and this war rumbled between 203 and 202. In 202/1, Nabis even felt strong enough to attack Messene. But Philopoemen took private action. Despite not holding any official post, he recruited warriors from Megalopolis, his birthplace, and with these troops he marched on Messene, where Nabis had taken control except for mount Ithome itself. The Spartans were surprised and fled at the sight of this unexpected opposition.

But in 207, the end of Machanidas certainly looked to the Aetolians like an awful disaster, pulling a pillar from their enterprise that might be enough to bring everything down; now the Achaeans would be free to turn on them with their victorious army. Other events were not helping either. The Roman Sulpicius attended a meeting in Aetolia but could not promise his allies anything much. The Aetolians had entered the fray with hopes of raiding the assets of a weak Symmachy, to recoup some of what they had lost in the Social War. But, although their allies had shown some muscle at times, their involvement had been essentially too weak or distracted to create a coalition that could bowl over the Macedonian state and its appendages. Now this had become clear to all parts of the Aetolian elite, it was possible for serious talking to begin. They were also getting harangued by desperate friends from Rhodes, concerned that their attitude was preparing the way for Roman enslavement of Greece. Fragments from Polybius indicate that envoys from Ptolemy, Rhodes, Byzantium, Chios and Mitylene addressed the Aetolians' assembly of autumn 207 at Heraclea, just as they had been doing for years. Now, however, it looked as if their efforts might pay off, that their line that this war was a fire consuming all Greece might be heeded. But Philip did not underestimate the capacity for stubborn Aetolian resistance, and showed that if they had needed a last persuasive argument he was prepared to make it. He persuaded King Amynander to let him go through Athamania, which outflanked Aetolian defences, and then taking the road to Lake Trichonis, Philip marched to Thermus. When there, he defaced the temples, particularly the ones he had not touched on his previous incursion. He was keeping at the forefront of his enemies' consciousness how vulnerable the Aetolian heartland was when the Macedonians determined to punch hard.

Aetolian fortunes had reached their nadir, and Philip's ambassadors were on hand to accept peace if Aetolia chose it. It became a rough house, showing how stressed matters had become. The people assembled even shouted down the response of their Roman allies after Greek ambassadors talked about the dangers of an Italian takeover of Greece. With the Achaeans militarily a new, bright force, Attalus long gone, and Philip flexing his muscles in central Greece, they had to call things to a close. They sued for peace, forced to contemplate the Macedonian king's terms in a way they would never have considered even a year before. He, as it turned out, would not press for the last drop of retribution in the negotiations. Agreement was reached in the autumn of 206 that the conflict between the Aetolians and Macedonians should end. With this decided, none of the bit-part players, Elis or Messene had the resources or inclination to carry on alone. The Symmachy members signed up too. They had to follow Philip's lead, and most were not reluctant; it was anyway their lands that usually saw the brunt of the fighting. The exact clauses are unclear. The Thessalian boundary between Macedonian and Aetolian holdings was rearranged, but the balance of power certainly favoured the Macedonians, even if Aetolia continued to hold sway across to Lamia, Heraclea and Thermopylae. Philip was even prepared to offer a face-saving formula over Pharsalus and some other Thessalian cities, which had the advantage for him that he could renege on what he had conceded at any time. Why he was prepared to be so reasonable in his demands is difficult to know, but it has been plausibly suggested that his desire for peace was to concentrate again on his Illyrian ambitions, to completely establish hegemony there while Rome was still tied up with their wars in Italy, Spain and Africa.

But, for the moment, a desultory war with Rome rumbled on. They had attended the peace conference, but that had been to try and keep her allies at the war with Macedonia. So they were not involved in this pan-Greek peace that was to be the last major Hellenistic power arrangement in which the Roman presence was not crucial. Still, these Romans, while they were hugely distracted by their Carthaginian enemies, were able the next year to keep up an Illyrian end to their game. An officer called Sempronius was sent to Epidamnus to make trouble for Philip. He began a siege of Dimale, but Philip responded by threatening their Romans friends in Apollonia. Sempronius soon gave up on Dimale, as he had not the strength to offer battle to Philip. In the end, it was the Epirotes who successfully brokered a termination of the war between Philip and the Romans, inviting the combatants to meet at the hill-girt town of Phoenice in the heart of the Chaonian country, which had been the centre for the Epirote confederation over the last few years and a long trek for all concerned. But up they eventually came. Philip met Sempronius, and others were included: Thessalians, Acarnanians, Epirotes, Illyrians, Achaeans, Phocians, Euboeans and even King Attalus. Most of these had not been actively belligerent for a while, but now it was possible they wanted to put a seal on the peace that had been creeping up on them for some time. Peace was made with Rome, and her presence in Greece, never mind east of there, was warranted no more. But if the kings and peace delegates from the Leagues and cities involved thought this was the end of the matter, they could not have been more wrong.

Chapter 8

Panion

In another empire, acrimony was still very much the order of the day. In Alexandria, no royal leader had established a robust ascendancy; there was only a stew of intrigue and internal rivalry. Since Raphia, the cracked edifice that had constructed that triumph had sustained itself, but in the year 203 decisive events took place and are described in the kind of detail that is extraordinary in this country, where what had gone on since the commencement of the third century can be discovered only from wisps of information.

The demise of Ptolemy IV in 205 or 204 brought matters into such a spotlight that it suggests our source heard it from a contemporary inside the court itself. A convocation was staged by Sosibius and Agathocles to announce the death of the old king and his wife Arsinoe, and to present the child Ptolemy V to his people. These two had been in power for years and been content to control a malleable monarch; in 13 years virtually nothing is noticed, and it is probable the government's greatest priorities had been to suppress a number of nationalist revolts that pitted these years.

Sosibius, the ultimate fixer, Agathocles, the guardian of a weak king's affection, and his relatives, had between them kept power in their hands. But, when Ptolemy IV's life started to slip fast away tensions came to the surface. Queen Arsinoe, the mother of the new king, now emerged as a potential threat as she never had been while Ptolemy IV lived. It was feared that she might manage her son in a way she never was able to do with her husband, so she had to be eliminated. It was not going to be easy but Sosibius and Agathocles had been at the game of bloody court politics for a long time. Philammon, an agent, did the actual deed, and the subtlety of their dealings is indicated in that it was not till some time later, perhaps not until the end of 203, that either the death of the former king or his wife was announced.[1]

A platform was erected in the largest court in the palace and the foot guards, officers of the other regiments and government officials crowded in from the corridors around. From their eminence, Sosibius and Agathocles announced the demise of the king and queen and placed the diadem on the head of the five- or six-year-old monarch. But, for a coronation, it was a strained business; the establishment was feeling far from completely secure in this interregnum. There are stories of urns with spices instead of ashes and turbulent crowds that do not suggest a well orchestrated event, instead the antics of desperate men hanging onto power. A will making Sosibius and Agathocles the guardians of Ptolemy V, but which later was exposed as a forgery, was paraded in an effort to give the old elite credibility in the new reign. Oaths were taken and donatives paid out to the soldiers, many of whom were then dispersed in upcountry garrisons while new troops recently raised by the guardians were posted round the key places in the city and palace. There was a whiff of a disintegrating government; potential competitors and backstabbers were either sent on foreign embassies – in one case to govern Cyrene – or on mercenary-recruiting missions.

Sosibius soon disappears from view, presumably dying. He would have been far from a young man by this time; his father had probably been a mercenary from Tarentum, who rose to be a captain in the royal guard of Ptolemy II. Some suggest he was got rid of by Agathocles, which if true did not work to his advantage, as he never after seemed to have the kind of grip they exercised when working in tandem. He just did not have the same skill in the ways of political survival; it had been in retaining the previous king's affections that he had excelled, rather than with a winning personality or political competence. Indeed, his subsequent behaviour only amplified this lack of nous, getting drunk with his friends and apparently debauching young bluebloods of both sexes.

Matters, unsurprisingly, began to come apart alarmingly swiftly. First, a man named Deinon, who had been strongly implicated in the death of Arsinoe, started bragging about what he knew and Agathocles had him silenced in the most ruthless fashion. But, more than this falling out at the top, threats from outside were developing. Tlepolemus, who had been made garrison commander at Pelusium, found this placement only whetted his appetite for greater power, and in about 202 began to make plans. He systematically began to subvert his officers and men. We are given vivid details of drinking parties where he flattered his followers and badmouthed Agathocles, as a weakling sybarite, until their favourable response gave him the confidence to reveal his intention to overthrow him. Loose talk inevitably reported to Agathocles and he replied in kind, to besmirch Tlepolemus' reputation, first as an agent of Antiochus, then as an aspirant to the throne itself. But to no avail. Indeed, it only made people aware there was a potential leader prepared to take up the gauntlet against the despised administration.

This treason discovered on the frontier made Agathocles desperate, but he knew the key demographic when it came to keeping power. In the year 202, in Alexandria, another extraordinary scene unfolded. A meeting of the Macedonian guards was called. They were the power behind the throne, the Praetorian Guard, and the ruler of Egypt intended to make the strongest play to ensure their support. Agathocles entered and led in his sister Agathoclea with the child King Ptolemy V in her arms. With tears in his eyes, taking the child from his sister's arms, he made a sentimental plea that showed how shaky his grasp on power had become:

'Take the child whom his father on his death-bed placed in the arms of this woman,' pointing to his sister, 'and confided to your faith, you soldiers of Macedon. Her affection indeed is of but little moment to ensure his safety, but his fate depends on you and your valour.'[2]

The sense of imminent danger was enhanced by eye witness evidence that there were, at that moment, outside ceremonies being prepared to crown another in the child's place. But, the response was not what those who had arranged matters had hoped for. The meeting had been a gamble, but it did not pay off. The Macedonian soldiers, officers and men, if they had feelings for the child king, had nothing but contempt for his guardian. They hooted derision after this tearful exhibition and the circumstances became so threatening that Agathocles and his party had to flee the room. The rest of the army was equally as disaffected. Many of them had come in from their upriver stations, postings they had resented. The civil populace was also in an ugly mood, although, tellingly, it is reported their motives were just as much fear of Tlepolemus' stranglehold on the city's supplies as their distaste for the government. That general had travelled in considerable strength from Pelusium and was now occupying the country around the capital with nobody opposing him at all.

Agathocles had lost most of the authority he once had, and disaffection had clearly spread throughout much of Alexandria. Desperate, he notched things up further by dragging Tlepolemus' mother-in-law off to prison, which only proved to be the catalyst for opposition to come out into the open. Soon, the people were holding meetings in the streets, they had at least expected the government would try and mollify the man who had the power to turn on and off the tap of provisions. Agathocles was completely unnerved; at one moment he prepared to flee and the next determined to remain and eliminate anybody he had a grudge against. A rival called Moeragenes was arrested and brought to a torture chamber, but the officer in charge, understanding the old power was losing its grip, was not inclined to be tainted as one of Agathocles' henchmen. He left, leaving the torturers with brands ready but without orders. These underlings then slipped away, and Moeragenes, at liberty, finding some breakfasting Macedonian troops encamped in the city, set out to inspire the population in tearing down his erstwhile persecutor. This was the spark that lit the fire, but when it was reported to Agathocles that Tlepolemus, himself, had arrived at Alexandria's gates it only led him back to his old ways.

There was rioting round the stadium and chaos in the city, while Agathocles, himself, kept at the wine jug. But alcohol could only sustain his nerve so long. Soon, completely spooked, he dragged the young king into the theatre with a small guard and most of his relatives, while the rebellious populace and soldiers took over every space in the city. When the Macedonian soldiers came to demand the king be handed over to them, he tried to bargain, offering to retire in exchange for his life. Aristodemus, an Acarnanian, is mentioned here as a go-between. It was risky role and the mob first tried to run him through, but he survived, and the report he made to his master ensured Ptolemy was handed over as the only possible hope of the Agathoclids escaping with their lives. While the people mounted Ptolemy on a horse and took him to the stadium, Agathocles and Agathoclea slipped away from the theatre to their houses. The king was then easily persuaded to agree to their summary punishment; a dénouement interestingly orchestrated by a powerful faction that included the son of Sosibius, presumably unhappy with his treatment since his father had died. All of the fugitives were delivered into the hands of the mob, and while Agathocles was stabbed to death, many of the others were literally torn to pieces. And, more than this, other grudges were paid off too; Philammon, who had killed Arsinoe, had arrived from Cyrene three days before and was himself massacred with his family by young women of the city. Much had led to this end, but Agathocles' fall had been made inevitable when he lost the support of the army. It was almost certainly the redistributing of regiments from the comforts of Alexandria into outlying garrisons that had first soured his relations with them.

Puffed up by the ease of his triumph, Tlepolemus took over at the helm as guardian of the child king, but it was not an easy task, and he was a young man with a penchant for ostentation, a good soldier with the common touch, but he just did not have a head for the details of government. He spent his time at play, fencing and drinking with his comrades, while the state went down the tubes. He was incorrigibly generous to soldiers, actors and Greek visitors. Keeping the soldiers happy made sense, but the sycophancy at court went to his head. It led to an arrogance that upset many, and when Ptolemy, another son of Sosibius, came back from an embassy to Macedonia, he found himself the focus of resistance for those at court who had a grievance against the new incumbent.

To add to their troubles, this unstable crew found they had a major war on their hands. The Great King of Asia had not been inclined to rest on his laurels. He was far from old and there is no suggestion that the hard road in the east he had recently travelled had taxed him physically to any great extent. Ancient kings who had their eyes on posterity either built cities or made war. The former does not seem a particular penchant of Antiochus III, but the latter certainly was. The administrative machine at Antioch had been re-infused by the return of the royal court and all that entailed in terms of energy and resource, and although they had listened for some time, more or less inattentively, to the rumbling echoes of discontent from Alexandria, now they pricked up their ears. Less than 1,000 miles to the south, this place looked like it was disintegrating. The feuds played out there did not initiate Seleucid ambitions of conquest; Ptolemaic hegemony still stretched over the Levantine coast up to Sidon and Tyre and inland to Coele Syria. They had an established ascendancy over local peoples, whether Jews, Arabs or Phoenicians, though how happily this dominion was received was anybody's guess. But in 203, after Ptolemy's death, as the vultures hovered, it was going to be tested.

An axis of exploitation had surfaced when the Macedonians and the Seleucids matched each other's eagerness to take advantage of the stumbling Empire centred at Alexandria, whose assets also included Cyprus, Hellespontine Thrace, Samos, and much more south from Ephesus along the south coast of Anatolia. Threats to the places in Asia Minor and on the blue Aegean waters had been played out for some time, but now Antiochus could taste old ambitions unsatisfied, and this would bring the thunder of war to the very borders of Egypt itself. Philip and Antiochus were up to complete partition in 204, if we are to believe Appian, but far more likely is that both had limited ambitions; the former having his eyes on just what he could pick up around the Aegean while the latter wanted what he always had, the Lagid Levant.[3]

The Seleucid army moved in strength in 202, with the royal regiments, mercenaries, local auxiliaries and elephants. They were intending a serious conquest, no mere foray. Their achievements are not detailed but were impressive, bringing Seleucid power to the margins of Egypt, although this was not the first occasion he had reached so far and last time it had ended at Raphia. The whole enterprise may have taken up two campaigning seasons, starting in 202.[4] With the southern offensive accomplished sure and steady, it was only in the winter at the end of 201 that they pulled the main army back, leaving garrisons to hold the towns they had taken, while the leadership and royal regiments returned to Antioch.

The Ptolemaic ship of state had been navigating stormy waters since Tlepolemus took the helm, and despoliation in Thrace and Anatolia had undermined what little muscle there was in this playboy's administration. But it was the invasion by Antiochus that eventually unseated him. Although affable and brave, he could not match what the despised Agathocles and Sosibius had managed in 217. So in another coup, of which we know nothing, there was a change at the power seat behind the child throne of Ptolemy V. The new man was Aristomenes, an Acarnanian officer of the royal bodyguard, who started up the greasy pole by playing sycophant in the entourage of Agathocles, but who, once given his chance at the head of things, showed great quality. Support by Scopas, the Aetolian marshal, must have been both crucial in his power bid and in maintaining supremacy afterwards. He had been, for a while, a key player in the military. Indeed, he had been perceived as enough of a threat for Agathocles to send him off on a recruiting mission when he was getting rid of rivals a couple of years before. Since then, he had returned and become a key performer in the intrigues that played out in the Alexandrine court. In the new arrangement, the Acarnanian guardian shored up the home administration while the Aetolian took responsibility for the Levantine front.

This was back to field command for Scopas, and it would eventually end in one of the decisive battles of the era. Even before the Social War, he had been one of the most significant of those leaders that had steered the fortunes of the Aetolian League. Always a front-foot fighter, he had started that war with an invasion of Thessaly, and in the twenty odd years since, he was a stalwart of the war party that took on Macedonia, the Achaeans and the rest of Symmachy. Perhaps, in the end, that had contributed to his undoing in Aetolia; associated with a couple of wars that had ended not so well and had driven many of his people into deep debt. Scopas had been *strategos* in 205/4, after the wars, and with another old warhorse, Dorimachus, he tried to propose reforms. The radical debts cancellation they pushed was not unheard of as a solution, and the reason was the same; to give relief to the infantry class that filled the army, not to mention some personal debts of his own. But, this was always a potentially dangerous road, as was made all too plain when his services were dispensed with by the people after being outmanoeuvred, and his reforms scuppered by a man called Alexander, who had recently held office as hipparch and was clearly on the up in the politics of the League. Like many a Greek before with a military reputation, when rebuffed at home, he took service in Egypt.

Polybius, for some reason, directs considerable ire at Scopas for being the epitome of greed, saying: 'he delivered his soul for money'. He castigates him for not being satisfied with his lot and compares him to a dropsy sufferer: 'the thirst of the sufferer never ceases and is never allayed by the administration of liquids from without, unless we cure the morbid condition of the body itself, so it is impossible to satiate the greed for gain.'[5] A charge that could be levelled at many a condottiere in the Hellenistic Age.

He clearly retained clout in Aetolia, as when he was sent back to recruit, 6,000 infantry and 500 cavalry enrolled under his standard.[6] Apparently, even then, he had to be pulled up short, or he would have emptied the country of soldiers altogether. It was with this considerable force, plus what the Lagid military had already mustered, that Scopas now marched.

It began as a winter war. Scopas reoccupied Coele Syria in the winter of 201/200 and retook most of what had been lost, including Jerusalem. The counter strike reached up as far as the Golan Heights, towards the Lebanon valley, and along the coast to Sidon. It comes over as something of a promenade, so perhaps Antiochus' previous triumphs had not been so complete, or perhaps many places still cleaved loyally to the Ptolemies and sprang back into their arms when they arrived in the region in force. Certainly, Scopas took some Jewish leaders back to Egypt to firm up Ptolemaic influence amongst those people. But finally, it was always down to who won on the battlefield, and so in the following spring of 200, Scopas was back in force and pushing on towards Lebanon. But this year would be no walkover; Scopas found himself faced with the main Seleucid army, with the Great King at its head and battle took place on the road from Lebanon to Palestine at Panion.[7]

Some have suggested the numbers involved in this encounter as approaching the magnitude of those at Raphia.[8] But this is problematic, as that was the culmination of an extraordinary Ptolemaic effort, and there is no evidence that this was the case before Panion. Certainly, Scopas had recruited in Greece, but we do not hear of the wholesale purchase of warlord and mercenary service that occurred in 217. Still, both sides must have been present in great force. The Ptolemaic army that navigated the well-trodden roads east from Pelusium would have comprised a large phalanx: those Thracians and Galatians who had been stalwarts in the Ptolemaic army for decades, the Aetolians and elephants too.

Josephus explains that Panion, although near, is not actually the source of the Jordan and, ever affable, lets us know that fishing is good in the area. The site of the battlefield is reasonably clear, despite the fact that our main source Polybius is once more sidetracked. Here, instead of giving the details of the battle, he devotes most of his description to a refutation of his source and contemporary, Zeno of Rhodes. Criticizing him for sacrificing accuracy for style, Polybius raises many pertinent points for a military historian, but somewhat spoils the effect by obsessing about a number of matters. The best example is his insistence that Antiochus had only one son at the battle, despite Zeno's clear statement that there were two. Young Royals frequently appear on the battlefield in command roles, supported by more experienced officers, so Polybius' obduracy on this issue is difficult to understand. Fascinatingly, Polybius actually wrote to Zeno, pointing out his geographical errors. Zeno, showing admirable forbearance beyond the point of duty, thanked him courteously for his criticism but replied that he had already published his work and it was too late to change anything. His real feelings may well have been considerably different. Be that as it may, Polybius' account does give us something of an idea of the terrain and flavour of the encounter.

Antiochus had advanced down the ancient Damascus-Egypt road and descended the Golan Heights to Panion, where he camped with the river to the west, between him and Scopas. Antiochus deployed at sunrise on the day of battle, and initially the Seleucids anchored the right of their battle line on the lower slopes of an adjacent mountain, presumably north of Panion. This force consisted of mixed infantry and horse, but it was just an outpost, and the main right wing was below on the plain. Most likely, the rest of the army formed conventionally, with the phalanx in the centre and another cavalry wing on the left, with the river across the front of the whole force. From this initial posting, the Great King had sent forward his elder son 'just before the morning watch' to occupy high ground that commanded the enemy camp, possibly a spur west of Panion, and the river above the open plain that lay south of there and east of the 1949 Israeli and Syrian armistice line. Then, at the signal to advance, the Seleucids lined up to offer battle and crossed over the river. Their dressing remained largely predictable; the phalanx of heavy-armed pikemen were in the centre and the cavalry took position on the flanks. One side, under the command of the king's younger son, also called Antiochus, probably was on the right, the position of honour. Who commanded on the left is uncertain, but in front of the whole – right, centre and left – were the elephants with their guards of archers and slingers, and there must have been a considerable number, probably as many as the 102 present at Raphia. Antiochus had lost some at that encounter, but equally had garnered many more during his recent *anabasis* to Bactria and India. And, more than this, an officer named Antipater led out the Tarentine light horse as a skirmish line in front of the elephants; 'while he [Antiochus] himself with his horse and foot guards took up a position behind the elephants.'[9]

So, the king himself was leading from the front of the phalanx with the Companions and footguards, a location for a commander-in-chief we do not hear of in any other encounter, and which would appear impractical as he might be crushed between friend and enemy when the phalanxes clashed. So, perhaps it should be understood that when the centres stepped forward to enter combat, these glittering staff men with their escorts would slip back through avenues left by the pike men before they closed up again for hostilities.

Scopas, a veteran now, on the other side, was well aware of what was afoot and broke his men out of camp at the double. He, too, deployed his well-drilled phalanx in a great block in the centre and presumably ranged his horsemen either side. The Ptolemaic army, too, must have had its elephant corps; after all, they won at Raphia, and had had nearly twenty years to recruit from Sudan to fill out the ranks of the veteran animals who had died of wounds or old age. But how many and how they fared in battle we do not know, although it is reasonable to assume, as at Raphia, that they did not do well against their bigger Asian cousins.

Events commenced on the Seleucid right, as was so often the case, and here Antiochus, the younger, had Cataphracts as his spearhead. They were armoured all over but without a shield, which most Hellenistic horsemen had started using over the third century. Again, their strength is unknown, but what is certain is that they must have been picked up by Antiochus III in the east as they are not heard of in the army before. Whatever the exact composition of this force, it was successful in routing the Ptolemaic wing opposite. Certainly, here Zeno's account as filtered through Polybius is difficult if, is as claimed, he says that they are firstly on level ground then charge downhill. What is clear, though, is that

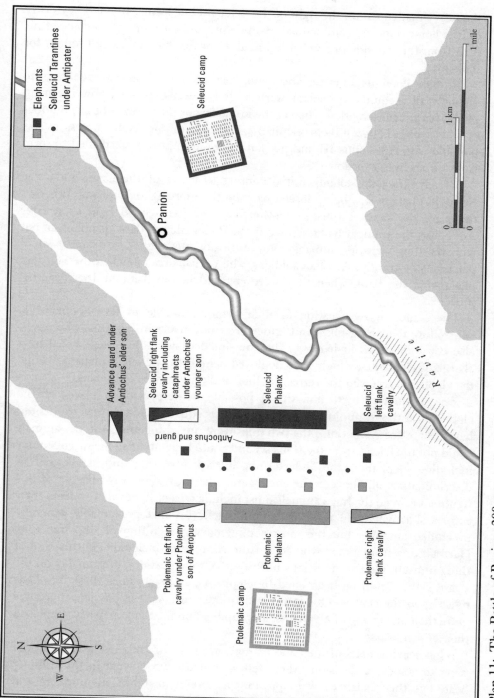

Plan 11: The Battle of Panion, 200 BC.

the heavy mailed fist on the right of the Seleucid line swung to hit. They drove off the horse opposite commanded by Ptolemy, son of Aeropus, but some of his men from the left side of the battle line did not flee but stayed and fought for their lives.

But here Polybius, in criticizing Zeno, does ask a question that is relevant to virtually all accounts of ancient warfare. It is never explained how the main phalanxes got at each other when in the initial layout there might be any number of other troops between them, elephants, light infantry or cavalry, unless, as was possible with Antiochus III and his staff, the phalangites were drilled to form lanes for them to exit down.

Already, after the bloody initial coming to blows of the *sarissa*-men, the Seleucid phalanx was being forced back by the more agile Aetolians. Whether these are the same Aetolians mentioned as making a good fight of it after Antiochus the younger had swept away the Ptolemaic left flank, is not clear, but whoever they were, presumably they were not phalangites but *thureophoroi/* peltasts, so typical of Aetolian soldiery, who perhaps had attacked the Seleucid phalanx in the flank when they were engaged in the front by the Egyptian phalanx.

These men were sweating in their armour, unable to face about while controlling their long pikes and under fire from men with javelins, who might also come in sword-in-hand on their unshielded side. They were saved by a charge of elephants, which were deployed behind the Seleucid phalanx; 'while the elephants received the retreating line' and tore into the Aetolians.

Zeno is quizzed as to how this is possible, as he previously placed all the elephants at the front of the phalanx, and he is equally taxed on how they could have been effective because the two lines were mixed together, and the animals could not tell friend from foe. This second could be contended in any encounter including elephants, and indeed, not infrequently they did fatally fail to discriminate at all between the enemy and their own side. Any imaging of this fighting between the huge animals must include tens of light infantry from their escorts skirmishing in the dust around their feet that presumably generally precluded anything but the most rudimentary recognition of who was who. Hard tasking from a man who is far from completely inculpable in this kind of thing himself. He also questions how some Aetolian cavalry, presumably on the Lagid right, could be frightened by elephants, as he assumes these Aetolians must be in the centre. This is all tendentious stuff, as it is possible there was more than one group of elephants; a group held on the flank may have panicked the Aetolian horse.

This heaving mass of men and animals in the centre of the battle could not seem to achieve a decision. Many fell wounded or exhausted in the summer heat, but the phalanxes were presumably evenly matched in numbers and quality, because it needed something else to separate them. And it came from the younger Antiochus, who returned from pursuing the enemy left, which his armoured troopers had trounced so soundly. The hot taste of glory meant that they plunged ahead to cut the enemy down, but enough officers among them kept cool heads and were able to make the decisive impact. Sufficient of them drew rein to allow a sizable force to cohesively form behind the unprotected rear of the Ptolemaic phalanx.

There are two different versions of Scopas' part in the attack, the first being: 'when he saw the younger Antiochus returning from the pursuit and threatening the phalanx from the rear he despaired of victory and retreated.'[10] So when Antiochus the younger's troopers crashed murderously into the back of the enemy line, the Aetolian was already looking to save his skin. Yet also, Zeno says: 'the hottest part of the battle began, upon the phalanx being surrounded by the elephants and cavalry, and now Scopas was the last to leave the field.'[11] Whether he was the first or last to flee once the Lagid phalanx had both enemy cavalry and elephants trampling down their rear rank, the contest was over.

A different description of the encounter has been effectively argued that sees the combat developing as a fight of two halves, separated by the river.[12] The benefit of this explanation is it does have a role for Antiochus' eldest son, who is envisaged holding the left of the Seleucid line on a hill to the east of the river, and this also being the sector in which the Aetolians are seen off by the elephants. And it very satisfactorily clarifies how Scopas both leaves the field as soon as the enemy gets behind the main phalanx and also fights to the very end. In this account, he leaves the left section of his army, when it is clear they are not going to win, and goes over the right side to try and make a difference there, and when it goes against him on that side too, he battles to the end in an effort to extricate the remains of his army and get them on the road to Sidon. But this account still accepts that the key victory that overwhelmed the Ptolemaic phalanx occurred on the small plateau west of the river. While this thesis is perfectly arguable, it is based on assumptions that we do not feel confident to make, and we find errors of reporting and transcribing just as likely to be enlightening on the inconsistencies in the story of the affray. Either account would fit what little we know, and our thinking is based on the fact that it would be very unconventional for a battle in this era to be fought in two parts separated by a river. But, then again, anybody interested in the world of the Hellenes and their heirs knows unconventionality is far from being unheard of. And, if an argument of numbers is made, then accepting that the sides were considerably smaller, perhaps a half or two thirds those at Raphia, this would allow all the combat to take place in the northern area west of the river, on the plateau, which it could not have done if the manpower had really been equivalent to the fight in 217. Whatever the exact details, the outcome was clear. 'Antiochus overcame Scopas, in a battle fought at the fountains of Jordan, and destroyed a great part of his army.'[13]

While 10,000 got away and followed Scopas to find refuge in Sidon, Antiochus was not going to let the fruits of this victory slip away. He chased them down with all the energy at his command. And, after the siege-lines were drawn round Sidon, it soon became clear that there was no absolute steel in the defence, and although the government at Alexandria sent a force under four 'famous' generals to relieve them, the attempt failed, and Scopas and the remnants of the Panion army were left to work out their own fate. It took empty bellies inside of Sidon to ensure an outcome, but Scopas at least ensured he got back to Alexandria as part of the deal. It is probable that as the siege had moved to its conclusion his eyes had become more and more focused on what was happening back in Alexandria. He was not egregious, but certainly egotistical, and looked now to the priority of securing of his own power base there.

After this triumph, the Seleucid army now marched south, intent on making their presence permanent in this region that had changed hands so often in the past decades. Antiochus took the Batanaea region, Abila and Gadara, Greek cities east of Jordan, and then the Samarians and Jews submitted. He had to fight to take the citadel of Jerusalem from its Ptolemaic garrison, but the king was clearly pleased with the Jewish authorities for their cooperation and solicitude in looking after his men and elephants.[14]

After this, it was onto the siege of Gaza, another of those epics of which we get only the faintest echo: 'It seems to me both just and proper here to testify, as they merit, to the character of the people of Gaza.'[15] Polybius admired this people's fidelity to the Egyptians who had ruled them for so long. Their overlord had been vanquished in battle, but they still defended their walls, despite there being no prospect of succour from Alexandria. It was a pattern; the Gazans had stood firm to the end against Alexander the Great 130 years before. But the latest besieger was irritated, not impressed, by their tenacity, and even knowing himself to be in a line with the Great Macedonian, did not mollify him, and Antiochus destroyed the place as soon as he took it.[16]

Scopas still had some juice in the tank, as would be expected for a man with his extraordinary career. Back at Alexandria, despite disasters in the Golan Heights and at Sidon, he had loyal regiments at his back, which was what counted. He was still well connected in the military, certainly best of friends with the officer in charge of the elephant hunts that recruited for the royal herds, and he apparently had access to the royal money as well. All this in a few years overcame any loss of confidence due to Panion, and he made a bid for supreme power in about 196. But Aristomenes did not have a pedigree in Agathocles' court for nothing. He was too sharp for the general, and had him arrested and tried in front of all the Greek diplomatic officials, including Aetolians, in the capital. Like Socrates, if lacking his cachet, he too was given a cup of poison to take him away from the troubles of a world in turmoil.

Conclusion

In 201, a huge war fleet launched off the east coast of Chios Island and manoeuvred into the strait between it and the mainland shore. This armada comprised 'fifty three of the heaviest class' warships with reinforced decks above the rowers, capable of carrying catapults, wooden towers and large numbers of soldiers. The biggest of them was a deceres, with 10 oarsmen a side on each bench, handling up to three banks of oars, and at least one enneres, several octeres, septiremes and sexiremes and the balance made up of quinqueremes and quadremes. With these battleships were '...undecked ones, and a hundred and fifty galleys and beaked ships.'[1] These were much smaller, lighter vessels with far fewer oarsmen and with only gangways and small deck sections, able to carry a limited number of marines. But they all had rams, and so could be effective in holing enemies and breaking off their oars; many may well have been *lembi* of Illyrian design, which were one of the preferred ships of pirates at this time.

The man leading them was the Macedonian King Philip V, who had been forced to leave the digging he loved to do in front of Chios' beleaguered city walls when an enemy fleet manoeuvred across his supply lines. This enterprise had anyway got bogged down to some extent, and Philip decided he needed to get away before the blockade began to really affect the efficiency of his forces. The aim was probably to get back to the island of Samos, where he might boost his chances by outfitting more of the Egyptian ships he found mothballed there when he took it over. Philip did not really want to fight as he led his squadrons out into the channel where an allied fleet from Rhodes, Pergamum and Byzantium were waiting, and it certainly seems they too were taken unawares. He had high hopes he might make an escape; although if he had to fight he was confident enough, having bested the Rhodians at Lade Island near Miletus not long before. However, they had now been strongly reinforced and the allies could deploy sixty-five decked warships, three triremes – un-decked vessels with three banks of oars but with only one man on each – and nine trihemioliae. These last were particularly associated with Rhodes as anti-pirate craft, about the size of a trireme, fast and manoeuvrable.

As Philip sailed out, the blockade picket ships put up the alarm and the allies prepared to launch in pursuit, ensuring the encounter took place in the strait between Chios and the Erythraean peninsula on the Asian coast. The Macedonians initially sailed parallel to the coast of Chios Island, heading south away from their enemy, but Attalus with the Pergamene fleet responded swiftly when he realized what was happening, hurrying in loose order after them. Making good speed, they soon had almost come up with the leading Macedonian vessels. Attalus, on the allied left, closed with his heavy cataphracts, mostly quadremes and quinqueremes. His ships were chasing the right of the Macedonian line, commanded by Philip himself. The Macedonian king responded and ordered his right wing to turn and face prow to prow, drawing up in the channel facing northeast, with his larger ships on the right, protected on one side by the Asian shore and in front of two small islands. But when a fight became inevitable, and indeed in some places had already been joined, he made an interesting choice, slipping away 'with a few light vessels' and landing himself on a nearby island 'in the middle of the strait' and settled down to see what happened.

The other half of the allied fleet, mainly Rhodians, got underway, and were soon cleaving the water with their usual impressive celerity. Some were already at sea when Philip initially emerged, but the faster ships were drawn up on the beach of the Asian shore to keep them dry. However, the trailing end of the Macedonian line, as it tried to withdraw, was within range of those Rhodians launching from the Erythraean peninsula, and 'by a vigorous use of their oars' they caught up with them. Well trained and nimble in this rundown, some of the Rhodians rammed the enemy in the stern or smashed through their oars. The pursued now turned and formed the left of the Macedonian line, while Theophiliscus, the Rhodian commander, brought up the balance of his fleet, including three older, heavier vessels that he personally commanded.

Battle had been joined all along the line, but those cruisers under Attalus were not well in hand and apparently attacked with little order. The old king of Pergamum was one of the first to engage; standing on the fighting platform of his flagship, he directed it at one of the enemy's heavy octeres and holed it below the waterline. There was hard fighting between the marines over the deck sides, but the damaged Macedonian vessel eventually sank beneath the waves. As well as royalty in the Pergamene line, two brothers holding high commands took a vigorous part. One of them, Deinocrates, drove at another octeres, but his crew were inexpert and found themselves rammed above the waterline and stuck fast to their victim. This commander in trouble was rescued by Attalus, arriving from his earlier triumph, who rammed the enemy, separated the ships, slaughtered the crew and took it. The other brother had, meanwhile, charged full pelt at another enemy but missed, and in the debacle lost his right side oars and turrets, and his maimed cataphract found itself surrounded by enemies

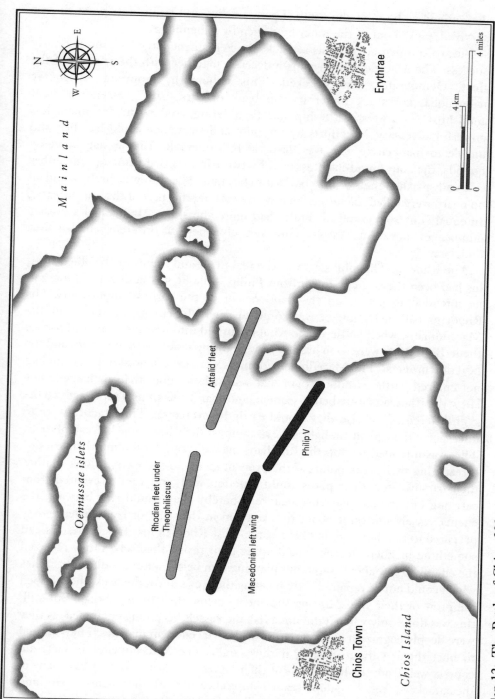

Plan 12: The Battle of Chios, 201 BC.

determined to be in at the death. Dionysodorus and two sailors were all that survived, picked out of the water by a friendly trihemiolia.

But, to compensate for this setback, the Pergamene navy had another early success. The Macedonian flagship, a deceres, together with the admiral of the fleet, Democrates, was wrecked. This behemoth, ramming an enemy trihemiolia, got stuck under its top bank of oars, having taken her right amidships. So a great battleship was floundering, wedged in this much less powerful adversary. No efforts by the pilot and steersmen could free her, and unable to manoeuvre, she was desperately vulnerable. Like a stag beset by hounds, the ship found itself assailed by two triremes that came up one either side and smashed their bronze beaks into her hull. The ship was disabled and all on board were killed, including Democrates. Along this part of the line of battle, an equal contest was waged. Philip had more ships, but Attalus had a greater number of powerful vessels. However, elsewhere a different combat was underway.

The Rhodian Theophiliscus was the real heart and brains of the allied fleet; his had been the strategy to confront Philip while he was besieging Chios, and he intended to get in on the dénouement at the earliest opportunity. His Rhodians had had a longer way to go to reach the enemy, but here too, the Macedonians, when battle was inevitable, turned into line and deployed to face them. Both fleets were soon head to head, fighting it out 'with loud cries and the peal of trumpets.' The Macedonian admirals were experienced officers and had not entered battle without a plan that was at least more than inchoate. They knew the Rhodians were better seamen, and that it was important to reduce the skill differential, or else they would easily be overcome. Their tactics were to intersperse their plentiful light galleys amongst their heavy–decked cataphracts. This was intended to stop the Rhodians manoeuvring by fouling their oars or threatening their weak points at the prow or stern. In these conditions, neither their oarsmen nor their pilots could function well, and were prevented from carrying out the *diekplous* manoeuvre, whereby they would row between the enemy vessels and came about to take them in the flank or rear. Instead, they prepared to ram head on, but here again, these Rhodian maritime tricksters had something up their sleeves. 'For dipping their prows themselves they received the enemy's blow above water, but piercing him below water produced breaches which could not be repaired.'[2] By pushing the crews down the deck, they dipped the prow of their ships, hitting the enemy below their bronze beaks. But still, this was done only when it did not a risk the vessels becoming entangled, as they were deeply cognizant of the prowess of the Macedonian marines. They wanted to hurt them without closing, if they could. The Macedonians, in fact, did contest well from the high decks of their larger vessels and kept at bay many of the attackers. Yet, by adept seamanship, shearing off the enemy's oars and catching them astern, the Rhodians still took a heavy toll.

Not that all went their way. One Rhodian holed a victim but left its beak in its target, and started taking water in the breach this created. Taking advantage, the Macedonian marines boarded, and though kept at bay for a time, when the pilot was wounded and knocked overboard the rest of his men were killed. Theophiliscus rode to the rescue, with three quinqueremes, but they could not save the flooded ship. But then this trio turned on the foe, they stove in two enemies straight away, forcing their crews and marines overboard. Soon they were surrounded by Macedonian galleys and decked ships, and it was hard fighting. Many officers and crew were killed and wounded, but they just won out when Philostratus came to their rescue. Theophiliscus, though wounded, was joined by the rest of his squadron and attacked again with desperate bravery.

This was a fissiparous business, an affair of two battles a considerable distance from each other in the three-mile channel. Philip's squadrons on the right wing, 'following out his original plan', although surely more probably driven that way, made for the shore, while the left wing, caught up by the Rhodians, had turned about and were fighting close by the island of Chios. As the ships of Attalus' fleet neared the mainland shoreline, they approached the island where Philip was stationed. He had not stayed there out of fear but to get an overview, and what he saw was worrying. One of his quinqueremes nearby was rammed and out of action, so he put to sea and led two quadremes to go to her assistance. The enemy disengaged and backed off towards the mainland shore; Philip gave chase, and it was then he noticed the exposed position of the Pergamene king. When the Macedonian fleet had turned to face the Rhodians, this seemed to have created a gap, and Attalus went for it, chasing some of Philip's ships in towards the Asian shore. In doing so, he passed near Philip's island. Philip, 'seeing that Attalus was widely separated from his own fleet, took four quinqueremes and three hemioliae and such galleys as were near him and, intercepting the return of Attalus to his own fleet, compelled him in great disquietude to run his ships ashore.'[3] The king of Pergamum was in trouble and, determined not to be captured, he abandoned his flagship and escort on the beach and legged it for Erythrae town, a feat he managed by decoying the Macedonians. He had his men hurry to pile up some obviously valuable treasure in full view on the deck of his vessel. The enemy took the bait, swarming round and allowing the human prizes to escape. But Philip, if he had lost the king, had the flagship to show, and put to sea with it in tow to rally his forces and claim a victory. A contention that was buttressed by the rumours that Attalus was dead. But Dionysodorus, the Pergamene admiral, whether aware of what had happened to his leader or feeling the need to find order out of chaos, hoisted a signal flag, regrouped his ships and sailed to the mainland harbour at Erythrae.

If the encounter between Attalus' and Philip's fleets had not been decisive, the Rhodians had trounced those opposed to them, and the Macedonians they were contending with now fled the fight, although later claiming they were heading off to help their comrades. The Rhodians did not pursue, but took control of the serviceable ships and sank, by ramming, those too damaged to be worth saving, then comfortably retired with their prizes to Chios town, which had been saved from the attentions of Philip by their actions. The whole butcher's bill, as reported, was formidably one-sided and must be open to question, considering a context in which both sides claimed victory. In the action against Attalus, Philip lost one deceres sunk, an enneres, a septireme, a sexireme, ten other decked ships, three trihemioliae and twenty-seven galleys with their crews. This was bloody stuff already, but worse was on the other flank. The Rhodians had done for ten decked ships, forty galleys sunk, two quadremes and seven galleys captured with their crews. On the allied side, we hear that Attalus lost one trihemiolia and two quinqueremes sunk, two quadremes and his flagship captured, while the Rhodians suffered the loss of only two quinqueremes and a trireme sunk, and none captured. Their crews suffered only 130 killed and 700 captured, while the Macedonians were decimated to the extent of 3,000 soldiers and 6,000 sailors, and 2,000 made prisoner.

Despite the disparity, Philip maintained victory on the grounds that he had driven Attalus ashore, captured his flagship and had retained the field, anchored among the wreckage off Argennus. But this show was dented the very next day, when Dionysodorus picked up the king of Pergamum, united the allied squadrons and sailed out to offer battle again. Having lost more men than ever before in his career, 'the whole strait was filled with corpses, blood, arms, and wreckage, and on the days which followed quantities of all were to be seen lying in confused heaps on the neighbouring beaches.'[4] Philip, who claimed to have triumphed, slunk away. However, it was not unalloyed rejoicing in the allied camp; the Rhodian admiral, Theophiliscus, died in his hour of triumph, only living one day after, although time enough to report home to Rhodes of the victory.

This collision between two great battle fleets is fascinating, allowing details seldom heard of how maritime melées played out. The account almost certainly comes in part from a Rhodian source, and while it is wonderful in its particulars, it falls into a tradition in which not a few sea fights in this era are confused as to outcome. Andros was the same, and if Lade was clearer in conclusion, it certainly is not in terms of sequence. And, apart from its intrinsic interest, the battle of Chios sits as the only great tableau in the process that brought Rome, like a great bull in a china shop, for good into the Hellenistic World.

After concluding a fizzling war at Phoenice in 205, Philip had turned east towards the Aegean and the Hellespont. He was following a long-held Macedonian imperative; controlling the Propontic corn trade was always lucrative and, at that moment, particularly useful for putting pressure on an Athens that was beginning to be difficult. The timing was the key; the Romans gone, Aetolia quiescent, other fronts reasonably quiet, and Ptolemaic influence in the area declining. A power vacuum called to those with the wherewithal to fill it. The sequence of events is obscure, but certainly Philip, with a convenient ally, had been entering the privateering business in the Aegean in a substantial way. He needed money, and he had friends in Crete who had dabbled in piracy for centuries, and with them he hoped to finance a ship-building spree that might make him dominant in these waters. We are told the Cretans had a pirate fleet of seven vessels, and it was their maritime depredations that provoked the Rhodians, who were determined to suppress these commerce raiders. In so doing, they instigated a Cretan war that started a timeline ending with armies from Rome marching deep into Macedonia and Anatolia.

Another couple of 'scoundrel' eminences now emerged in Philip's entourage: a Tarentine called Heracleides with a CV of frequent double dealing in Italy, and an Aetolian called Dicaearchus. The former both acted for Philip as incendiary in the Rhodian shipyards and as high admiral at the battle of Lade.[5] The latter led a campaign of freebooting and tribute collection that seemed part of a general outbreak of waterborne criminality that even included Nabis, the tyrant of Sparta. Philip began to stir the cauldron in person, rather than through Cretan clients, when he moved both his army and an illicitly-funded fleet east towards the Propontis. In 202, he forced Lysimacheia and Chalcedon, allies of Aetolia, into the Macedonian fold. Perinthus, an ally of Byzantium, was captured, then he ventured deep into the sea of Marmaris to take Cius. This was deeply troubling for many. The Aetolians, for one, sent envoys to the Senate in Rome to appeal for someone to muzzle this rabid ruler, and the Byzantines were sufficiently distressed to commit their navy against the intruder.

At sea, things had also gone well, as the Macedonian navy, built on pirate gold, even before the nettle of Chios, had attacked and captured the island of Thasos in 202, before moving through the Cyclades and seizing the Ptolemaic naval base at Samos, boosting the fleet to over 200. They had then gone on to beat the Rhodian navy in a battle off the island of Lade, of which the only details are that two Rhodian quinqueremes were captured and a Rhodian craft that had been rammed raised studding-sail to flee, the rest following suit, leaving the Rhodian admiral with no choice but to join in. They had to withdraw to Cos, allowing the Macedonians to plunder their camp, and although Philip's commander, Heracleides, won many plaudits, there was still enough dispute about who had won the victory to allow Polybius an opportunity to take a pop at Zeno (again) and Antisthenes of Rhodes, contemporaries who had the temerity to hold a different view from him.

Sometime during this period, Euromus and Pedasa in Caria, Bargylia, Iasus opposite Chios, and Abydos up by the Hellespont, were all brought into the Macedonian camp and either accepted or had garrisons imposed. Somewhere along the line, Attalus felt threatened enough to enter the fray again, and Philip was apparently so taken aback (which is surprising, considering their past history) that he turned to hit back. He bearded the old man himself in Pergamum, and not only attacked the city, but also cemented his vandal reputation by despoiling some temples outside the walls. It was a destructive proclivity the people of Peraea also witnessed, although they were not sworn enemies, but only linked in amity to the Rhodians. This conquest is noted when Philip took Prinassus, in Peraea, by an act of deception. Such was Philip's reputation for mining that, despite the place being built on solid rock, by bringing earth from elsewhere and piling it in front of a contrived mine entrance, he conned the garrison into surrendering. But still, it was far from plain sailing all round. At some point, Philip was required to be rescued by Zeuxis, Antiochus' veteran provincial governor in the region, when his corn supply ran out. His fleet was at Cos at the time, but clearly could not bring him what he needed. And, more than this, after the battle at Chios, Philip found himself for a time blockaded in Bargylia and then hanging on with a discouraged army in Caria.

But finally, it was not what he did, but the reactions of the enemies Philip had stirred up that made the real change. Envoys were piling up in Rome, trying to drag in these Italians as the answer to what was seen as an awful regional threat. It was not a new thing for rival powers to look for outside support against more potent neighbours, or indeed even domestic opponents. The Great King of Persia had entertained plenty of Hellenes who wanted money to fund their wars. The Aetolians had been first, but Attalus joined in, and Rhodes soon followed, feeling they needed outside aid both to ensure the Macedonians did not get too powerful in their backyard and that the high seas were safe for commerce. But what they wanted was a return to business as usual; they as much as anybody else would not have believed what would be the result of their pains in just the next ten or eleven years. They all had made themselves hostages to fortune to a people not just happy to meddle in their neighbours' affairs, but who would take them over altogether.

But Aetolia, Pergamum, Rhodes and Byzantium were not the only communities whose feathers Philip had ruffled. A name hardly mentioned for years, Athens showed some grit when Roman backing was in the wind, and became part of the kindling that ignited the second Macedonian War. It has been strange describing action in Greece without some of the big players from centuries before. Sparta, Oreus, Chalcis, Corinth; the king and his armies had been all over them, but Thebes and Athens are hardly noticed. It is a totally different political geography from the Classical World. But now, for a moment, she was centre-stage again. It came about innocuously enough, when an Athenian crowd lynched a couple of Acarnanian tourists for sacrilege, a people who had long been allies of Philip. The bad feeling was compounded when the Athenians dissolved the tribes named for two Antigonid kings, Antigonus the One-eyed and Demetrius the Besieger, and named a new one for Attalus of

Pergamum. Ambitious men in Rome had been pumping themselves up to despoil the ruler who had had the gall to make an alliance with Hannibal, and their inclination was kept fuelled by Philip, who came back from his Anatolian foray intent on roughing up the Athenians. His officers caused such damage that she sent envoys griping to the Senate. The Macedonians even kept pillaging the Attic countryside when Roman representatives were present in town. With this brinkmanship reported, the atmosphere changed, and ambassadors, some of whom had been lounging in the atriums of Rome for years, suddenly found their cause taken up by belligerent men with a taste for war and the loot and fame it brought. The less affluent Romans who would have to fight the Macedonian War were less convinced, but here, as so often in history down to the present day, those in charge have never been adverse to lying through their teeth to ensure nothing stops them doing what they had determined on all along.

These Romans were not universally loved. As Appian says of the Greeks 'the greater part of them preferred the alliance of Philip and sided against the Romans on account of certain outrages against Greece committed by Sulpicius.'[6] They were a bloody people, but Greeks on the wrong side of a beating just could not resist calling them in. The communities who did so knew there were risks; in the last ten years of the third century there had been several debates reported that revolved around the imminent danger, like those at Naupactus and Sparta. In the latter, a deliberation developed as to whether that city should join the new Aetolian axis along with the Romans. Polybius here, through the long-winded speech of an Acarnanian, visualizes the Aetolians bringing in Rome first as an ally, but in reality they were 'men of a foreign race who intend to enslave her [Greece].'[7] The Romans were even compared as a threat to the Persians, against whom the Spartans so famously fought. And at Naupactus at the end of the Social War, the danger from the victors of the latest Punic War was famously articulated. Now Rome was coming, but still Philip's eyes were firmly directed east. These Italians were still not high on his agenda; we do not even hear of precautions on the Illyrian front. It was back round the Hellespont that the final slide to war commenced. The king was besieging Abydos when the Roman Lepidus arrived in the siege lines with an ultimatum that he get back to his starting line. This he would not do, instigating the struggle that ended with the newcomers arriving for good.

But, this was not the only thread as the old century wore down. A familiar figure, not a king, and old by now, cemented a reputation that few Hellenes won in a Tiber-centric age. Philopoemen, the victor of Mantinea had, by 200, started a lean to Rome. His relationship with the Macedonians had badly corroded; there is even talk of Phillip trying to have him poisoned. So when Cycliadas, an old pro-Macedonian, was elected *strategos*, Philopoemen found it convenient to accept an invitation from Gortyn in Crete and return to his old trade as mercenary. He returned as an Achaean power player later, and understanding how the world had changed, he found the wriggle room to finally crush Spartan independence and incorporate the city into the Achaean League. But it was a local war in Messene that saw the end of him in 183. He was captured (the prison cell where he is supposed to have been kept can still be seen, a highlight of this extensive wall-girt site) and, like Scopas before, while incarcerated, he was given poison to drink.

What gives an imbalance is that much in the last decade of the third century is glimpsed through Livy's eyes, and he always gives Rome centre stage, even when their contribution may not warrant it. These years to the end of the century were still essentially about Hellenistic performers bustling in a Hellenistic World, but by the time the extant Polybius returns in meaty detail, the Romans really have arrived. Consular armies are prowling the borders of Macedonia, and the Romans are no longer an auxiliary, but the major player in a war with Philip. The whole question was becoming what the Achaean attitude would be towards Rome. What would Aetolia do? Stay friends with the Senate or gamble in a different diplomatic direction? Even accepting that history is written or dictated by the winners and most tales of overwhelming victory and irresistible influence should be toned down a good deal, it is impossible not to realize that from then on, the place where the heirs of Alexander the Great had lorded was becoming a Roman world. From now on, it was all revolving around Rome, this much was transparent; whether it was Philip going down at the battle of Cynoscephalae in 197, much trimmed but with a kingdom to hand to his second son, or Antiochus finding a Roman war impossible to avoid and losing much of Anatolia after campaigns in Greece and decisive defeat at Magnesia in 190. The Ptolemies remained centred on their old interests, and the war in Coele Syria entered its fifth round, but they also soon found they required an Italian counterweight to throw in against an heir of Antiochus III who was pressing on their very front door.

Whatever the active elements in these streams of time, economic, social, military or personal, one of the pleasures of detailing these years is how familiar are the *olio* of people we come across: a Ptolemaic queen being sniffy about the lower orders indulging in bring-a-bottle parties, or prolix and dissentient academics scoring points off one another's lack of topographical expertise. It is all so accessible, and on the continuum of attractiveness, the move from Hellene to Roman sees a real greying, with the occasional Greek experiments in direct assembly democracy replaced by a Roman pattern. This was a process whereby one model of communal activity was subsumed and another advanced, with effects that resonate well down to our own times. It might seem romantic to deplore the impact of representative democracy seeded by the Tiber city over direct assembly democracy, whatever its faults, but there is a core there. And if the huge differences between people from the recent past and those of Rome or Greece must not be forgotten, still it is difficult not to see that these early Italians always had Mussolini in their eye, possibly in a way that was not true of their cousins east of the Adriatic.

Notes

Introduction

1. There are now numerous general histories of the Hellenistic period, such as those of R.M. Errington, *A History of the Hellenistic World, 323–30 BC* (Oxford, 2008), P.M. Green, *From Alexander to Actium* (London, 1991), G. Shipley, *The Greek World after Alexander, 323–30 BC* (London, 2000) and FW Walbank, *The Hellenistic World* (London, 1981). All have value and some are excellent, notably the magisterial, if occasionally wrong-headed, Green. But recent books on the main characters are noticeable by their absence, save for Grainger's partial account of Antiochus. The omnipotent Walbank's books on Philip V and Aratus are now both more than 70 years old and Errington's book on Philopoemen dates back to 1969.

2. Polybius, *The Histories, Volume I*, translated by W.R. Paton (Massachusetts, 1922), 2.38.6.

3. Polybius, *The Histories, Volume I*, 2.38.7.

Chapter 1

1. Hieronymus of Cardia was allegedly an incredible 104 years old when he died at Gonatas' court. A general, ambassador and historian, he had marched with Alexander the Great. In the chaos of the Diadochi Wars he hitched his fortunes to that of his fellow countryman Eumenes. Antigonus Monopthalmus pardoned him and he served the Antigonids, grandfather, son and grandson, faithfully as court historian. He wrote a history of the Diadochi Wars, upon which the main source Diodorus Siculus is based. Unfortunately, none of Hieronymus' work has survived.

2. Most of Plutarch's Lives are Parallel Lives where he compares and contrasts (often somewhat artificially) the vices and virtues of prominent Greeks and Romans. Aratus, the Roman emperors Galba and Otho, and the Persian Artaxerxes are all the subject of individual lives. Why this should be is unknown.

3. See, for example, Polybius, *The Histories, Volume I*, 1.3.2–4 and Plutarch, *Aratus*, translated by B. Perrin and included in *Parallel Lives XI* (Massachusetts, 1926), 3.2.

4. Polybius, *The Histories, Volume I*, 2.40.4.

5. Plutarch, *Aratus*, 5.3.

6. Plutarch *Aratus*, 11.2 actually states the money is from the king of Egypt, but all commentators seem to think that Antigonus is meant (e.g. see FW Walbank, *Aratos of Sicyon* (Cambridge, 1934), p. 35 and note). In addition, the whole chronology of this period is somewhat confused and disputed, but we will not be detained by it.

7. Pausanias in the second century AD apparently saw a statue above the stage of the theatre in Sicyon. It was identified to him as being that of Aratus. Pausanias, *Guide to Greece, Volume I, Central Greece,* translated by P. Levi (London, 1971), II 42.
8. Plutarch, *Aratus,* 16.4. This is from the translation in 1683 by the English poet and playwright John Dryden.
9. Plutarch, *Aratus,* 18.3.
10. Plutarch, *Aratus,* 22.5.
11. Plutarch, *Aratus,* 29.5.
12. Plutarch, *Aratus,* 31.3.
13. For contrasting views of the reasons for this alliance, see FW Walbank, *Aratos of Sicyon,* pp. 57–69, and contra J.D. Grainger, *The League of the Aitolians* (Leiden, 1999), pp. 217–43. In reality, the sources are so meagre and the chronology so vague and confused that they cannot completely bear the weight of any interpretation. We have chosen to use the conventional chronology, with the view that whichever one is chosen, the position at the start of Antigonus Doson's reign, when our real story starts, is clearer and essentially the same.
14. Plutarch, *Aratus,* 27.2.
15. Plutarch, *Aratus,* 34.3.
16. There is also an extant Athenian inscription bestowing an honorary citizenship on a Bithys, which is almost certainly this general, which suggests an anti-Aratus feeling amongst the populace.
17. See RM Errington, *A History of Macedonia* (Berkeley, 1990), p. 175, although contra P.M. Green, *From Alexander to Actium,* p. 154 and 252.
18. Plutarch, *Aratus* 34.4.
19. Polybius, *The Histories Volume III,* translated by W.R. Paton (Massachusetts, 1923) 5.106.7–8.

Chapter 2

1. Just to emphasize the singularity of Sparta, apparently, some descendants of the Ancient Spartans still speak a separate language called Tsakonian, which is derived from the Spartan language. Though in danger of extinction, a small number of speakers exist a few miles east of Sparta itself.
2. In the last few years there has been a three-part series on the ancient Spartans on mainstream British TV, hosted and created by Bettany Hughes, but based on the book by P.A. Cartledge, *The Spartans, An Epic History* (London, 2002). It aired on Channel 4 in Britain in 2003.
3. Lycurgus was the legendary lawgiver of Sparta who established the military-oriented reformation of Spartan society in accordance with the Oracle of Apollo at Delphi. However, there is some doubt as to whether he was an historical figure at all. See for instance P.A. Cartledge, *The Spartans, An Epic History,* pp. 5–7, and G.L. Huxley, *Early Sparta* (London, 1962), pp. 41–52.
4. Aristotle, *The Politics,* Book II, part IX.
5. Plutarch, *Agis,* translated by B. Perrin and included in *Parallel Lives X* (Massachusetts, 1921), 7.3.
6. In fact, the land was divided up into two portions, "that which lay between the water-course at Pellene and Taÿgetus, Malea, and Sellasia, into forty-five hundred lots, and that

which lay outside this into fifteen thousand," Plutarch, *Agis*, 8.1. The 15,000 plots were subsequently divided into equal lots and given to the remaining *perioeci* who could bear arms.

7. Naomi Mitchison *The Corn King and Spring Queen* (London, 1931).
8. Plutarch, *Cleomenes*, translated by B. Perrin and included in *Parallel Lives X* (Massachusetts, 1921), 1.2.
9. The Aetolians' motive for giving the towns to Sparta is, as with all aspects of the Aetolian League, much disputed. The reference to the event in Polybius, *The Histories, Volume I*, 2.46.2 is vague enough to allow almost any interpretation.
10. Plutarch, *Cleomenes*, 6.3.
11. Plutarch, *Aratus*, 38.1.
12. Pausanias, *Guide to Greece, Volume I, Central Greece*, 2.9.1.
13. Polybius, no friend of Cleomenes and his political reforms, has no doubts and puts the blame squarely on Cleomenes. Plutarch, on the other hand, blames those who had put Agis to death and is ambivalent about Cleomenes' role in the whole affair. Whatever the motives or reasons, one senses some blackening of Cleomenes' character in all this, as it is problematic to see how he could have been behind both the murder of Eudamidas and Archidamus V. Polybius, *The Histories, Volume III*, 5.37, also has Archidamus fleeing, originally because of Cleomenes, not his brother's death. See also B. Shimron, 'Polybius and the Reforms of Cleomenes III' in *Historia*, 13 (1964), pp. 147–155.
14. Diogenes Laertius in his (exceedingly brief) *Life of Sphaerus* tells us that Sphaerus became pre-eminent at the court of Ptolemy IV in Egypt, presumably going into exile with Cleomenes. He was apparently admired for the accuracy of his definitions (Cicero, *Tusclulan Disputations*, 4.24). Stoicism itself was founded by Zeno of Citium and was regarded as a way of life, believing that the best indication of an individual's philosophy was not what a person said but how he behaved.
15. Plutarch, *Cleomenes*, 11.2.
16. Polybius, *The Histories, Volume I*, 2.58.4.
17. Plutarch, *Aratus*, 39.2.
18. See for example, F.W. Walbank, *Aratos of Sicyon*, pp. 96–7.
19. Plutarch, *Cleomenes*, 19.2.
20. Plutarch, *Cleomenes*, 19 4.
21. The position of the Aetolians in all this is again exceedingly obscure. Whatever arrangement they had with Antigonus in 228 must have fallen away for them to block Thermopylae. J.D. Grainger, *The League of the Aitolians*, pp. 244–8, suggests they were in alliance with the Spartans but, in any event, they played no part in the Cleomenean War.
22. Plutarch, *Aratus*, 43.1–2.
23. Plutarch, *Cleomenes*, 20.3.
24. For contrasting views of this see Plutarch, *Aratus*, 44.4, who castigates Aratus, and Polybius, *The Histories, Volume I*, 2.59–61, who, criticizing Phylarchus, goes on at interminable length about what a fitting punishment it was.
25. The size of the manumission fee has prompted some amazement. F.W. Walbank, *Aratos of Sicyon*, p. 108, rejects the story, which appears only in Plutarch, *Cleomenes*, 25.1, altogether. P. Green, *From Alexander to Actium*, (London, 1991) p. 260, finds the fee puzzling and prohibitive, but P.A. Cartledge and A.J.S. Spawforth, *Hellenistic and*

Roman Sparta: A Tale of Two Cities, (London, 2001), pp. 51–2, find it a feasible amount. None of them attribute the move to Cleomenes' desire for helot equality and brotherhood!

26. Plutarch, *Aratus*, 45.5.
27. Polybius, *The Histories, Volume I*, 2.58.12.
28. Plutarch, *Philopoemen*, translated by B. Perrin and included in *Parallel Lives X* (Massachusetts, 1921), 5.2.
29. Polybius, *The Histories, Volume I*, 2.64.6–7.
30. Polybius, for all his faults and biases, could be an extremely impressive historian at times and his tirade against Phylarchus and his account of the Ptolemy withdrawal of funds is worth quoting at length.

   "What he tells us next is still more astounding; after this assertion about the booty, he states that just ten days before the battle an envoy from Ptolemy reached Cleomenes informing him that that king withdrew his subvention and requested him to come to terms with Antigonus. He says that Cleomenes on hearing this resolved to stake his all on a battle before it reached the ears of his troops, as he had no hope of being able to meet their pay from his own resources. But if at this very time he had six thousand talents at his command, he could have been more generous than Ptolemy himself in the matter of subventions; and if he could only dispose of three hundred talents it was enough to enable him to continue the war against Antigonus with absolute financial security. But to state in one breath that Cleomenes depended entirely on Ptolemy for money and that at the very same time he was in possession of such a large sum, is a sign of the greatest levity and want of reflection." Polybius, *The Histories Volume I*, 2.63.1–6.

31. Plutarch, *Cleomenes*, 22.7.
32. J. Pietrykowski, *Great Battles of the Hellenistic World*, (London, 2009), p. 172, wonders whether Doson was influenced by the tactics of Pyrrhus of Epirus at the battle of Asculum in 279, where similar deployment was tried. As he points out, there were of course Epirote troops at Sellasia. Apart from Pietrykowski's account, we have also used P. McDonnell-Staff, 'Sparta's Last Hurrah; The battle of Sellasia (222 BC)', in *Ancient Warfare*, Volume 2, Issue 2 (2008), pp.23–29, to great profit.
33. Polybius, *The Histories, Volume I*, 2.66.9.
34. It is noticeable that Plutarch glosses over Sellasia in his life of Aratus in just five words! Aratus was not *strategos* that year, but given his close relationship with Doson it seems probable that he was present at the battle to give him the benefit of his knowledge. However, Plutarch's account of the battle is somewhat lacking and exemplifies his general lack of interest in warfare. He could have described it in three of his lives, *Aratus*, *Cleomenes* and *Philopoemen*, but he adds comparatively little to the excellent account of Polybius, which he was well aware of and indeed quotes in *Cleomenes*.
35. Plutarch, *Philopoemen*, 6.5.
36. Polybius, *The Histories, Volume I*, 2.68.2. Plutarch, *Philopoemen*, 6.7, tells a similar tale, with Antigonus laughing and saying, "That young man behaved like a great commander."
37. It should be noted that Plutarch (following Phylarchus) retells a story of treachery, which was apparently the main reason why Cleomenes lost the battle. In this version, the secret flanking movement of the Illyrians and Acarnanians round the flank of Eucleidas'

hill is known about, but its implications are dismissed by Cleomenes' chief of secret police, Damotoles, who had been bribed by Doson. Though possible, the whole scenario sounds unlikely.

Chapter 3

1. For a full discussion of the origins of the League and its reputation, see J.D. Grainger, *The League of the Aitolians*, in particular chapters 2 and 3.
2. J.D. Grainger, *The League of the Aitolians* is a much needed attempt to rehabilitate the Aetolians' reputation, though, as with all such efforts, it perhaps goes too far the other way. For examples of modern historians' bias against the Aetolians, see F.W. Walbank, *The Hellenistic World*, p. 153, and P. Green, *From Alexander to Actium*, p. 140.
3. Polybius, *The Histories, Volume II*, translated by W.R. Paton (Massachusetts, 1922), 4.11.1.
4. Polybius, *The Histories, Volume II*, 4.25–36, does not make it clear whether these 'known friends' took over and were then deposed and murdered or whether they did not have time to take up the reins of power before the revolution that led to the accession of Lycurgus. As for the legitimacy of Lycurgus and possible Polybius bias, see P.A. Cartledge and A.J.S. Spawforth, *Hellenistic and Roman Sparta: A Tale of Two Cities*, p. 57.
5. Polybius, *The Histories, Volume II*, 4.73.6.
6. Polybius, *The Histories, Volume II*, 4.65.11.
7. Polybius, *The Histories, Volume II*, 4.67.6.
8. Apparently, the brazen shields of the hoplites made them think this, as Antigonus Doson had re-equipped the soldiers of Megalopolis some years before.
9. Polybius, *The Histories, Volume II*, 4.69.6–7.
10. Polybius, *The Histories, Volume II*, 4.71.9–11.
11. Polybius, *The Histories, Volume III*, 5.2.2–3.
12. Polybius, *The Histories, Volume III*, 5.17.6.
13. Polybius, *The Histories, Volume III*, 5.18.10.
14. Polybius, *The Histories, Volume III*, 5.22.3–4.
15. But all this must be understood as very hyped from Aratus' own memoirs. The reality was probably one where Aratus was an important local ally but not the predominant mentor that is claimed.
16. Polybius, *The Histories, Volume III*, 5.16.6–7.
17. Polybius, *The Histories, Volume III*, 5.26.12.
18. The Athenian authorities shut the gates on Megaleas, forcing him on to Thebes.
19. Polybius, *The Histories, Volume III*, 5.27.6.
20. Polybius, *The Histories, Volume III*, 5.28.5.
21. Polybius goes on at great length about Philip's lack of planning, but we can perhaps be more understanding; for if he intended a surprise attack he would not have sent in engineers to estimate the height of the defences and thus warn the defenders of his approach.

Polybius mentions the episode again, later in his histories (*The Histories, Volume IV*, 9.18.5–9), where he suggests the failure was just as much to do with the attackers arriving before partisans in the city had activated a coup to let them in.

22. Polybius, *The Histories, Volume III*, 5.101.2.
23. Polybius, *The Histories, Volume III*, 5.101.3–4.
24. Polybius claims that 2,000 were made prisoners and 400 killed, which is more than the original force!
25. Polybius, *The Histories, Volume III*, 5.95.10.

Chapter 4
1. Polybius, *The Histories, Volume III*, 5.46.12.
2. Polybius, *The Histories, Volume III*, 5.48.9.
3. Polybius, *The Histories, Volume III*, 5.54.2.
4. For details of Pithon's intrigues, see B. Bennett and M. Roberts, *The Wars of Alexander's Successors, 323–281 BC, Volume One: Commanders and Campaigns* (Barnsley, 2008), particularly pp. 64–75.
5. Polybius, *The Histories, Volume III*, 5.59.6.
6. Polybius, *The Histories, Volume III*, 5.62.3.

Chapter 5
1. Ptolemy Euergetes had paid him every honour – as one soldier to another – and had put up a statue of him at Olympia, the base of which has been discovered.
2. The Adulis inscription was copied in the sixth century by a monk called Cosmas Indicopleustes. The anonymous text tells that Ptolemy set out for Asia with an army and elephants (both Troglodyte and Ethiopic). That they reached Babylon is confirmed by the local chronicles. Justin, *Epitome of the Philippic History of Pompeius Trogus*, translated by J.S. Watson (London 1853) (27.1.5ff) confirms a war where many communities in Asia, incensed by Laodice's treatment of Berenice, went over to Ptolemy. Polyaenus (*Stratagems*, 8.50.) suggests Ptolemy took control as far as India by a trick when his people claimed Berenice and her son had survived a fatal attack and were preparing to return to power sponsored by the Egyptian king.
3. The evidence for this battle is just two brief sources, neither of which date the battle or even who fought. It is not even clear which Antigonus is meant. For a recent brief summary of the latest thinking see P. Green, From *Alexander to Actium*, p. 772.
4. Polybius, *The Histories, Volume III*, 5.69.1.
5. Polybius, *The Histories, Volume III*, 5.70.5.
6. See R. Post, 'Alexandria's Colourful Tombstones, Ptolemaic Soldiers Reconstructed,' in *Ancient Warfare*, Volume 1, Issue 1 (2007), pp. 38–43.
7. The meaning of the term Neocretan is exceedingly obscure. Some, including F.W. Walbank, *A Historical Commentary on Polybius (Vol. 1)* (Oxford, 1957), think it may mean simply soldiers sent by Knossos, whereas others such as C. Fischer-Bovet, 'Counting the Greeks in Egypt' in *Princeton/Stanford Working Papers in Classics* (2007), thinks it refers to a special type of soldier, perhaps light-armed soldiers with small, round *pelte*. Yet others think it is the nomenclature of young Cretans in organizations called *neoi*!
8. According to Diodorus Siculus, *Universal History X*, translated by R.M. Geer (Massachusetts, 1954), 19.80.4, Egyptians were present at the battle of Gaza in 312, although not as frontline troops: 'but a great number were Egyptians, of whom some

carried the missiles and the other baggage but some were armed and serviceable for battle.'

9. Polybius, *The Histories, Volume III,* 5.80.3.
10. So thinks B. Bar-Kochva, The *Seleucid Army, Organization and Tactics in the Great Campaigns* (Cambridge, 1976), pp. 132–3.
11. Polybius, *The Histories, Volume III,* 5.84.2–6.
12. It has been suggested that Ptolemy actually had some Indian elephants as well. See M.B. Charles, 'Elephants at Raphia: Reinterpreting Polybius 5.84–5.' in *Classical Quarterly,* New Series 57 (2007), pp. 306–311.
13. Polybius, *The Histories, Volume III,* 5.85.2.
14. See J. Pietrykowski, *Great Battles of the Hellenistic World,* (Barnsley, 2009) p. 194.

Chapter 6

1. Polybius, *The Histories, Volume III,* 8.16.5.
2. Polybius, *The Histories, Volume III,* 8.23.5.
3. See Justin, xli. 4.9.
4. W.W. Tarn, *The Greeks in Bactria and India,* (Cambridge, 1938).
5. There is an acute lack of literary evidence for this time in Bactria and much has been tentatively reconstructed on the basis of coins (numismatics). W.W. Tarn, *The Greeks in Bactria and India,* has been heavily criticized by some academics, for instance F.L. Holt, *Thundering Zeus: The Making of Hellenistic Bactria* (California, 1999). For an interesting review of the coin evidence, see K.L. Rappe, 'The Greco Bactrian Mirage: Reconstructing a History of Hellenistic Bactria', in *Archive: A Journal of Undergraduate History* 4 (2001).
6. Polybius, *The Histories, Volume IV,* translated by W.R. Paton (Massachusetts, 1925), 10.49.9.
7. Polybius, *The Histories, Volume IV,* 10.49.13.
8. 'For those authors... find it necessary to place before their readers all the devices, all the daring strokes, and in addition to this describe at length the capture of Tarentum, the sieges of Corinth, Sardis, Gaza, Bactra [Balkh], and above all Carthage.' Polybius, *The Histories, Volume VI,* translated by W.R. Paton (Massachusetts, 1927), 29.12.7–8.
9. Polybius, *The Histories, Volume IV,* 11.39.15.

Chapter 7

1. Polybius, *The Histories, Volume III,* 5.108.1–2.
2. Polybius, *The Histories, Volume III,* 7.9.12–13.
3. Polybius, *The Histories, Volume III,* 5.10.1.
4. Plutarch, *Aratus,* 49.2.
5. Polybius, *The Histories, Volume III,* 7.12.2–3.
6. Plutarch, *Aratus,* 52.2.
7. Plutarch, *Aratus,* 52.3.
8. Polybius, *The Histories, Volume III,* 8.14.6–7.
9. Livy, *The History of Rome, Books 21–45,* translated by Canon Roberts (London, 1912), 26.25.15.
10. Livy, *The History of Rome, Books 21–45,* 27.30.8.

11. Polybius, *The Histories, Volume IV,* 10.26.1.
12. Livy, *The History of Rome, Books 21–45*, 27.32.3.
13. See Livy, *The History of Rome, Books 21–45*, 27.32.4. He calls these Tralles Illyrians, but in fact it seems they were from Thrace.
14. Livy, *The History of Rome, Books 21–45*, 27.32.6.
15. Livy, *The History of Rome, Books 21–45*, 28.5.8.
16. Polybius, *The Histories, Volume IV*, 10.43–47, goes into great detail regarding this system, which he considers a great advance. He also mentions his own part in developing the code and how the alphabet is split into five parts and used in five different tablets, which are then indicated by torches (10. 45.6–12).
17. See Frontinus, *Stratagems*, translated by C.E. Bennett (Massachusetts, 1925), 1.4.6.
18. F.W. Walbank, *Philip V of Macedon* (Cambridge, 1940), p. 96 and 302, thinks Achaea had control over Olympia, so Machanidas was attacking on behalf of his allies. But see contra R.M. Errington, *Philopoemen* (Oxford, 1969), p. 60, who thinks that Sparta is attacking Elis.
19. This is Polybius, *The Histories*, 11.11.7, but in the translation by E.S. Shuckburgh (London, New York, 1889). We have not used the usual Loeb translation as it is translated as 'the mercenary cavalry in close order,' which is significantly different. F.W. Walbank, *A Historical Commentary on Polybius (Vol. 2)* (Oxford, 1967), p. 287, points out this is an incorrect translation.
20. Polybius, *The Histories, Volume IV,* 11.13.1.
21. Polybius, *The Histories, Volume IV,* 11.14.7.
22. Polybius, *The Histories, Volume IV,* 11.16.2.
23. Polybius, *The Histories, Volume IV,* 11.18.4.
24. Plutarch, *Philopoemen*, 10.6–7.

Chapter 8

1. So E.R. Bevan, *The House of Ptolemy* (London, 1927), p. 252.
2. Polybius, *The Histories, Volume IV,* 15.26.3–4.
3. Appian, *The Foreign Wars*, translated by H. White (New York, 1899), The Macedonian Wars 1. Fragment YR 554.
4. See B. Bar-Kochva, The *Seleucid Army, Organization and Tactics in the Great Campaigns*, p. 146.
5. Polybius, *The Histories, Volume IV,* 13.2.2.
6. See Livy, *The History of Rome, Books 21–45*, 31.43.5.
7. See Flavius Josephus, *Antiquities of the Jews*, translated by W. Whiston (New York, 1895), 12.132.
8. Again, see B. Bar-Kochva, The *Seleucid Army, Organization and Tactics in the Great Campaigns*, in particular p. 19 and p. 153. See also J.D. Grainger, *The Roman War of Antiochus the Great* (Boston, 2002), pp. 25–26 and 316–317.
9. Polybius, *The Histories, Volume V,* translated by W.R. Paton (Massachusetts, 1926) 16.18.8.
10. Polybius, *The Histories, Volume V,* 16.19.10.
11. Polybius, *The Histories, Volume V,* 16.19.11.
12. This is taken from B. Bar-Kochva, *The Seleucid Army, Organization and Tactics in the Great Campaigns*, pp. 146–157, and his fascinating and ingenious account of the battle.

13. Flavius Josephus, *Antiquities of the Jews*, 12.131.
14. See Flavius Josephus, *Antiquities of the Jews*, who reproduces an alleged letter from Antiochus to Ptolemy, where he praises the Jews and grants them their freedom in a barbed rebuke to the Egyptian monarch (12.136–145).
15. Polybius, *The Histories, Volume V,* 16.22.A.
16. The chronology of the siege of Gaza and whether it takes place before or after the battle of Panion is very unclear. Both E.R. Bevan, *The House of Ptolemy*, pp. 256–258, and F.W. Walbank, *A Historical Commentary on Polybius (Vol. 2)*, pp. 523–527, place the siege before the battle. The evidence for Polybius, which is just a fragment (16 IV 22 a), is not conclusive, and it could be argued that his description of a brave defence made in the face of impossible odds would better fit a time after the Lagids had clearly been bested in battle.

Conclusion

1. Polybius, *The Histories Volume V,* 16.2.9.
2. Polybius, *The Histories Volume V,* 16.4.12.
3. Polybius, *The Histories Volume V,* 16.6.4.
4. Polybius, *The Histories Volume V,* 16.8.9–10.
5. See Polyaenus, *Stratagems*, translated by R. Shepherd (London, 1793), 5.17.2.
6. Appian, *The Foreign Wars*, The Macedonian Wars 1. Fragment YR 554.
7. Polybius, *The Histories, Volume IV,* 9.37.7.

Bibliography

Ancient Sources

Appian, *The Foreign Wars*, translated by H. White (New York, 1899).

Arrian, *The Campaigns of Alexander*, translated by A. De Selincourt (London, 1958).

Diodorus Siculus, *Universal History X*, translated by R.M. Geer (Massachusetts, 1954).

Flavius Josephus, *Antiquities of the Jews*, translated by W. Whiston (New York, 1895).

Frontinus, *Stratagems*, translated by C.E. Bennett (Massachusetts, 1925).

Justin, *Epitome of the Philippic History of Pompeius Trogus*, translated by J.S. Watson (London, 1853).

Livy, *The History of Rome, Books 21–45*, translated by Canon Roberts (London, 1912).

Pausanias, *Guide to Greece, Volume I, Central Greece*, translated by P. Levi (London, 1971).

Plutarch, *Agis*, translated by B. Perrin and included in *Parallel Lives X* (Massachusetts, 1921).

Plutarch, *Aratus*, translated by B. Perrin and included in *Parallel Lives XI* (Massachusetts, 1926).

Plutarch, *Cleomenes*, translated by B. Perrin and included in *Parallel Lives X* (Massachusetts, 1921).

Plutarch, *Philopoemen*, translated by B. Perrin and included in *Parallel Lives X* (Massachusetts, 1921).

Plutarch, *Moralia, Volume III*, translated by F.C. Babbitt (Massachusetts, 1931).

Polyaenus, *Stratagems*, translated by R. Shepherd (London, 1793).

Polybius, *The Histories, Volume I*, translated by W.R. Paton (Massachusetts, 1922).

Polybius, *The Histories, Volume II*, translated by W.R. Paton (Massachusetts, 1922).

Polybius, *The Histories, Volume III*, translated by W.R. Paton (Massachusetts, 1923).

Polybius, *The Histories, Volume IV,* translated by W.R. Paton (Massachusetts, 1925).

Polybius, *The Histories, Volume V,* translated by W.R. Paton (Massachusetts, 1926).

Polybius, *The Histories, Volume VI*, translated by W.R. Paton (Massachusetts, 1927).

Modern Authors

Bar-Kochva, B., *The Seleucid Army, Organization and Tactics in the Great Campaigns* (Cambridge, 1976).

Bennett, B., and Roberts, M., *The Wars of Alexander's Successors, 323–281 BC, Volume 1: Commanders and Campaigns* (Barnsley, 2008).

Bevan, E.R., *The House of Ptolemy* (London, 1927).

Bowman, A.K., Egypt *after the Pharaohs* (Oxford, 1990).

Cartledge, P.A., *The Spartans, An Epic History* (London, 2002).

Cartledge, P.A., and Spawforth, A.J.S., *Hellenistic and Roman Sparta: A Tale of Two Cities* (London, 2001).

Cary, M., *A History of the Greek World from 323 BC to 146 BC* (London, 1951).

Casson, L., *The Ancient Mariners* (Princeton, 1991).

Chaniotis, A., *War in the Hellenistic World* (Oxford, 2005).

Charles, M.B., 'Elephants at Raphia: Reinterpreting Polybius 5.84–5' in *Classical Quarterly*, New Series 57 (2007), pp. 306–311.

Errington, R.M., *Philopoemen* (Oxford, 1969).

Errington, R.M., *A history of the Hellenistic World 323–30 BC* (Oxford, 2008).

Errington, R.M., *A History of Macedonia* (Berkeley, 1990).

Ferguson, W.S., *Hellenistic Athens* (London, 1911).

Fields, N., *Tarentine Horseman of Magna Graecia* (Oxford, 2008).

Fischer-Bovet, C., 'Counting the Greeks in Egypt' in *Princeton/Stanford Working Papers in Classics* (2007).

Gaebel, R.E., *Cavalry Operations in the Ancient Greek World* (Norman, 2002).

Grainger, J.D., *The League of the Aitolians* (Leiden, 1999).

Grainger, J.D., *The Roman War of Antiochus the Great* (Boston, 2002).

Green, P.M., *From Alexander to Actium* (London, 1991).

Habicht, C., *Athens from Alexander to Antony* (Cambridge, Massachusetts, 1997).

Hansen, E.V. The *Attalids of Pergamon* (New York, 1947).

Head, D., *Armies of the Macedonian and Punic Wars* (Cambridge, 1982).

Holt F.L., *Thundering Zeus: The making of Hellenistic Bactria* (Berkeley, 1999).

Hooker, J.T., *The Ancient Spartans* (London, 1980).

Huxley, G.L., *Early Sparta* (London, 1962).

Lane Fox, R., *The Classical World* (London, 2005).

Macurdy, G.H., *Hellenistic Queens* (Baltimore, 1932).

McDonnell-Staff, P., 'Sparta's Last Hurrah; The Battle of Sellasia (222 BC)' in *Ancient Warfare*, Volume 2, Issue 2 (2008), pp. 23–29.

Nossov, K., War *Elephants* (Oxford, 2008).

Pietrykowski, J., *Great Battles of the Hellenistic World* (Barnsley, 2009).

Post R., 'Alexandria's Colourful Tombstones, Ptolemaic Soldiers Reconstructed' in *Ancient Warfare*, Volume 1, Issue 1 (2007), pp. 38–43.

Pritchett W.K., Studies *in Ancient Greek Topography, Part II, Battlefields*' (Berkeley, 1969).

Rappe, K., 'The Greco Bactrian Mirage: Reconstructing a History of Hellenistic Bactria' in *Archive: A Journal of Undergraduate History* 4 (2001).

Shipley, G., *The Greek World after Alexander, 323–30 BC* (London, 2000).

Shimron, B., 'Polybius and the Reforms of Cleomenes III' in *Historia*, 13 (1964), pp. 174–155.

Shimron, B., 'The Spartan Polity after the Defeat of Cleomenes III' in *Classical Quarterly*, New Series, 14 (1964), pp. 232–239.

Tarn, W.W., *The Greeks in Bactria and India*, (Cambridge, 1938).

Walbank, F.W., *Aratos of Sicyon* (Cambridge, 1934).

Walbank, F.W., *Philip V of Macedon* (Cambridge, 1940).

Walbank, F.W., *A Historical Commentary on Polybius, Volume I* (Oxford, 1957).

Walbank, F.W., *A Historical Commentary on Polybius, Volume 2* (Oxford 1967).

Walbank, F.W., *The Hellenistic World* (London, 1981).

Wilkes, J., *The Illyrians* (Oxford, 1992).

Yalichev, S., *Mercenaries of the Ancient World* (London, 1997).

Index